TO THE OTHER

Purdue Series
in the History of Philosophy

General Editors

Arion Kelkel

Joseph J. Kockelmans

Adriaan Peperzak

Calvin O. Schrag

Thomas Seebohm

TO THE OTHER

An Introduction to
the Philosophy of
Emmanuel Levinas

Adriaan Peperzak

Purdue University Press
West Lafayette, Indiana

Printed in the United States of America

Book and cover design by Anita Noble

Library of Congress Cataloging-in-Publication Data

Peperzak, Adriaan Theodoor, 1929–
    To the other : an introduction to the philosophy of Emmanuel Levinas / Adriaan Peperzak
      p.   cm.   —(Purdue University series in the history of philosophy)
    Includes French text and English translation of: La philosophie et l'idée de l'infini.
    Includes bibliographical references and index.
    ISBN 1–55753–023–8 (alk. paper). —ISBN 1–55753–024–6 (pbk. : alk. paper)
    1. Lévinas, Emmanuel. I. Lévinas, Emmanuel. Philosophie et l'idée de l'infini. English & French. 1992. II. Title. III. Series.
B2430.L484P46 1992
194–dc20
                                             91–44845

In memory of
my parents

Margareta Catharina Teppema
and
Adriaan Peperzak

CONTENTS

Since 1961 the work of Emmanuel Levinas has slowly acquired a pivotal position in the world of philosophy. Notwithstanding a sort of radical simplicity, its textual difficulty resists any quick or facile understanding. Having taught several courses on Levinas's thought in various schools of Europe and America, I wrote this book in order to facilitate a fruitful reading of his main philosophical texts. Although even the greatest thinkers have elicited criticisms from their students—and are not the best students, like Aristotle, Spinoza, or Hegel, the sharpest critics of their masters?—in this book I have not tried to follow the example of their attempts to transform what they received from their masters into a new, original philosophy but restricted my commentary, as much as possible, to an explanation of the position, the main perspectives, the background and the structure of Levinas's central texts.

In the hope that this introduction, thus, will be able to open doors to a thought that must be heard and meditated upon, I want to thank all those who collaborated in the process of its coming-to-be, especially Joe Flay, David Gandolfo, and Matthew Pacholec, who refined my English; Peter Rijnhart, who indefatigably typed the different versions of my manuscript; Margaret Hunt, who edited it with great care and skill; and Anita Noble, who gave my book its handsome appearance.

Some parts of this book are translations, revisions, or new versions of former articles. Permissions to (re)print were graciously extended by Kluwer Academic Publishers for permission to reprint "Philosophy and the Idea of Infinity" (from Emmanuel Levinas, *Collected Philosophical Papers*, © 1987 by Martinus Nijhoff Publishers: 47–60) with some slight changes, and my article "The One for the Other," *Man and World* 24 (1991): 427–59,

© 1991 Kluwer Academic Publishers; to Librairie philosophique
J. Vrin for permission to reprint "La philosophie et l'idée de
l'Infini," from *En découvrant l'existence avec Husserl et Heidegger;* to the *Revue de Sciences Philosophiques et Théologiques*
for permission to print an English version of my article "Une
introduction à la lecture de *Totalité et Infini: Commentaire de
'La philosophie et l'idée de l'Infini,'" Revue de Sciences Philosophiques et Théologiques* 71 (1987): 191–217; and to *Research in
Phenomenology* for permission to print a revised English version
of my "Beyond Being: On Emmanuel Levinas, *Autrement qu'être
ou au-delà de l'essence," Research in Phenomenology* 8 (1978):
239–61, whose first, German version appeared in *Philosophische
Rundschau* 24 (1977): 91–116.

Chicago, May 1, 1992

I Works of Levinas

AE   *Autrement qu'être ou au-delà de l'essence,* Phaenomenologica, vol. 54 (The Hague-Boston: Nijhoff, 1979²) (see *OB*).

CPP   *Collected Philosophical Papers,* Phaenomenologica, vol. 100, translated by Alphonso Lingis (Dordrecht-Boston: Nijhoff 1987).

DDVI   *De Dieu qui vient à l'idée* (Paris: Vrin 1982).

DL   *Difficile Liberté: Essais sur le judaisme* (Paris: Albin Michel 1976²).

EDHH   *En découvrant l'existence avec Husserl et Heidegger* (Paris: Vrin, 1974²).

EE   *De l'existence à l'existant* (Paris: Vrin 1978²) / *Existence and Existents* (translation by Alphonso Lingis) (The Hague-Boston: Nijhoff, 1978).

EI   *Ethique et Infini: Dialogues avec Philippe Nemo* (Paris: Fayard, 1982).

HAH   *Humanisme de l'autre homme* (Montpellier: Fata Morgana, 1979²).

OB   *Otherwise Than Being or Beyond Essence* (translation of *AE* by Alphonso Lingis) (The Hague-Boston: Nijhoff, 1981).

PhII   "La philosophie et l'idée de l'Infini," *EDHH* 165–78; *CPP* 47–60.

TA   *Le temps et l'autre* (Paris: Quadrige-PUF, 1983²).

TH   "Transcendance et hauteur," in *Bulletin de la Société Française de Philosophie* 56/3 (1962): 89–101.

TI   *Totalité et Infini: Essai sur l'exteriorité*, Phaenomenologica, vol. 8 (The Hague-Boston: Nijhoff, 1961¹, 1974⁵) / *Totality and Infinity: An Essay on Exteriority* (translation by Alphonso Lingis) (The Hague-Boston: Nijhoff, 1979²)

❙ Works of Other Authors

Ak   Kant's gesammelte Schriften, herausgegeben von der Königlich Preußischen Akademie der Wissenschaften (Berlin, 1910ff.).

AT   Œuvres de Descartes publiées par Ch. Adam & P. Tannery, Paris, nouvelle présentation (Paris: Vrin, 1973ff.).

GA   Martin Heidegger, Gesamtausgabe (Frankfurt/M: Klostermann, 1975ff.).

GW   Georg Wilhelm Friedrich Hegel, Gesammelte Werke (Hamburg: Meiner, 1968ff.).

The One for the Other

| Thought and Existence

In 1963 G. Deledalle and D. Huisman published a collection of texts in which most of the outstanding French philosophers presented their life and work: *Les philosophes français d'aujourd'hui par eux-mêmes: Autobiographie de la philosophie française contemporaine.* Emmanuel Levinas's self-presentation is found on pages 325–28. Under the title "Signature," this text also forms the closing pages (321–27) of his own book *Difficile Liberté (Difficult Liberty)*, which appeared in the same year. For a Dutch collection of his work, *Het menselijk gelaat (The Human Face)*, in which "Signature," under the title "Handschrift" (handwriting), figured as the opening section, Levinas added a few paragraphs (29–34), and the French text of this version appeared in the second edition of *Difficile Liberté.*[1] Its sober enumeration of facts and thoughts calls for additional information and profound meditation on his works in order to grasp the full meaning of his modest statements. On the course of his life and his intellectual development, one can now consult a large number of interviews, especially those

---

1 *Difficile Liberté: Essais sur le judaisme,* Présences du judaisme, 2d rev. ed. (Paris: Albin Michel, 1976), 373–79; *Difficult Liberty: Essays on Judaism,* trans. Sean Hand (Baltimore, Md.: The Johns Hopkins University Press, 1991). The first translation of "Signature" into English was by W. Canavan in *Philosophy Today* 10, no. 1 (1966): 31–33; a second one, by M. E. Petrisko and annotated by A. Peperzak, was published in *Research in Phenomenology* 8 (1978): 175–89. *Les philosophes français* was published by the Centre de Documentation (Paris, 1963); the first edition of *Het menselijk gelaat* was published by Ambo (Baarn, 1969); the seventh edition was published in 1987.

| 1

printed in *Emmanuel Levinas: Qui êtes-vous?*[2] and *Ethique et Infini.*[3] Whereas the former tells us many interesting things about his life, the latter one, by concentrating on the starting points and the evolution of his thought, has become an excellent introduction to his work.

Without resolving the general problem of the relations between thought and existence, it can be safely stated that at least some acquaintance with the personal and cultural background of Levinas's thinking is useful, if not necessary, to understand his criticism of the Western philosophical tradition as well as his own, very original thought. I will therefore start by approaching his work in a rather external way in order to ask to what extent the mentioned facts are relevant for a correct and sympathetic understanding of his texts. One of the advantages of this approach is that it can reveal a great variety of traditions or histories toward which Levinas had to take a stand by wholly or partially integrating, rejecting, or transforming them. It will enable us to ask what, in his case, it meant to become human amidst or "under the influence" of such different traditions.

Born in 1906 of Jewish parents in Kaunas, Lithuania, Levinas had been initiated very early into Jewish orthodoxy. Being a Lithuanian Jew, he was soon confronted with the surrounding Christianity—a Christianity not free from antisemitic tendencies and actions—and with the Russian language and culture, which dominated the school system. His father had a bookshop, and besides the Bible, which he learned to read in Hebrew, it was above all the great Russian poets and novelists Pushkin, Gogol, Lermontov, Dostoyevski, Tolstoy, etc., read in the original language, that formed his mind.

In 1923 Levinas left Russia for Strasbourg to study philosophy. Because of the political freedom and the philosophical tradition found in France, he came to love that country, and, shortly after having published his dissertation in 1930, he became a French citizen. University studies familiarized him with classical texts of antiquity and modern philosophy as well as with the French tradition of psychology and idealist

---

2 F. Poirié, *Emmanuel Levinas: Qui êtes-vous?* (Lyon: La Manufacture, 1987).

3 *Ethique et Infini: Dialogues avec Philippe Nemo* (Paris: Fayard & Radio France, 1982).

philosophy. Hegel did not belong to the normal curriculum and certainly not Marx, Nietzsche, or Freud. A decisive turn was his introduction to Husserl's phenomenology.[4] Although Husserl's reception in France would still take a long time, Levinas decided to write a dissertation on the fundamental concepts of his phenomenology. In 1929 he published a still-classical review of Husserl's ideas: "Sur les 'Ideen' de M. E. Husserl"[5] and in 1930 his dissertation, *La théorie de l'intuition dans la phénoménologie de Husserl,*[6] which received a prize from the French Academy.

In the meantime, however, Levinas had come to recognize that, more than Husserl, the author of *Sein und Zeit* was the radical renewer and master of philosophy. Heidegger's lectures in Freiburg (Breisgau) were the main reason why Levinas spent the academic year 1928–29 in that town. Heidegger's influence is clear in Levinas's interpretation of Husserl as proposed in his dissertation, and for many years Levinas would be an outstanding interpreter of Heidegger's *Sein und Zeit.* After the completion of his studies, Levinas returned to France. He taught at the Ecole Israélite Orientale du Bassin Méditerranéen, whose director he would later become, and he participated in the Parisian philosophical life inside and outside the Sorbonne. But aside from some articles on Husserl and Heidegger and a series of reviews,[7] his philosophical production remained modest. Apart from some very short pieces of a more religious character, Levinas wrote

---

4 According to Levinas's own statements, it was Gabrielle Peiffer who drew his attention to Husserl's philosophy, which he began to study in 1927–28 together with Jean Héring, who wrote the first French book on phenomenology: *Phénoménologie et philosophie religieuse* (Paris, 1925). Cf. *Emmanuel Levinas: Qui êtes-vous,* 73 and "Signature" in *DL* 373.

5 *Revue Philosophique de la France et de l'Etranger* 54 (1929): 230–65.

6 Paris: Alcan, 1930¹; 2nd and 3rd eds., Vrin, 1963 and 1970. English translation by A. Orianne: *The Theory of Intuition in Husserl's Phenomenology,* Northwestern University Studies in Phenomenology and Existential Philosophy (Evanston, Ill.: Northwestern University Press, 1973). Together with Gabrielle Peiffer, Levinas translated also Husserl's *Cartesian Meditations* (Edmond Husserl, *Meditations Cartésiennes: Introduction à la phénoménologie* [Paris: A. Colin, 1931]), and he wrote the article "Freiburg, Husserl et la phénoménologie" in the *Revue d'Allemagne et des pays de langue allemande* 5 (1931): 402–14.

7 Some of these reviews were published in the short-lived review *Recherches Philosophiques,* founded in 1931, in which several émigrés, such as Eric Weil, A. Koyré, and K. Löwith, published.

only one thematic essay: "De l'évasion" ("On Evasion"), in which, however, some main lines of his later work are already visible.[8]

In the early 1930s, Levinas was preparing a book on Heidegger, but only fragments of it were finished. Heidegger's collaboration with the Nazis and his rectoral address of 1933 were a shock and turning point for the young Levinas. Although he always continued to see his master as the greatest philosopher of our century and *Sein und Zeit* as one of the five greatest books of Western philosophy,[9] from then on Levinas developed a critical attitude toward Heidegger. Initially still mild, his criticism developed slowly into a sharper polemic against the "pagan" inspiration of Heidegger's thinking.[10] Even Hitler did not provoke Levinas to violent criticism during these years. His article "The Philosophy of Hitlerism"[11] is a relatively mild attack, and Levinas later left it out of his list of publications because he regretted that he had honored his target by naming it a "philosophy."

The victories of Nazism, the mobilization, and the war brought Levinas to silence. As a French citizen and military officer, Levinas, once captured, was not brought to a concentration camp but to a prisoners' camp, where he had to do forced labor as a member of a Jewish labor force.[12] His wife and daughter could hide in France, but his wife's mother was deported from France, and his own parents and brothers, who had stayed in Eastern Europe, were murdered by collaborators of the German Nazis.

When Levinas returned to Paris after the war, he published a small book with the programmatic and provocative title *From*

---

8 "De l'évasion" was published in *Recherches Philosophiques* 5 (1935–36): 373–92, and republished, with a letter from Levinas and an introduction and notes, by J. Rolland in book form by Fata Morgana (Montpellier, 1982).

9 The other four are Plato's *Phaedrus*, Kant's *Critique of Pure Reason*, Hegel's *Phenomenology of Spirit*, and Bergson's *Essai sur les données immédiates de la conscience* (Paris, 1888).

10 For the development of Levinas's critique of Husserl and Heidegger between 1920 and 1951, see "Phenomenology—Ontology—Metaphysics: Levinas's Perspective on Husserl and Heidegger," *Man and World* 16 (1983): 113–27.

11 "Quelques réflexions sur la philosophie de l'hitlerisme," *Esprit* 2 (1934): 199–208.

12 A glimpse of the situation is given in "Nom de chien ou le droit naturel," *Difficile Liberté* (1976[2]), 199–202.

Existence to Existents.[13] In it he presented for the first time a—
albeit still fragmentary—phenomenology of his own. The title
announces a reversal of Heidegger's enterprise. Whereas the
latter started from a reflection on beings (*Seiendes, l'étant,* or
l'existant) in order to discover Being (*das Sein, l'essence,* or *l'existence*), Levinas described the way of truth as a movement from
"essence" or "existence" (*Sein*) to "existents" (*Seiendes*). *From
Existence to Existents* attracted little attention because the style
of the phenomenological analysis practiced was so difficult, its
orientation so uncommon, and the author so unknown. Twenty
years later, the first edition was not yet sold out.

Not having obtained a *doctorat d'Etat*[14] and without an academic position, Levinas remained marginal to the philosophical
scene in the French universities; his relations to Maurice Blanchot,
Gabriel Marcel, and Jean Wahl did not make him well known
outside of a small circle of experts. Wahl, who himself was a full
professor at the Sorbonne, invited Levinas to give talks at the
lecture series organized by Wahl under the name *Collège Philosophique.* A series of four lectures delivered there on "Time and the
Other" were published, together with texts of Wahl, Alphonse De
Waelhens, and Jeanne Hersch under the title *Choice-World-
Existence.*[15]

Although Levinas's philosophical production between 1947
and the publication of *Totalité et Infini*[16] in 1961 remained modest, some important articles from this time showed a very independent and forceful but difficult thinking. Besides six new

---

13 *De l'existence à l'existant,* Collection Exercice de la pensée (Paris:
Editions de la Revue Fontaine, 1947). A part of the book had been
published under the title "Il y a" in *Deucalion: Cahiers de Philosophie*
1 (1946): 141–54. The book was taken over by J. Vrin, who, in 1978,
published a second edition with a new preface by Levinas. The English
translation by A. Lingis was published as *Existence and Existents* by M.
Nijhoff (The Hague-Boston, 1978).

14 The *doctorat d'Etat* is the doctor's degree granted by the nation,
not by a university. It often leads to a professorship at a French
university.

15 "Le temps et l'autre," J. Wahl et al., *Le Choix-Le Monde-
L'Existence,* Cahiers du Collège Philosophique (Paris: Arthaud, 1947),
125–96. The text was published again separately, and with a preface
by Levinas, by Quadrige-PUF (Paris, 1983).

16 *Totalité et Infini: Essais sur l'extériorité,* Phaenomenologica, vol.
8 (The Hague: Nijhoff, 1961[1]; 1974[5]). English translation by Alfonso
Lingis: *Totality and Infinity: An Essay on Exteriority,* Philosophical
Series, vol. 24 (The Hague: Nijhoff, 1969[1]; 1979[2]).

articles on Husserl and / or Heidegger,[17] one on Proust,[18] and one on Lévy-Bruhl,[19] he published a three-page draft for the 1948 International Congress of Amsterdam[20] and five very dense thematic studies, in which an original philosophy became visible.[21] The distinction between Levinas's studies of other authors and his own thematic reflection is a rather superficial one, since his rendering of another's thought is simultaneously a profound and original meditation on the questions treated by the others. His very important article on Heidegger, "Is Ontology Fundamental?" ("L'ontologie est-elle fondamentale?") not only gives a critical interpretation of Heidegger's thoughts on Being but also sketches another orientation from which new lines of thought should be developed. "Freedom and Command"[22] and "The Ego and the Totality"[23] anticipate parts of *Totality and Infinity*, whereas "Philosophy and the Idea of the Infinite"[24] already exposes the main coordinates of that book.

In addition to these philosophical studies, Levinas's renewed concentration on his Jewish roots is evident in a multitude of essays on various aspects of Judaism, which he sometimes calls

---

17 "L'ontologie dans le temporel" (1948), "De la description à l'existence" (1949), "L'ontologie est-elle fondamentale" (1951), "La ruine de la représentation" (1959), "Réflexions sur la 'technique' phénoménologique" (1959), and "Le permanent et l'humain chez Husserl" (1960).

18 "L'autre dans Proust," *Deucalion: Cahiers de Philosophie* 2 (1947): 117–23; also in Levinas, *Noms propres* (Montpellier: Fata Morgana, 1976), 149–56.

19 "Lévy-Bruhl et la philosophie contemporaine," *Revue Philosophique de la France et de l'Etranger* 82 (1957): 556–69.

20 "Pluralisme et Transcendance," *Proceedings of the Tenth International Congress of Philosophy* (Amsterdam 11–18 August 1948) (Amsterdam: North-Holland Publishing Company, 1949), 1:381–83. With a few modifications, and under the title "La transcendance et la fécondité," this text has become a part of *Totalité et Infini* (251–54).

21 "La réalité et son ombre" (1948), translated by A. Lingis as "Reality and Its Shadow" in: Levinas, *Collected Philosophical Papers* (Boston: Nijhoff, 1987), 1–14. "La transcendance des mots: A propos de 'Biffures' de Michel Leiris" (1949), "Liberté et commandement" (1953), "Le moi et la totalité" (1954), and "La philosophie et l'idée de l'Infini" (1957).

22 *CPP* 15–24, translation of "Liberté et commandement," *Revue de Métaphysique et Morale* 58 (1953): 236–41.

23 *CPP* 25–46, translation of "Le moi et la totalité," *Revue de Métaphysique et de Morale* 59 (1954): 353–73.

24 *CPP* 47–60, translation of "La philosophie et l'idée de l'Infini," *Revue de Métaphysique et de Morale* 62 (1957): 241–53; reprinted in *EDHH* 165–78.

"parochial essays" to distinguish them from the philosophical ones. From 1947 to 1960, he published more than fifty of these more religious essays.[25]

It was only in 1961 that Levinas gained international renown by publishing his main thesis for the *doctorat d'Etat: Totalité et Infini.*[26] After this, an apparently inexhaustible stream of publications, interviews, and talks made him famous throughout the Western hemisphere. Together with the translations, Burggraeve's bibliography counts more than nine hundred publications through 1985, and many others were to follow.

Although Levinas was already fifty-five when he obtained his *doctorat d'Etat,* soon after which he became a full professor at the University of Poitiers, he had not yet reached the end of his philosophical evolution. The next landmark was *Autrement qu'être ou au-delà de l'essence.*[27] This book, the result of intense meditations that parted from *Totality and Infinity,* expressed not so much a "turn" or *Kehre,* as some commentators have said,[28] but rather an intensification and radicalization of the thoughts reached in 1961. The adherence to the language of ontology, still maintained in *Totality and Infinity,* has been transformed into a more consequential style, and the considerable difficulties as well as the necessity of the attempt to think beyond ontology are now thematized with greater force and lucidity than before. However, one cannot say that *Otherwise Than Being or Beyond Essence* represents the final stage of Levinas's development; for, although most of the topics treated in his publications after 1974 are already contained in it, they can be seen as preparations for a new and independent book on time as diachrony, which seems to be a focal topic of Levinas's recent efforts.

---

25 See the numbers 34, 42, 43, 46, 47, 48, 49, 51, 52, 54, 55, 56, 57, 58, 59, 60, 62, 64, 65, 66, 68, 69, 70, 71, 72, 73, 74, 75, 78, 79, 83, 84, 85, 86, 87, 88, 92, 93, 96, 97, 98, 100, 101, 102, 103, 105, 106, 107, 108, 109, 604, 606, 816 of R. Burggraeve, *Emmanuel Levinas: Une bibliographie primaire et secondaire (1929–1985)* (Leuven: Peeters, 1986).

26 Instead of a second book, as formerly prescribed by the statute of the *doctorat d'Etat,* Levinas was allowed to present and defend the totality of his preceding philosophical studies.

27 Phaenomenologica, vol. 54 (The Hague: Nijhoff, 1974). The English translation by Alfonso Lingis was published by the same publisher under the title *Otherwise Than Being or Beyond Essence* (The Hague, Boston, London: Nijhoff, 1981).

28 Cf., for instance, St. Strasser, *Jenseits von Sein und Zeit: Eine Einführung in Emmanuel Levinas' Philosophie,* Phaenomenologica, vol. 78 (The Hague: Nijhoff, 1978), 219–23.

| Roots and Traditions

Many writers on Levinas present his work as a synthetic, hybrid, or paradoxical result of Greek and Jewish culture, denying thereby the importance of other traditions like the Roman, Russian, Christian, or Germanic ones.[29] Such an interpretative scheme has the advantage of all simplifications: by approaching a limited number of aspects from partial perspectives, it illuminates them against an obscure background into which other aspects may have disappeared. As an initial orientation, it may nevertheless be helpful *if* it indicates its own partiality and oversimplification.

The scheme of "Jewgreek or Greekjew" has the advantage that—in opposition to a mighty but forgetful tendency in contemporary philosophy—it does not neglect the overall importance of the Bible and its many Jewish and Christian interpretations for the social and spiritual history of Western civilization. There will be various occasions to show the impact of a certain Judaism on Levinas's thinking, which does not thereby become less philosophical than, for example, Heidegger's philosophical interpretations of Parmenides or Hölderlin. For the moment, I only want to stress the fact clearly contained in the above references to his life that, as a Lithuanian-born Jew, a Russian, a French-educated citizen of Europe, and a philosophical member of contemporary humanity, Levinas is not only heir to (a certain) Greece and (a certain) Israel but also to the Roman Empire with the medieval and modern transformations of its law, to the Slavic and Germanic elements that entered into his formation, and even to a certain form of Christianity that has marked and impregnated two thousand years of European history. All these elements have some independence vis-à-vis one another; and although the ways in which they have become aspects of the common culture cannot be considered the most genuine or pure, it is impossible to reduce Rome to Greece, the Germanic traditions to nothing at all, and Christianity to a subordinate heresy of Judaism or to an amalgam of Jewish faith and Hellenistic philosophy. Characterizations of Western culture as "Platonic" or "Greek" or "Christian" presuppose that the histories to which we belong form one history

---

29 A clear example of such a treatment is J.-F. Lyotard, "Oedipe Juif," *Critique* 21, no. 277 (1970): 530–45 (review of J. Starobinski, *Hamlet et Freud* (Paris, 1967); E. Levinas, *Quatre lectures talmudiques* (Paris, 1968); and *Humanisme et Anarchie* (Paris, 1968); see also J.-F. Lyotard, *Dérive à partir de Marx et Freud* (Paris: Union Générale d'Editions, 1973), 167–88.

whose life belongs to one single spirit; but they are too primitive from a historical point of view to be taken as serious attempts at characterizing twenty-five hundred years of human thought and action. At best, such titles can give a first hint of the real orientation, but even then we have to ask first what "Greek," "Jewish," "Christian," etc. may mean.

The name "Greece," for instance, as used in this context, is far from clear. We all know that Plato and Aristotle produced their philosophy after the "Golden Age" of Pericles, and that the great period from Parmenides to Sophocles was not the Greece that the many European Renaissances enlisted in their efforts to renew, uproot, or overcome their own Roman and Christian traditions during the twelfth, thirteenth, fifteenth, seventeenth, eighteenth, and nineteenth centuries. To which Greece do we refer when we call some tendency of our culture, some work of a great author, or some strain of thought "Greek"? Is it the Greece of Homer, Aeschylus, Socrates, Zeno, Epictetus, Philo, Origines, Pseudo-Dionysios, Thomas, Erasmus, Winckelmann, Goethe, Hölderlin, Keats, Hegel, Burckhardt, Nietzsche, Heidegger . . . ? Many different Greeces exist, as many perhaps as there are Europes or Occidents. Do we all share one Western world? Is not one of the features by which our civilization is simultaneously great and weak precisely its ability to maintain a more or less peaceful community of radically divergent traditions and histories? The price paid for our moral and ideological pluralism seems to lie in the superficiality or even the emptiness of our general culture as illustrated by the media. Is this price too high for peace?

As a philosopher, Levinas is not *and is* Jew, Roman, Russian, European, and therefore also "Christian" in a certain way. The specificity of his participation in the history of thought is marked by all the "nonphilosophical" traditions in which he lived *and* by the peculiarities of the factual situation (the constellation of institutions, teachers, texts, ways of discussion, colleagues, publishing policies, etc.) in which he has come to find himself.

Levinas's French philosophical formation familiarized him with those philosophers who, during the first half of the century, were considered great: Plato, Aristotle, the Stoics, Plotinus, Descartes, Spinoza, Locke, Leibniz, Berkeley, Hume, Kant, Fichte, Comte, etc. The tradition of French philosophy that confronted Levinas as a student was a special form of idealism (Félix Ravaisson, Octave Hamelin, Léon Brunschvicg) in touch with mathematics and psychology. Good historical studies of ancient and

modern philosophy as well as the great tradition of the "explication de texte" gave a solid orientation in the history of philosophy. Henri Bergson had fought against the prevailing position
of the sciences, but a Bergsonian school did not exist. Hegel was
not read much; Marx and Nietzsche still less.

The most striking feature of the picture of philosophy given
at the universities of France was the total absence of all philosophies produced by Christian thinkers from the beginning of our
chronology until Descartes and Pascal. Of the first five centuries,
only writers like Plotinus and Porphyry counted as philosophers;
neither Philo nor Origenes, Augustine or Pseudo-Dionysios were
treated as examples of independent thinking. No medieval philosophers were taken into consideration because they were "theologians." The eighteenth-century ignorance about the "Dark
Ages" was still the prevailing view. The period between Plotinus
and Descartes (a period of thirteenth hundred years) was simply
ignored—a practice still found in some philosophical circles—as
if Christian faith had prevented all brilliant people from thinking
for themselves.[30] Even after Étienne Gilson and others had
proved that one can hardly understand anything of Descartes,
Leibniz, Kant, or Hegel without being acquainted with scholastic
philosophy, the general conception of philosophical history did
not change noticeably.

Like every other student of philosophy, Levinas had to make
choices in his readings and meditations. He answered the beneficial challenge of Husserlian and Heideggerian phenomenology
by becoming a pupil of Heidegger, but soon the suspicion became
almost inevitable that Heidegger's thought was somehow vul-

---

30 Before giving a diagnosis or criticism of "Western philosophy,"
we should first ask what we know about the two thousand years thus
summarized in two words. Since it is physically impossible to have
read all the original and important texts of these millennia (it is even
impossible to select them without reliance on the authority of others
who may have read them or depend themselves on others), the representation of "Western philosophy" is a risky extrapolation based on a very
restricted selection of works. On the basis of the texts we possess of
Heidegger, Levinas, and Derrida, we may say that their situation is
roughly the same as that of the French university sketched here. Patristic and medieval philosophy plays hardly any role in their diagnosis.
Philosophy tends to consist, for the three authors, of Plato, Aristotle
(4th century B.C.), and Plotinus (4th century A.D.) on the one hand, and
the philosophers of the last four centuries (from Hobbes and Descartes
to the present) on the other hand.

nerable or even kin to the immorality of Nazism. The long incu-
bation of Levinas's own thought might be related to the difficulty
in finding a way amidst the contradictory tendencies he experienced in the twenties and the thirties. As a Jew and a philosopher, he not only shared the general crisis of European
intellectuals but experienced intensely the apparent incompati-
bility between Israel and a certain Europe (or was it Europe as
such?). Did this opposition and that crisis have anything to do
with one another?

Who were and remained his favorite authors? As far as his
works show certain relations, for Levinas the main philosophers
are Plato (whose *Phaedrus, Republic, Gorgias,* and *Phaedo* are
often quoted), Descartes (mainly as the writer of the *Meditations*),
Kant (the first and second *Critiques*), Hegel (*The Phenomenology
of Spirit*), Husserl, and Heidegger. Of these, Plato and Heidegger
are certainly the most important ones. In the summary of *Totalité
et Infini* published by the *Annals of the Sorbonne,*[31] Levinas even
goes so far as to say that a renewal of Platonism belongs to the
task of contemporary philosophy. As far as Hegel is concerned,
we must be aware of the Parisian scene of the years during
which Levinas prepared his first opus magnum. In the fifties and
sixties, it was still dominated by Alexandre Kojève's interpretation of the *Phenomenology of Spirit.*[32] In his courses of the thirties
at the School of the "Hautes Etudes," this Russian émigré transformed Hegel's book of 1807 into a philosophy of history close
to Marx's interpretation of world history. It became thereby a
main source for postwar existentialism.[33] Jean Hyppolite's much
more adequate interpretation of the *Phenomenology*[34] had cor-
rected Kojève's distortions, but the latter's more easily under-

---

31 "Résumé de 'Totalité et Infini,' " *Annales de l'Université de Paris*
31 (1961): 9–10.

32 The first French author who renewed the traditional portrait of
Hegel as an extremely abstract and "speculative" philosopher was Jean
Wahl, whose book *La conscience malheureuse,* published in 1928, tried
to show that young Hegel was very close to Kierkegaard.

33 On the basis of these courses, Raymond Queneau published in
1947 the famous book A. Kojève, *Introduction à la lecture de Hegel:
Leçons sur la Phénoménologie de l'Esprit* (Paris: Gallimard). *Introduction
to the Reading of Hegel,* trans. J. K. Nichols (Ithaca, N.Y.: Cornell
University Press, 1980).

34 J. Hyppolite, *Genèse et structure de la Phénoménologie de l'Esprit
de Hegel,* 2 vols. (Paris: Aubier, 1946). This book had been accepted as
the main thesis for the *doctorat d'Etat,* whereas the second book was
Hyppolite's translation (with notes) of the *Phenomenology* into French.

stood and "nicer" interpretations have continued to exercise a
strong influence in France and elsewhere.[35] Levinas's explicit
and implicit references to Hegel must therefore be read with this
background in mind. Rather than being considered the last great
metaphysician, Hegel was considered to be the first philosopher
of history. According to this view, history would be the absolute
power that decides the destiny of humankind and has the final
judgment on its meaning. As we will see, *this* Hegel has been
so powerful that he sometimes penetrated Levinas's interpretations of Heidegger's philosophy.

A Global Characterization of Levinas's Attitude toward Heidegger's Thought

Already in his dissertation of 1930 on intentionality, which
for Husserl was "the principle of principles,"[36] Levinas showed
his preference for Heidegger's existential ontology over and
above Husserl's transcendental phenomenology of consciousness. His first articles on Heidegger testified to a deep admira-
tion and contained no criticism. Even after 1933, he did not
sharply attack Heidegger, but Heidegger's collaboration with
the Nazis demanded an explanation in which National Socialism's relations to Heidegger's thought could not be ignored.
Levinas's own philosophical approach and style remained, however, much closer to Heidegger's than to those of Husserl or
other phenomenologists.

The first article to manifest Levinas's growing distance is
the long essay "De l'évasion" ("On Evasion") of 1935, in
which Levinas asks how thinking can escape an all-penetrating
domination of Being. It is the reverse of the question whether
and how *transcendence* is possible—a question that, from now
on, will inspire and dominate all his reflections. As a questioning beyond Being, it names its point of orientation by
different terms such as "the other," "the infinite," "the metaphysical," "God." Many titles testify programmatically to this
orientation by opposing Being (which, as all-embracing, is
connected to totality) to something else: *Totality and Infinity,*
Other(wise) Than Being, "Beyond Being," "Thought of Being

---

35 For example, on Merleau-Ponty's essay "L'existentialisme chez
Hegel," *Sens et non-sens,* 109–22.
36 See E. Husserl, *Ideas,* vol. 1, section 24.

and the Question of the Other," "The Ontology of the Same and the Search of the Other."[37] On the other hand, the discussion with Heidegger's meditation on Being always accompanies Levinas's search not only as a target but also and primarily because the question of the Being of beings and Being itself constitutes an essential element in any radical thought. In Levinas's interpretation, Heidegger's "ontology" is a splendid renewal of the Western philosophical tradition inherited from Parmenides. A thorough critique of Heidegger is therefore necessary if one wants to know where we stand as heirs of the tradition who experience the crisis of contemporary civilization.

The attempt to characterize Western philosophy as a whole from a critical distance in order to grasp its principle(s) or spirit is a metaphilosophical topos practiced by most of the great philosophers since Kant's *Critique of Pure Reason* and Hegel's *Phenomenology of Spirit.* Although Levinas's diagnosis shows similarities with Heidegger's critique, the latter's thought is seen as an example—albeit a revolutionary one— of the Western mode of existence and thinking. This mode should not, however, be called "metaphysical," as Heidegger claims, but rather "ontological." Against the constant attacks of contemporary philosophy on "Platonism" and their attempts to overcome "metaphysics," *Totality and Infinity* tries to rehabilitate simultaneously a new form of metaphysics and the most profound inspiration of Plato's philosophy. Better than "ontology," the word "metaphysics" expresses the transcending movement of a thinking that goes beyond the realm of Being. Indeed, if we accept Heidegger's interpretation of the Greek *physis,*[38] it should not be translated by the word "nature" but rather by "Being." In that it grants to all beings their emergence and unfolding into the truth of their phenomenality, the *physis* is the all-embracing source to which all beings owe their coming to the fore. According to Levinas, however, the ultimate toward which all thought and existence are oriented coincides neither with any being or with the totality of all beings nor with Being as that which gives them generation,

---

37 Cf. *Totalité et Infini* (1981), *Autrement qu'être ou au-delà de l'essence* (1974), and "La pensée de l'Etre et la question de l'Autre," *Critique* 29 (1978): 187–97.

38 Cf. M. Heidegger, "Vom Wesen und Begriff der Φύσις: Aristoteles, Physik B,1," *Wegmarken,* GA 9, 239–301 (309–71).

growth, and corruption. The ultimate does not manifest itself to a *logos* whose perspectives are confined to the horizons of beingness and Being; in order to be heard or contacted, it demands another transcendence; it is another Beyond.

Just as Heidegger's thought of Being cannot be understood if it is cut off from the classical texts and traditions present in its retrievals, Levinas's philosophy cannot be separated from its polemical connections with Western ontology and its greatest contemporary representative in particular. An intrinsic reason for this lies in the impossibility of simply rejecting or abolishing ontology, since it is an essential element of all philosophy. This statement, in which I summarize a connection that—as I will argue below—underlies many passages of Levinas's work, sounds rather Hegelian. Did Hegel not understand every single philosophy of the past as a necessary but partial half-truth, the real truth being possible only as the ultimate whole of all truth(s)? In order to become truly (i.e., fully) true, every single philosophy had to be integrated, subordinated, relativized, and thus redeemed from its falsehood by becoming a functional moment of the complete and final truth represented in the absolute knowledge of the ultimate philosophy. Levinas's "integration" of ontology, however, differs no less from Hegel's *Aufhebung* than from Heidegger's *retrieve*. More than Heidegger's thought, Hegel's systematic "completion" of Western philosophy is the symbol and summary of the Western tradition. This may be the reason why Levinas sometimes seems to Hegelianize Heidegger's thought. If, however, this impression were the whole truth about Levinas's interpretation of Heidegger, the question would arise whether they are not allies in their anti-Hegelian attempt to renew the paths of philosophy, or even whether Levinas does not simply continue Heidegger's search for a beyond of totality.

| Phenomenology

Husserl's renewal of philosophy through phenomenology can be summarized in the word "intentionality." He saw not only that all consciousness is a *cogito of* something (*cogitatum*), but also that the intentional structure of consciousness cannot be characterized as the relation between a representing subject and objects met by that subject. Feeling, walking, desiring, ruminating, eating, drinking, hammering, too, are intentions—or rather clusters of intentions, related in a specific, nonrepresentational way to specific correlates. The task of philosophy involves the intentional analysis of all the modes of phenomenality in which the whole variety of different intentions is given to consciousness, that is, it involves an adequate description of their givenness and peculiar structure. Such analyses show that every single intention is composed of, supported by, and embedded in other intentions, whose interwovenness with yet other intentions should be analyzed in their turn. A complete analysis would reveal the specificity of all real, necessary, and possible phenomena in their correlatedness to all the real, necessary, and possible intentions constituting human consciousness. Since nothing can be given outside of those intentional correlates, such an analysis would encompass a complete description of an all-embracing consciousness and of the totality of all beings capable of manifesting themselves. The criterion for the authenticity and truth of all statements that can be justified on the basis of this approach to the phenomena is the evidence of their being given in "bodily presence." The impossibility of denying the immediate experience of their givenness was considered the solid rock on which Husserlian phenomenology established its hope for the final promotion of philosophy to the dignity of a valid and rigorous science.

Although Husserl recognized the fact that, in addition to objectifying, presenting, and representing intentions, consciousness is also constituted by affective and practical intentions, he maintained—at least in his earlier works—the primordial and exemplary role of the theoretical or doxic intentions. Notwithstanding his effort to purify consciousness from all contingent and particular features in order to reach a truly transcendental perspective, consciousness remained a panoramic review of a universe of presently given, remembered, or anticipated phenomena. All forms of nontranscendental consciousness were parts of this universe, and the spirit of this phenomenology remained faithful to the modern urge for autonomy. Following the path of Descartes and Hegel, it strove toward the absolute self-possession of a transcendental ego including the truth of all givens in the knowledge of itself.

An extension of the structure of doxic intentions to other species of intentionality by multiplying—as Max Scheler did—the analysis of emotional experiences is not a sufficient remedy against the "egological" illusions of Husserlian phenomenology. Those intentions, too, can be interpreted as partial structures of a universe that opens up for a central and all-encompassing consciousness. However, the experience of our existence, and, in general, every experience, shows that consciousness is never so universal as to embrace also the whole of its own being and beginning. Every single experience includes, besides an element of self-consciousness, also the acceptance of a surprising element that is irreducible to a spontaneous production by ego itself. And not only knowledge but all intentions and consciousness as such affirm the surprising otherness of an a posteriori element that cannot be reduced to a moment of the cogito or its well-controlled panorama. Self-consciousness discovers itself as an original and irreducible relation to some "other" that it can neither absorb nor posit by its own, a priori capacities. The origin is not to be found in a transcendental I; it is the absoluteness of an ultimate *relation*.

Heidegger's transformation of phenomenology has taught us that consciousness is rooted in deeper levels of being-there that precede all sorts of objectifying knowledge and representation. Hammering, caring, being busy, being thrilled, etc. are specific ways of understanding the being of beings before any thematization. *Dasein* is openness and transcendence toward the truth of beings; it is enlightened by the original light that allows them to appear. The understanding of Being implied in our ways of existence is the horizon allowing the coming into being and phenomenality of all phenomena and their interwovenness.

Notwithstanding Heidegger's constant insistence on the distinction to be made between the totality of beings (*das Seiende im Ganzen*) and Being itself (a distinction that in his later works was complicated by the distinction between the beingness of beings and Being itself), and notwithstanding his contrasting *Dasein* with the autonomous subject of modern philosophy, Levinas is convinced that Heidegger *in the end* does not escape from the totalitarian and egological tendencies of the Western tradition.

A first line of attack characterizes Heidegger's thought as an attempt to identify the ultimate instance as an all-embracing horizon. Although Levinas, at least in oral discussions,[39] clearly stated that Heidegger's *Sein* does not signify a totality, various passages of his work seem to say or suggest that Being is so intimately united with the universe of beings that it cannot

---

39 For example, in a seminar I gave with him in May 1983 at the Instituto Superiore di Filosofia in Naples. In the fifth "Conclusion" of *Totalité et Infini* (270 / 294–95), Levinas seems to affirm very clearly that Heidegger's ontology is a panoramic thought and a philosophy of totality.

be freed from its totalitarian character. As an all-encompassing horizon within which all beings (humans, gods, and God included) are allowed to be, Being is the ultimate "universal." Even if it were possible to distinguish it from beings and their inherent beingness without making Being itself into an ultimate, originary, and fundamental being, it would not be possible, according to Levinas, to conceive of it as a nontotalizing instance.

In this discussion, the ontological difference is at stake. Can we distinguish clearly between beings (including modes of their being) and Being itself? In the first chapters of *Autrement qu'être,* Levinas, through an original retrieval of Heidegger's thought, gives his own interpretation of the beingness of Being; but neither there nor in *Totalité et Infini* does it seem to be different from the beingness of beings (*to on hei on*). In evoking Heidegger's ontology, Levinas most often uses the word *"être"* to indicate two things at once: (1) that by which all beings are given as what and how they are ("Being itself"), and (2) (the whole of) reality as such, that is, (all) beings insofar as they exist. If the distinction between these two cannot be made in a comprehensible way, how then can we escape from identifying Being as the monistic horizon or source of universal participation?

More detailed study of the relationship between Heidegger and Levinas must revise, correct, and refine the summary given here as a provisional orientation. By way of anticipation, it might be stated already that the very perspectives of both authors are so radical and so radically different that it may remain doubtful whether we can understand their thoughts as answers to one and the same question.

In Levinas's view, the central and all-mastering position of the modern ego is also retained in Heidegger's analysis of *Dasein,* notwithstanding its profound transformation of any philosophy of consciousness. Even if it is true that the fundamental "passivity" of *Befindlichkeit,* mortality, and contingency is stressed and that the initiative of discovery and truth is more and more attributed by Heidegger to Being itself, the subject of truth acceptance and "letting-be" is still the center of a panoramic universe, an open space well protected against the invasions of other humans, other histories, or God. If gods exist, they are there for men. Other humans are mentioned only as companions within anonymous communities, not as disturbing forces that rob me of my central place.

Heidegger's radicalization of phenomenology has established the domination of the most radical and original of all intentions: the essence of the human being-there is transcendence toward the enlightening clearing of Being, to which all phenomena owe their truth. From their "beginning," "always already" (*je schon*), all beings are caught in the fundamental understanding of a subject that, thereby, has "always already" been familiar to them. According to Levinas, Heidegger's insistence on this prepredicative familiarity is a new version of Plato's interpretation of knowledge as remembrance and of Hegel's claim that the core of all empirical givenness can be deduced from self-evident principles.[40]

Besides the rather abstract considerations just summarized, Levinas's oeuvre contains passages in which he attacks certain analyses of Heidegger from a strictly phenomenological point of view. Levinas understands Heidegger's attempt to think Being in the light of the expression *es gibt* (the normal German equivalent of the English "there is" and the French *"il y a"*) as the celebration of a profound generosity by which Being would bestow light, freedom, truth, and splendor to all beings. The *il y a* does not, however, strike Levinas as particularly generous but rather as an indeterminate, shapeless, colorless, chaotic, and dangerous "rumbling and rustling." The confrontation with its anonymous forces generates neither light nor freedom but rather terror as a loss of selfhood. Immersion in the lawless chaos of "there is" would be equivalent to the absorption by a depersonalizing realm of pure materiality. With regard to this "Being," the first task and desire is to escape or "evade" it (cf. "On Evasion"). The source of true light, meaning, and truth can only be found in something "other" than (this) Being.[41]

In his preface to the 1978 edition of *De l'existence à l'existant*, Levinas singled out the description of the "there is," as presented in its first edition of 1946, as a portion of his former thought that he still defends.[42] Without denying it, he described the essence of Being in *Autrement qu'être* as an *"interesse"* or "interestedness" ruling all beings and connecting them together by a reciprocally interested self-interest. Positing every being as a center for itself, it is in the "act of being," characterized by Spinoza as a *conatus essendi*, that all beings participate in one community of self-preservation. Being as universal interestedness makes all beings,

---

40 Cf. T. Sheehan, "Excess, Recess, Access," *Tijdschrift voor Filosofie* 41 (1979): 635.

41 The description of the *"il y a"* was the prepublished part of Levinas's first thematic book, *De l'existence à l'existant* (1947). However, the opposition to Heidegger's "description" of Being was already present in "De l'évasion," of 1935–36.

42 He alludes to it also in *TI* 116, 117, 165–66; cf. 132–34.

and especially the living ones, mutually dependent. Their needs relate them to one another and create an "economic" system of mutual satisfaction as well as a political network of resistance, tension, war, and peace for the sake of satisfaction. Ruled by universal interest, human history is an alternation of war and peace on the basis of needs.

| Otherness

The preceding pages have argued that if all knowledge presupposes the experience of something that can be neither given nor wholly integrated by consciousness as such, then there must be something other than Being. Against the thesis that all truths and values can ultimately be reduced to the transcendental activity of an autonomous subject, Levinas insists forcefully on the irreducible moments of heteronomy. Instead of seeing all realities as unfolding or surrounding elements of one basic and central instance called "the Same," which realizes itself by appropriating them, the irreducibility of all Otherness must be recognized. This recognition supplants the overt or hidden monism of ontology by a pluralism whose basic ground model is the relation of the Same (le Même) and the Other (l'Autre).

The otherness of the Other is concretized in the face of another human. The proof for Levinas's basic "principle" lies in the most ordinary, simple, and everyday fact of another facing me. I *can* see another as someone I need in order to realize certain wants of mine. She or he is then a useful or enjoyable part of my world, with a specific role and function. We all belong to different communities, in which we function more or less well on the basis of reciprocal needs. I *can* also observe another from an aesthetic perspective, for example, by looking at the color of her eyes, the proportions of his face, and so on. But none of these ways of perception allows the otherness of the other to reveal itself. All aspects manifested by a phenomenological description that starts from these perspectives are immediately integrated by my self-centered, interested, and dominating consciousness. These ways of looking at them transform the phenomena into moments of my material or spiritual property. The sort of phenomenology based on these and similar observations is a form of *egology*.

Another comes to the fore *as other* if and only if his or her "appearance" breaks, pierces, destroys the horizon of my egocentric monism, that is, when the other's invasion of my world destroys the empire in which all phenomena are, from the outset, a priori, condemned to function as moments of my universe. The other's face (i.e., any other's facing me) or the other's speech (i.e., any other's speaking to me) interrupts and disturbs the order of my, ego's, world; it makes a hole in it by disarraying my arrangements without ever permitting me to restore the previous order. For even if I kill the other or chase the other away in order to be safe from the intrusion, nothing will ever be the same as before.

When Levinas meditates on the significance of the face, he does not describe the complex figure that could be portrayed by a picture or painting; rather, he tries to make us "experience" or "realize" what we see, feel, "know" when another, by looking at me, "touches" me: *autrui me vise;* the other's visage looks at me, "regards" me. Similarly, the word "language," often used in this context, evokes the speech addressed to me by some living man or woman and not the linguistic structures or anonymous meanings that can be studied objectively or practiced by a style-conscious author. *Autrui me parle:* primordially, it is not important *what* is said; even if the words are nonsensical, there is still their being addressed. Neither is it relevant *who* speaks to me; any other is the revelation of *the* Other, and peculiar features deserving special attention would only lead me away from the "absolute otherness" that is at stake. In order to concentrate on the other's otherness, Levinas often stresses the *nakedness* of the other's face: if I am touched, if I am conscious of being concerned, it is not because of the other's beauty, talents, performances, roles, or functions but only by the other's (human) otherness.

As disrupting the horizon of my egological—and thus, onto-logical—ways of handling and seeing the world, the others resist a description that would present them as a particular sort of phenomenon among other phenomena within a universal order of beings. Since they "show" and "present" precisely those realities that do not fit into the universal openness of consciousness, they cannot be seized by the usual categories and models of phenomenology. The other transcends the limits of (self-)consciousness and its horizon; the look and the voice that surprise me are "too much" for my capacity of assimilation. In this sense, the other comes toward me as a total stranger and from a dimension that surpasses me. The otherness of the other reveals a dimension of "height" (*hauteur*): he / she comes "from on high."

Husserl's theory of intentionality, based on an adequate and symmetric correlation between noesis and noema, no longer fits. A forgotten element of Descartes's analysis of consciousness, however, offers a formal structure much closer to the relation meant by Levinas. According to Descartes's third *Metaphysical Meditation,* all human consciousness contains not only and not primarily the idea of itself but also and preceedingly the irreducible "idea of the infinite," that is, an immediate and a priori given relation of the conscious subject to a reality that can neither be constituted nor embraced by this subject. This means that the cogito from the outset is structured by a bipolarity other than the bipolarity of the noetico-noematic relation of phenomenology, in which an idea and its *ideatum* fit one another adequately. Descartes still knew (as all great metaphysicians before him) that consciousness "thinks more than [or beyond] that which it can think." The infinite is different from any noema or *cogitatum,* for it essentially surpasses our capacity for conception and embracing. Although Descartes identifies "the infinite" with "God" (i.e., the God of the traditional, late scholastic philosophy), we can consider the formal structure he discovers to be the structure of my relation to the other in the form of another human being. When I am confronted with another, I experience myself as an instance that tries to appropriate the world by labor, language, and experience, whereas this other instance does not permit me to monopolize the world because the Other's greatness does not fit into any enclosure—not even that of theoretical comprehension. This resistance to all integration is not founded on the other's *will; before* any possibility of choice and *before* all psychological considerations, the mere fact of another's *existence* is a "surplus" that cannot be reduced to becoming a part or moment of the Same. The Other cannot be captured or grasped and is therefore, in the strictest sense of the word, incomprehensible.

In all his works, Levinas has endeavored to show that the (human) other radically differs from all other beings in the world. The other's coming to the fore cannot be seen as a variation of the general way of appearance by which all other beings are phenomenal. This is the reason why Levinas reserves the word "phenomenon" for realities that fit into the totality of beings ruled by egological understanding. Since the other cannot become a moment of such a totality, it is not a phenomenon but rather an *"enigma"* not to be defined in phenomenological terms. If visibility, in a broad and metaphorical sense, is a feature of every being that can become a phenomenon, Levinas may even call the other "invisible."[43]

The way the other imposes its enigmatic irreducibility and nonrelativity or absoluteness is by means of a command and a prohibition: You are not allowed to kill me; you must accord me a place under the sun and everything that is necessary to live a truly human life. This demands not only the omission of criminal behavior but simultaneously a positive dedication: the other's facing me makes me responsible for him / her, and this responsibility has no limits.

We meet here with an exceptional or extraordinary *fact*: a fact that is at once and necessarily a *command* and a *norm*. By seeing another looking at me, or by hearing a voice, I "know" myself to be *obliged*. The scission between factuality (*be*) and normativity (*ought*)—a scission many philosophers since Hume have believed in—has not yet had the time to emerge here. The immediate experience of another's emergence contains the root of all possible ethics as well as the source from which all insights of theoretical philosophy should start. The other's existence as such reveals to me the basis and the primary sense of my obligations.

| The Other and I

The abstract structure that was opposed to the tautology of egocentric monism has now been concretized into a relation between the selfhood of an ego and the otherness of the other person who comes toward this ego. This relation posits a certain connection, still to be qualified, and a separation. The latter is necessary in order to avoid the consequence that the independence and difference of both the other and me are drowned in a fusion. The connection lies in the fact that the other's emergence answers the deepest desire motivating me. This *desire* differs radically from all forms of *need*. A need can be satisfied. The radical human desire is, however, too "deep" or "great" to be fulfilled; it wants the absolute and infinite, which does not fit into the "comprehension" and capacity of the desiring subject. The answer given by the absolute in the form of the "invisible" other is not a species of satisfaction but rather an infinite task: the task of my responsibility toward everybody I shall meet.

---

43 Cf., e.g., *TI* 4.

To endure this responsibility, I must, however, be someone: an independent being with an initiative and a concrete existence of its own. What are the conditions for this independence? In the unfolding of his answer to this question, Levinas proceeds like an accomplished phenomenologist. He analyzes thoroughly the intentions through which the I constitutes itself as an independent subject or "self." In doing so, he criticizes the Heideggerian analyses of *Dasein's* being-in-the-world as found in *Sein und Zeit*. Human selfhood is due to a specific way of commerce with the surrounding reality: to be an ego means to rise out of the elements and dominate them from an independent perspective, for example by eating or drinking. The character of this commerce is not primarily utilitarian; indeed, the world is not primarily a context of useful or instrumental tools and references but rather an enjoyable place in which we live to enjoy the pleasures it offers. We stand on the earth and walk from place to place; we bathe in water, air, and light. Food and drink are not primarily sought out of rational considerations but because they are good, that is, pleasurable. If we did not establish a home in which to dwell, we would be lost and without orientation. Only a home—which fits no better than food and beverage into Heidegger's category of the "ready-at-hand"—enables us to dedicate ourselves to labor and to produce works. This would not be possible were there not a certain distance between the material reality and the subject enjoying it and therewith a possibility of objectification. This objectification is made explicit and thematized in the scientific consideration of the reality from and on which we live.

The description of "being in the world," as given in *Totality and Infinity*, has features of an earthly paradise. To love and to enjoy by eating, drinking, being at home, etc, are activities that have not drawn much attention from Western philosophers. By way of his phenomenology of terrestrial existence in light of an all-embracing hedonism, Levinas shows that our search for happiness is not bad at all but rather a necessary condition of the possibility of the self-possession through which the I acquires its autonomous substantiality. In this still-solitary dimension, the law of life is: Enjoy life as much as possible.

Appropriation, integration, and assimilation are constitutive and thus necessary elements of the realization of human individuality. It would be possible to systematize Levinas's descriptions of this existential dimension and to range all the aspects thus revealed as organized elements of an ontological hierarchy, but such an enterprise is not the purpose of his analytical style. For instance, it is not immediately clear from his different texts how exactly the bathing in the elements of light, water, and air relates to our immersion in the "there is" (*il y a*). After opening up new paths, Levinas attempts again and again to determine how he can hold them open and prolong or adjust them. He also asks how different paths may converge or meet, but his goal is not the full description of a complete map wherein all ways and crossings have received their places and proportions. Although certain sorts of totality are good and necessary, Levinas is much more concerned about the relevance of the Other's disruption of all horizons than about the systematic construction of wholes.

Through his analyses of a paradiselike existence, Levinas legitimizes the egocentrism that is at the heart of all forms of hedonism. The enjoyment of a corporeal and terrestrial existence constitutes an ego: the I establishes itself as a self by the absorption of elements, things, and events or by submitting them to the I's government. Without this egocentrism, there would be no relationship to other persons because the encounter of unfree, dependent beings can result only in a fusion or confusion. To the extent that the world of dwelling, eating, and drinking, sleeping, labor, and so on, satisfies the needs of the ego and confirms its position of ruler and owner, it can be called, in a broad sense of the word, the world of "economy." The law (*nomos*) by which this dimension is ruled is the law of being at home in the world as one's own home (*oikos*).

A human being is, however, more than a cluster of needs. Desire points beyond the horizon of "economy." That is why the legitimization of egocentric hedonism is not absolute but relative. If it does not submit itself to a higher law, it loses its innocence. The consciousness of an ego protecting itself against all non-"economical" realities is a bad conscience (*mauvaise conscience*).

The encounter with another reveals the supreme law: my selfhood must bow before the absoluteness revealed by another's look or speech. My home, my food and beverage, my labor, and all my possessions of the earth that I enjoy receive their definitive meaning by being put into the service of another who, by her unchosen "height," makes me responsible. All commandments together form one single order: the other makes me accountable for his life. I must feed my body and arrange my house in order to receive the foreigner knocking at my door; if I possess a home, it is not for me alone. Expressions such as "After you" or "Make yourself at home" say quite well that the person who enters is respected as Other. "Here I am" does not, then, signify that I am the most important being of the world but, on the contrary, that I am at your disposal. The French "*me voici*" expresses it even better by putting the "I" in the oblique form. Indeed, the entering of another in "my" world produces suffering for the I that has abandoned itself to hedonism: the claims implied in the Other's existence put limits on my right to satisfy myself; the limits are so exorbitant that they even threaten to reduce my claims to zero. Insofar as I have not yet awakened from the dream of my paradiselike innocence, the Other awakens, accuses, and judges me.

The absoluteness revealed by the other's visage causes an earthquake in my existence. The justification of my nestling in the world—and the appropriation, labor, and consumption by which it is accompanied—does not lie in the necessity of my satisfactions but in the dedication to others that thereby becomes possible. To realize my responsibility for the Other, I myself must be free and independent; but the sense of my selfhood is my being-for-the-Other. The law before which the economical existence must bow is not primarily the autonomy of my own reasonability; neither is it the voice of Being that I should hear and obey; nor is it a range of prescriptions that would have descended from heaven; it is the needs of the Other who, as a foreigner, disrupts my being at home with myself.

| The-One-for-the-Other

From the perspective of the "metaphysical" relation, which has thus replaced the foundation (*archè*) or the principle (*primum principium*) sought by philosophy from its Greek beginning, Levinas has developed a very original interpretation of human existence and, in the first place, of the human subject, which since Descartes has been primarily understood as an *ego* or an I. In contrast with those French philosophers who resolutely abolished human subjectivity and autonomy without wondering whether the traditional way of problematizing them perhaps should not be profoundly transformed, Levinas tries to show that the human self (*le soi* or *le moi*) has a structure other than the one that was presupposed by the tradition.

Oriented by the desire that directs me to the Other, and thus by the Other that I cannot assimilate, I am a human body of flesh and blood, simultaneously independent and pertaining to the Other. Only on the basis of this fact—but not as the most basic truth—can a human being be defined as a "living being that is reasonable" or as a "unity of body and spiritual soul." The whole of my concrete—corporeal, sensible, kinetic, emotional, contemplative, striving—existence is determined by my orientation toward the Other: I am demanded, disposed, obsessed, and inspired. As a partial elaboration of this thesis, *Totality and Infinity* and *Otherwise Than Being* offer extensive and refined analyses of human corporeality and sensibility not contaminated by any dualism. From the outset, being human is a concrete and physical sensitivity to the claims revealed by the Other, a being-delivered to the Other and a substitute. Since the fact of others' existence makes me infinitely responsible, I am a hostage even before I may know it. The accusative of the accusation in which I find myself when I try to live for myself alone reveals itself in the unrest of a bad conscience. If I open myself to the Other's speech, the meaning of that accusative changes, although I must continue to plead guilty because I will never finish performing my endless obligation. As substitute and hostage, I am no longer master of the situation but vulnerable and possibly persecuted.

No more than the body is "the spirit" a constitutive part of a composition called "man." Corporeality, to have giving hands and a consoling mouth, is itself the concrete way of being human, that is, of being-for-the-Other; and spirit is nothing other than the inspiration due to which corporeal existence has a meaning.

The consequences that this overcoming of dualism has for philosophical anthropology, and especially for a philosophy of the senses and feelings, are not yet fully seen. In this point, too, a certain affinity with Heidegger is undeniable, although the latter did not give much attention to the simplest aspects of everyday life, such as eating and drinking. A great difference lies, however, in the fact that Levinas insists on the primordially moral meaning of human life, whereas Heidegger concentrates on the contemplative and poetic aspects.

| Equality and Asymmetry

A first, rather obvious objection raised by readers and nonreaders of Levinas in various forms says: If it is true that the existence of another human being obliges me and makes me infinitely responsible, this thesis is also valid for everyone other than me;

everybody is an I for whom I and all other humans are others. All human beings are therefore equally and reciprocally obliged, and everybody is master and servant at the same time.

This objection is formulated from a perspective that places itself outside or above the relation of the other(s) and me; it considers all others and me as similar cases of one and the same species or genus of beings: both (or all of us) are human beings, who, as humans, appear to one another (and to all people) as commanding and demanding beings. It is, indeed, possible—it is even inevitable—that we treat the relation between you and me as a singular case of the universal concept "interhuman relationship" and that we look at human individuals as singularizations of a universal "essence": being human.

All the works of Levinas testify to this possibility, which is a necessity. By thematizing all here-and-now-concrete realities, the language of reflective discourse transforms them into single cases of general possibilities. Not always, however, does the content of such a discourse—its "Said" (le dit)—adequately render what it wants to say. What Levinas tries most of all to express in the "Said" of his writings is the unicity of a unique experience that cannot be universalized: I—not an other ego, but I myself, named so and so, born there and then, having lived until now this life story in connection with these and those relations, friends, etc, who here-and-now, in these particular and contingent situations—find myself confronted with, and thereby occupied, demanded, and obsessed by, this Other here-and-now. But is this sentence itself not a statement that can be applied to all egos, among which I am only one case of "ego-ness"? Indeed, I should have written: "I, Adriaan Peperzak, born 3 July 1929 in Malang" and so on by way of a summary pointing at the unrepeatable features of one unique life. But are there unique features? And if I write such a phrase—not by way of promise, contract, or vow but in a philosophical treatise on ethics (which might be an ethics in the situational style)—have I not already betrayed the intention of saying something unique? By using such a phrase as an example, I state through it a general truth valid for any ego. What I say in recognizing my being-for-you and your having rights on me is thematized and thereby converted into a universal truth as soon as I write down "I," "here," "now," "thus," "am obliged," "you," etc.

When we read Levinas's writing about the unicity of a singular Other or a singular I that cannot be universalized, we understand what he wants to express, but at the same time we are aware of the abyss separating the Said, which sounds like a universal truth, from the experience of Levinas's discovering himself as the one who is totally and uniquely responsible for a determinate Other, who also, but in a different way (as obliging Levinas), is unique. The generalizing language of the thematizing discourse that has become the language of philosophy is not able to express the uniqueness of such a unique experience. Levinas calls this uniqueness "election." I have been chosen, neither by myself nor by another's will or decision but by some thing or some no-thing that is present through the Other who shows me his/her face. I have been chosen to be responsible for anybody whom I shall meet. I cannot refuse this election, for it has appointed me as an irreplaceable servant who cannot put this burden on others. The Other's existence reveals to me the uniqueness of a task that constitutes the meaning of my life. Only through reflection—and not by way of experience—do I discover that every human being experiences the same responsibility as I do and that I, too, impose an infinite responsibility on each one of them. The discovery of our similarity in this respect— and therewith of a fundamental equality between myself and all other people—is the fruit of a reflective comparison; it is not simultaneous with, but comes after, the revelation of a more original *asymmetry*. This original asymmetry should not be obscured or forgotten by concentration on the secondary truth of our equality and its realm in which I myself, like all other people, am a replaceable instance of one universal "being-human" (cf. Kant's *Menschheit*).

An answer by which Levinas has tried more than once to cope with the objection exposed above runs thus: "It is not I, but the other, who should state and recognize his/her infinite responsibility toward me." This answer confronts us with several difficulties. For now it may suffice, however, to stress the core of the issue. This lies in the difference between, on the one hand, the recognition in the first person of my responsibility—I and only I am responsible for any other—and the universal imperative, on the other hand, formulated from an Archimedean point of view unengaged in the situation, the body, and the time in which I, here and now, without choosing them, find myself involved. The radical standpoint that I can neither abolish nor deny (although I can forget, ignore, or neglect it) is I myself *as* claimed and taken into hostage by the Other with whom I, quite contingently, happen to meet. I discover myself as radically different from any other, namely as a *"me"* in the oblique, subjected to and unable to escape from my being regarded, touched, and disposed of by my encounters.

The "passivity" involved in this structure is opposed to a way of being that could be characterized as an autonomous initiative or self-projection. My speaking, for example, is not primarily a magisterial discourse in which I expose my themes from an independent perspective; on the contrary, it is a speech that goes from me to an interlocutor without permitting me to have an overview of our relation and my speech; it is an "apo-logy." In addressing myself to another, I cannot detach myself from this address and orientation *from* me *to* this other in which I am engaged. I am not capable of leaving behind or overcoming my finite and obliged selfhood by a transcendental stepping back nor by a sublation (*Aufhebung*) that would establish me as a master of myself and the whole situation of my involvement.

In *Otherwise Than Being*, Levinas insists on the inner coherence between, on the one hand, the fundamental passivity at the bottom of substitution and suffering for another and, on the other hand, the Saying (*le dire*) that precedes and can never coincide with any Said (*le dit*). In complete distinction from those who are inclined to see language as an anonymous power not only ruling but also producing all writings and speeches of all (pseudo-)authors, Levinas insists on the absolute irreducibility and incomprehensibility of speaking as such, in which something—someone—comes to the fore "before" its Said is understood. Speaking itself cannot be defined or determined as a content ("said") within the framework of conceptual discourse. It is surely possible to talk to a speaker in order to reach him / her through language, but that by which the other is someone evaporates as soon as my language thematizes the utterance of a speech.

Whereas the *Saying* breaks all the limits of philosophical language, the *Said* belongs to the dimension of things that are objectifiable. Among them are also the technical, the political, and the aesthetic works and performances through which people realize history. The Other, the Self, and Speaking, however, cannot enter the realm of the Sayable because in all their vulnerability and humility they are too originary for a thetic thought that would try to thematize them. And yet we hear them continuously. Before a philosopher submits the Other, herself, or speaking to the categories and structures of her discourse but also in the course of her reflection, there is, behind her back, an "I" that addresses itself through that reflection. Discourse addresses itself to another, presenting certain contents ("Saids") that can be objectified and talked about. The horizon formed by you who listen to me, and by me who speak to you, cannot be surpassed by the horizon of a universe in which you and I are parts or participants only. All linguistic totalities are transcended by, and owe their existence to, the relation of speaking—a relation that escapes from all attempts to reduce speech to an object, a topic, or a theme.

| Intersubjectivity and Society

A second objection often made against Levinas's insistence on the relation of you and me can be stated in the following way: If the existence of one Other already condemns me to an unlimited responsibility and dedication, how, then, can I cope with the fact that I, during my lifetime, am confronted not only with one or a few men, women, and children but with innumerable others? How would I be able to be totally dedicated to all others?

This difficulty, too, presupposes a point of view that is no longer confined to the unique relation of me-here-and-now to this unique other-here-and-now. The objection is therefore a particular version of a fundamental question probably never answered in a satisfactory way: How exactly are face-to-face relations related to collective structures?

Classical social philosophy has always seen people as real or potential parts, role takers, functionaries, or citizens of different sorts of social formations. In developing a theory of society, the philosopher (just like his reader or student) is present twice: once as one of the constitutive elements of the social whole upon which he is reflecting, and a second time as the master of a conceptual game, that is, as an imaginary and theoretical summit from which that social whole is unrolled. If he, for example, stresses the equality of all human beings, he maintains, in addition to his equality as fellow person, the inequality of himself and the others, since he sits at the top, overseeing the human community of which he, with and like all others, is a part. This view does not do justice to the structure of the intersubjective relation described above, in which I am the servant and "subject" of the Other. And yet such a panoramic overview is—for Levinas, too—inevitable and beneficial if limited to a certain dimension. The moral perspective itself, the very relation of intersubjective asymmetry, not only demands an infinite respect for somebody who confronts me as (a) You; it also imposes a general care for all human others whose face and word I cannot perceive personally.

We cannot claim that Levinas has deduced a complete social philosophy from the intersubjective relation he analyzed so often and so well. Neither does one find in his numerous publications an exhaustive treatment of the relations between the intersubjective relation and the categories of social and political life. He does, however, give a number of important indications for the determination of those relations.

Already in "The Ego and the Totality" ("Le moi et la totalité," 1954) Levinas stated that the encounter with the Other cannot limit itself to the intimacy of love because this would exclude all people except my intimate friends from my attention and responsibility. Other others stand beside and behind this other who obliges me here and now through his/her presence. Since the obligation is not attached to a particular feature of this other but only to his/her entrance into my world, all others oblige me as much as this one. In this other's face, I see the virtual presence of all men and women. Since I cannot, however, behave in any concrete way as everybody's servant, the situation makes it necessary for me to gather all others by means of a universal category that allows me to speak about them in general terms.

It is, however, not enough to speak about all humans; we are urged to take measures and to follow rules according to which the concrete dedication of everyone to all others will be realized. This demands a social organization—Levinas often uses here the word "administration"—in which mutual respect and equality of rights are guaranteed by mores and other institutions. At this point, Levinas's thinking converges with the mainstream of modern social philosophy. But the inspiration of his thought and his philosophical legitimation of a just and liberal society find their source exclusively in the original relationship of the-(unique-) one-for-the-(unique-)Other, that is, in the moral "principle" explained above. Administration and politics have their true source in the high esteem of individuals for other individuals. All social tasks are consequences of, and preparations for, the possibility of adequate face-to-face relationships and good conversations. If they are not directed toward this end, collective measures lose their human meaning because they have forgotten or masked real faces and real speech. This forgetfulness is the beginning of tyranny. If the infinite dignity of concrete individuals whom we love has been obscured, the only outcomes are universal war in the name of innumerable conflicting needs, or the dictatorship of an ego who happens to be the handiest of all, or an inhuman system in which war and dictatorship are repressed and outbalanced by other aggressors no less fond of one day becoming dictators in their turn.

| Language and Thought

In rendering some central topics of Levinas's philosophy, I have borrowed many key terms from the tradition of Western ontology, such as *fundament, principle, origin,* and so on. Levinas, too, has used similar terms in his writings. *Totality and Infinity,* for example, abounds in such words as "experience," "being," "phenomena," "absolute," "the infinite," etc. In later works, he tries to avoid, as much as possible, the terminology of ontology and those thoughts that can hardly be separated from it. Due to this attempt, *Otherwise Than Being* has become a book exceptional in its surprising categories and language, and the language of ontology is avoided as much as possible. From the perspective of this later development, Levinas deems his earlier work until and including *Totality and Infinity* to be "still too ontological." Yet there is no radical abyss between the two main books—and we cannot speak of a real "turn"—but rather a difference of degree. In the later writings, ontological language and conceptuality are still irresistible: as long as we philosophize, they confirm their universal domination. And in earlier works, too, we are confronted with "heterology" breaking its way through the armature of ontological and phenomenological "evidences."

In calling the relation to the Other the "principle" or the "fundament" of this philosophy, we connect it with a whole constellation of foundational concepts characteristic of the way in which thought has been practiced since Plato and Aristotle. Western thinking has always been a questioning from the perspective of possible foundation, principle, origins, or grounds. Using the Greek word *archè* (beginning, principle, "ground," or that from which something "starts"), we could characterize that way of thought as an "archeology." A thought that would not follow its patterns and methods could then be called "groundless" or "an-archical." In this sense, Levinas's thought is a philosophy of anarchy.

Levinas's critique of the primacy of foundational thought is part of his attack on the conviction that the reality of human existence could be summarized by reconstructing it as a panoramic totality on the basis of solid and self-evident foundations. The search for foundation—a search that can never stop until it reaches the one and absolute Principle or Ground of all grounds— is an intrinsic moment of the striving for the great Synthesis, which is as wide as reality. That search itself is founded on the idea that thought and reality correspond adequately to each other and ultimately are identical.

| Time

When classical ontology uses such terms as "principle," "origin," "end," "a priori," "precedence," "primary," "before," "first," and so on, it mostly understands them in a nontemporal, "logical," or "ontological" sense. Heidegger has pointed out that the distinction between time and being presupposed in that usage is not at all clear and that we cannot separate the temporal dimension from being by a simple abstraction. Levinas, too, hears in all those terms a reference to temporality. As key concepts in the search for a well-constructed and complete world picture on the basis of a first and last foundation, they enable us to represent the universe as an orderly whole that can be comprehended here and now. Such a representation poses the universe, and the time "in" which it unfolds itself, as a present totality. The past and the future are presented as secondary forms of the present; remembrance and expectation bring them back or reduce them to the presence of a thought that ties all faces of temporality together in a supratemporal, eternal "Now." This Now, then, is immovable because it transcends all mobility by encompassing it within the limits of an imaginary superpresence.

Presence and presencing characterize the time of the overall visions sought by Western ontology. The analyses of the encounter and of ego's subjectivity as summarized earlier showed, however, that we are not able to find one unique absolute origin, archè, or principle. If it is true that I, in the relation to the Other, discover myself from the outset as already "occupied," claimed, and made hostage, then it is impossible to conceive of myself as a true beginning. Before any free choice can be made and before any possibility of a contract or any acceptance of an obligation, I have—"always already"—been chosen, delivered over to the Other. To be an ego is to have been exercising—well or badly— the service that constitutes me as a subject. The meaning of human life has begun and established itself in my doings long before I became aware that there was a question or an obligation. We cannot go back to the time where our subjectivity started to exist; imagination and thought are not able to reach the beginning of "what it is all about."

The attempt to precede our "having-originated-before-we-discovered-it" by postulating the ultimate, that is, the most primordial and absolutely transcendental Ego, is a reflex of systematic ontology. It is refuted by the Other's transcendence, to which my passivity corresponds. Although I neither contracted nor wanted anything—without my consent—I am obliged with regard to the Other. Although I never committed a crime, I am always already in your debt and responsible as well for my *and your* misery as for your failures and guilt. Not being able to be the origin of my responsibilities and obligations—not even by a reflection in the style of Plato's remembrance—I am aware that the past from which I stem is more past than any past that can be recalled to memory: an *immemorable* past.

From the perspective of relation, the dimension of everybody's future appears as threatened by death. Death is not—as Heidegger would have it—the ultimate possibility of existence but an alien power that destroys every possibility of wanting or willing anything. Instead of the possibility of impossibility—which still suggests too much freedom—it is the impossibility of all possibilities. This impossibility receives, however, a positive meaning from the Other's claims which dedicate me to an endless task whose performance costs me my life.

The future of a more just world, for which we cannot give up hoping, has also another time structure than that of a teleological projection in which history is produced as the collective maturation and completion of humanity. Again and again, Levinas insists that time cannot be understood as a continuous extension back and forth from the present because, in a multiplicity of ways, we are surprised and overwhelmed by events that cannot be seen as moments of an intelligible totality. Against the Hegelian interpretation of history, according to which all people, events, and works receive their meaning from their being necessary moments in the self-unfolding of anonymous Reason, Levinas defends the humanism of another, hidden, and invisible history—a history that respects the absoluteness of every other in every here-and-now. The *eschaton* of this secret history is the just world of those who indeed feed and clothe the others before they take care of their own possessions.

| God

The keystone of all systems produced by Western philosophy has always been a being that simultaneously was origin, support, end, and horizon of the existing universe: as ground of all grounds, it existed because of its own essence; autarch and self-sufficient, it did not need other beings but rather made them exist by giving them being. It is certainly not true that this Ultimate and First was simply represented as a highest being or cause; all great metaphysicians have insistently argued that "God" cannot be compared to any being and does not coincide with beingness, either. It is, however, true that the God of medieval and modern philosophy and theology has been marked by the ontological and systematic concerns and horizons of Hellenistic philosophy.

This God is not the God of Levinas. Our language about or to God should be in agreement with the relation of me to the Other, who is the only "place" where God is revealed. Only from this perspective can one approach God prudently and respectfully. Not, however, simply as an enlargement of the human Other; for God is not an other *Autrui,* but still other than the human Other. Of course, God is also no thing and, least of all, an anonymous "essence." The strange ways by which this enigma touches us via the human Other is the reason why our attempts to talk about God are necessarily full of uncertainty and guessing, unable as we are to capture God by thetic and dogmatic discourse. By following certain suggestions, philosophical thinking can try to name God as the One who has left a trace behind in the Other who knocks at my door. Is he not the one who chose me before any engagement on my part and ordered me to welcome the unexpected visitor as guest? The immemorial past from which I stem suggests that the One who placed me on my way as one-for-the-Other has always already passed away, leaving me to my responsibility. Since God is essentially the One who has passed, "He" has never been present. If we get in touch with "Him," it will be only his back of which we receive an inkling. God has always already escaped, not only from every form of phenomenological experience and description but also from all ways of evoking the human Other.

To indicate the incomprehensible character of the great enigma that is neither a thing or you or being, nor a big or small Neuter, Levinas uses the neologism "illeity," formed on the Latin or French form for "he" (*ille, il*). That responsibility and justice exist is due to "him," but the unnamable can neither present himself in our time nor be represented as a Presence in another, supernatural, or heavenly world outside the real one. As always already passed away, God is an abyss, not a ground (*archè*), a foundation, a support, or a substance but "he" who left a trace in *an*archical responsibility. This, and not the happiness of a total satisfaction, is the way in which the Good reveals itself on earth.

∎ Method

The difficulties of Levinas's enterprise are great. The two main problems it must try to overcome seem to be the following. Rather than being two different problems, they are two sides of one central difficulty.

1. The revolution by which the constellation of the philosophical tradition undergoes a radical transformation or even a "destruction" cannot escape from the necessity of itself using the traditional terminology and conceptuality.

2. The unfolding of the new departure also needs the old perspectives, language, and logic because of their own relative truth, which should neither be abolished nor forgotten. They must, however, receive a new function and meaning from the new (and very old) perspective revealed by the Infinite. Thus, Levinas's oeuvre develops—as does Heidegger's oeuvre—by an ongoing critique and retrieval of the past, which must be remembered and transformed in order to understand the meaning of the new.

All the descriptions of the Other, the I, and the relation between the Other and me, all terms for unicity, singularity of the here-and-now, etc., are *general* terms one cannot protect against universalization. So, too, the attempt to replace the typical logic and language of ontology and phenomenology by another logic can never become a full success. All thematizing discourse converts itself, as soon as it has been uttered, in a "Said" that obeys the constraints of a constellation in which objectification, universalization, representation, consciousness, experience, phenomenality, givenness, and presence orient and—at least to a certain extent—dominate its thought. It is not possible to destroy that constellation completely; neither is it possible to eliminate a few of its elements. It is, however, possible—and this is what Levinas tries to do—to speak and to write in such a way that our Said itself eases our transcending it toward another invisible and incomprehensible dimension from the perspective of which the meaning of all the Said is revealed to be relative only. What we proffer about otherness, the self, the metaphysical relation, God, and time changes immediately in a moment of systematic patterns and structures, betraying thus the truth at which we aimed. This justifies a certain skepticism with regard to all philosophies. However, we can take the time to deny or "unsay" (*dédire*) what we just said (*le dit*)—a piece of ontology produced by our saying (*le dire*)—and be clearly aware that our denial, in its turn, will immediately change into a Said, which must be criticized again. If thinking means to do justice to "reality as it (really, truly) is," it is an interminable work of self-correction, a diachronical saying, unsaying, saying again, leaving all syntheses behind in a succession of dictions and contradictions without end.

A Commentary on "Philosophy and the Idea of the Infinite"

Having taught several courses on the thought of Emmanuel Levinas as expressed in *Totality and Infinity* and *Otherwise Than Being or Beyond Essence,* I have found no better introduction to the reading of these books, especially the first, than the 1957 article "Philosophy and the Idea of the Infinite."[1] Not only does this essay show clearly how Levinas's works sprang from a profound meditation on the very roots of Western philosophy; it also indicates the path by which his thought separates itself from the Husserlian and Heideggerian versions of phenomenology, to which he is nonetheless heavily indebted. In comparing this article with *Totality and Infinity,* one gets the strong impression that it was the seed from which Levinas developed the book. Indeed, it is notable that the argument of the essay follows in almost all points the argument of the summary of *Totality and Infinity,* which Levinas, after defending his book as a dissertation for his *doctorat d'Etat,* published in the *Annales de l'Université de Paris.*[2] The one notable difference is that the essay deals with the face (section 4) before speaking of desire (section 5), while *Totality and Infinity* and its summary reverse this order. The purpose of the running commentary on "Philosophy and the Idea of the Infinite" that follows here is primarily didactic and introductory: through a series of notes on the article, the main lines of *Totality and Infinity*'s argument will emerge, as well as its important connections with the sources of Western thought.

---

1 "La philosophie et l'idée de l'Infini," *Revue de Métaphysique et de Morale* 62 (1957): 241–53, collected in *EDHH* 165–78; *CPP* 47–60.
2 Cf. *Annales* 31 (1961): 385–86.

| Autonomy and Heteronomy

Without indulging in the despair of the skeptics or the cynicism of the sophists, Levinas begins with what could pass for a platitude, were it not the point of departure for all Western philosophical and even cultural undertakings: the passion for truth realizes itself through inquiry. The sciences themselves would lose all nobility if they did not, in their own fashion, inquire after the truth of things.

In calling the philosophical passion *eros,* Levinas refers, at the very beginning of his study, to the father of philosophy. In some way, and beyond Nietzsche's critique, we must "recover Platonism," as the end of the aforementioned summary clearly states.[3]

The idea of truth presents itself as an idea with two faces, both of which have called forth the reflection of thinkers since the beginning of wondering. Truth is looked for and understood, on the one hand, as something that the thinker does not yet know—to find it one must have an *experience,* that is, one must be surprised by an encounter with the unexpected. On the other hand, truth only gives itself to someone who appropriates and integrates it, becoming one with it as if it had always been present in the depths of the soul.

In later texts, Levinas claims that "truth," as the ideal of Western philosophy, already leans too much in the latter direction, that of integration, anamnesis, and freedom, while the former aspect—contact with the most "real" reality—is then characterized as a relation that surpasses *being* and *truth.* "Truth" then is considered to be equivalent to the truth of Being. Even the word "experience," which serves here to indicate the surprising aspect of the discovery of truth,[4] will later be reserved for the world of integration and totalizing autonomy.

---

3 Cf. *Annales* 31 (1961): 386. Cf. also *HAH* 55–56 for a new Platonism as antidote against a world disoriented and "dis-occidentalized."

4 The French expression "vers l'étranger" (*EDHH* 167), synonymous with the immediately following "vers là-bas," has been translated as "toward the stranger" (*CPP* 47). This might, however, hide an aspect that is crucial to Levinas's thought, who again and again insists on the fact that truth comes from the outside, from afar and *abroad. L'étranger* has two meanings and is intentionally ambiguous; it expresses simultaneously the foreign country from which the truth comes to me and the stranger who knocks at my door in order to receive the hospitality of my home.

In *Totality and Infinity,* the word "being" (*être*) is mostly used in a sense close to that of traditional ontology. "Experience" indicates, for the most part, a phenomenological experience, for example, a "concrete moral experience" ($TI24^{17}/53^{20}$); the experience of the infinite is called "experience *par excellence,*" and the Other (*Autrui*) is the correlate of an "absolute experience" ($194^{32}/219^{10}$), but this absolute experience is a "revelation" (*révélation*) in contrast to an "unveiling" (*dévoilement,* a translation of Heidegger's *Enthüllung* [*TI* 37^{22}, 39^4, $43^7/65^{37}$, 67^{12}, 71^7]). Sometimes, however, the universality of experience is disputed, as, for example, when it is contrasted with the relation to the Infinite ($xiii^{33}/25^{20}$; cf. $167^{37}/193^{13}$), where Levinas contrasts "sensible experience" with transcendence, or when it is distinguished from sensibility as enjoyment ($110^{26}/137^{12}$). In *Totality and Infinity,* the word "truth" is used in two different senses. In many places, it indicates the goal of philosophy as the search for truth (31–35, 54–56, $59^{35}/60$–64, 82–84, 87^{24}), the absolute other of transcendence ($xvii^{27}/29^{15}$), truth as the revelation beyond the unveiling of being (31^{37}, $76^{14}/60^{25}$, 103^3) and above the judgment of history ($225^{15}/247^{13}$). In other places in the same book, truth is contrasted with the Good ($xii^{27}/24^{18}$) or with the moral dimension preceding it (55^{31-39}, 75^{11}, 175^{18}, 177^1, 195^{33}, $196^{22-26}/83^{30-38}$, 101^{31}, 201^1, 202^{19}, 220^{25}, 221^{19-23}).

The book *Otherwise Than Being or Beyond Essence* in its entirety, from its double title to the last page, sets out to show that the language of ontology—in which being and essence, experience, phenomenality, showing (*monstration*), the present, and truth occupy center stage—is a secondary language dependent on a Saying (*Dire*) that precedes it, pierces it, and transcends it (cf. Levinas's own statement at the end of his autobiographical "Signature": "After *Totality and Infinity* it has become possible to present this relation with the Infinite as irreducible to 'thematization.'. . . The ontological language still used in *Totality and Infinity* . . . is thereafter avoided. And the analyses themselves do not refer to the *experience* in which a subject always thematizes what it equals, but to the *transcendence* in which it is responsible for that which its intentions do not encompass" (*DL* 379/"Signature," 188).

In Husserlian language, the beginning of the article can be rendered in the following manner: the two aspects of truth, which together constitute the "noema" of philosophical intentionality, are linked to two aspects of inquiry (*recherche*). The relation between "noesis" and "noema" is thought by Husserl to be a perfect correspondence between an element of consciousness and an element of phenomenal givenness. However, Levinas immediately criticizes several presuppositions of phenomenology and, notably, Husserl's theory of intentionality. Even the word "phenomenon" loses its universal significance, ceding the primary place to something other than that which shows itself "in flesh and bone." In *Totality and Infinity,* for example, the author rejects intentionality's universal claim while preserving the primordial importance of "experience."[5] "Phenomenon," which is opposed to revelation and epiphany, is criticized together with "unveiling" as a nonultimate reality.[6]

The foreignness and the alterity essential to the surprise element of all genuine experience are evoked with an expression used by Vladimir Jankélévitch in a few Plotinian pages of his book *First Philosophy,* the subtitle of which is *Introduction to a Philosophy of the Almost.*[7] The "absolute otherness"[8] that characterizes the Plotinian One separated from everything else is understood by Levinas before all else as something that surpasses all "nature." Because "nature" since Aristotle has been the "object" treated by "physics," one could also say that the "absolutely other" is something "beyond" the physical, and so something "meta-physical." Thus, we read on the third page of *Totality and Infinity* that "metaphysical desire tends towards something totally other," "towards the absolutely other," while "Transcendence and Height" refers to "Kierkegaard's entirely other."[9]

That which we experience surpasses nature in two ways. First, in that it does not belong, as a moment already known or anticipated (if only by a Heideggerian *Vorverständnis* or "precomprehension"), to the being of someone who has the experience. That which is given in experience surpasses that which is natural to us; it cannot be extracted like a part of something we possess from birth. In this, empiricism will always win out against the defenders of innate ideas.

Experience also leads us beyond the whole of nature, whether this is understood in the sense of the Aristotelian *physis,* which Heidegger tried to reconstitute through his

---

5 *TI* xv[12-15], xvi n. 1, xvii[5-9,22], 62[20-21], 81, 94–95/27[7-10], 28 n. 2, 28[25-30], 89[39-90,2], 109, 122.

6 *TI* xvi[6-9], 157[2], 187[25-26], 190[12-14]/27[38]–28[1], 181[34], 212[19-21], 215[5-7].

7 V. Jankélévitch, *Philosophie première: Introduction à une philosophie du presque* (Paris: P.U.F., 1954).

8 Cf. Jankélévitch, 120–22.

9 Cf. TH 94 and, for example, S. Kierkegaard, *Philosophical Fragments by Johannes Climacus,* trans. Howard V. and Edna H. Hong (Princeton, N.J.: Princeton University Press, 1985), 45.

commentaries,[10] or in the Spinozian sense, where it is equivalent to the entire universe. For in both instances, nature cannot really resist the human wish to dominate or integrate it as a medium, an instrument, or an extension of human existence. The second chapter of *Totality and Infinity* describes the manner in which nature is made to submit by the ego through consumption, dwelling, manipulation, work, and technology, as well as through aesthetic contemplation. If it is true that we are not strong enough to dominate nature effectively, knowledge (*connaissance*) still manages to accomplish its goal: the natural universe bends and is delivered to the power of the human gaze and to the theory in which a human perspective is developed through operations of the intellect. The material resistances that nature opposes to human attempts at mastering it provide us the same service: one can use them to construct lodgings where one feels "at home" (*chez soi* or, as Hegel puts it, *zu Hause in der Welt*) and to convert them into energy for replacing human labor in submission to our plans.

With regard to Levinas's discussion of Heidegger's "ontology," which will be made more explicit in section 2, it is important to notice the close affinity, or even the identity, between "nature," "*physis*," and "Being" (*être*) as suggested here. A text in which they are identified even more clearly is the paper delivered at the seventeenth World Congress of Philosophy, "Détermination philosophique de l'idée de culture," printed in *Philosophie et Culture. Philosophy and Culture,* Montréal 1986, 75–76.

The first characteristic of the discovery of the true—the fact that truth is in some way "super-natural" (*sur-naturelle*), i.e., meta-physical—is followed by a determination borrowed from Plato; the true is not only *other* than she/he who has an experience of it and *exterior* to the nature wherein the human subject has settled but it is also *more* than exterior, it is "over there" (*là-bas*) and "up there." Indeed, the alterity and foreignness of the true are distinguished by a special quality that must be described as a type of highness (*hauteur*)[11] and

---

10 Cf. Heidegger, "Vom Wesen und Begriff der Φύσις: Aristoteles, Physik B,1" ("On the Essence and Concept of Physis in Aristotle's Physics B1"), in *Wegmarken,* GA 9:239–301.

11 *Hauteur* should be rendered, in everyday language, as "height." The slightly antiquated and solemn "highness" has been used here in order to express the venerable character of the Other and to maintain the connection with the frequently used adjective

divinity. Absolute otherness comes to me and surprises me from on high.

At this point, a thorough reading of the pages where Plato refers to the region of truth and true being can show how their retrieval by Levinas transforms them into a vision that, notwithstanding profound differences, continues their deepest inspiration. In the *Republic* 484c, Plato shows that political wisdom can only be founded on a movement of the gaze to "over there" (*ekeise*), where the truly true (*to alèthestaton*), that is, pure being, is offered as the grand paradigm of the soul desiring to care for the social realm. According to Plato, that which is over there (*enthade*), the dimension of the ideas or the ideal, finds itself contrasted with the world here below.

In the *Symposium* (211d–212a), the difference between a trivial life (*bios phaulon*) and the life of somebody who enjoys the contemplation of the ideal Beautiful, unmixed and in all its purity, is described as a gaze that directs itself over there (*ekeise blepōn*), which is only possible after a long ascension of different stages comparable to the ascension toward the Good described in the *Republic* VI–VII. That this ascension is not only a difficult voyage requiring an ascetic life but also a very serious and radical "moving" from one place to another (*a metoikèsis*) can be seen most dramatically in the *Phaedo,* where philosophy is presented as a meditation on death and as a journey (*apodèmia*) that leads from here below (*enthende*) toward another land over there (*ekeise*), which is the land of the living gods (117c; cf. 61de and 66bd). The search for truth is an uprooting brought about by the experience of absolute otherness, which will not allow itself to be reduced—neither by a simple empiricist or rationalist logic nor by dialectic—to the world that is familiar to us. All of the movement of Plato's thought in these dialogues proves that for him the "over there" is equivalent to the "up there." That which is revealed to experience as foreign is the ideal, the high, the divine. The search for truth is not uniquely a discovery of the exterior but a transcendence or—as *Totality and Infinity* expresses it—a "transascendence"[12] toward a dimension that commands us, in a certain sense, as superior.

---

haut, "high." Another related term, *là-haut,* could not be rendered with a cognate of "high" and has been translated as "up there"; its literal connection to the notion of highness should still be borne in mind.

12 Cf. *TI* $5^{28}/35^{25}$ and my commentary on pp. 132–34 of this book.

In light of Levinas's later analyses, the Platonic image of a voyage that transports us toward another country must neither be interpreted as a symbol of a transcendence toward a "world" or "heaven of Ideas" beyond our world nor as petition for a new type of netherworld. The elimination of any kind of *Hinterwelt* is taken seriously.[13] However, the circular odyssey of all Greek and modern philosophies is replaced by the uprooting of Abraham, forced to leave the intimacy of his home and his country to go toward an unknown somewhere-else (cf. Genesis 21:1). The conversion required by Plato (*Republic* 515c–e, 518b–519c) must be reinterpreted in line with the alienation of this uprooting; as one becomes different through contact with absolute otherness, one never returns to the exact point of departure.

Thus one sees, in the structure of all true experience, the law of alterity and heteronomy, which can never be reduced to autonomy or the law of the Same; nevertheless, the latter is *also* essential to the search for truth. In choosing the word "metaphysics" to characterize this search, Levinas announces his critique of Heideggerian ontology and of the critique of metaphysics, which is its reverse side. Against the project of the overcoming of metaphysics characterized as onto-theo-logy, Levinas defends the deepest intention of metaphysics while refusing to return to an onto-theo-logy in which the Divine is conceived as a first cause or supreme being. All of this is summarized in the first three sentences that, after the preface, open *Totality and Infinity*.[14]

The second aspect of the way toward truth is determined by the fact that truth gives itself only to the person who appropriates it in total freedom. In the fourth *Meditation*, Descartes brought to light the moment of free will that is part of all true judgments. Of course, it is not necessary to be a Cartesian to recognize the free character of all theory if what one means by freedom is the absence of all exterior constraints and victory over all alienation by the appropriation and possession of all that at first seems astonishing and foreign. As Aristotle expressed it at the beginning of the *Metaphysics*, the project of traditional philosophy wanted, as much as possible, to go beyond the astonishing (*thaumasia*) by a comprehension for which the phenomena show themselves self-evident in their being such as they are. And Plato, in

---

13 Cf. *HAH* 57.
14 "'La vraie vie est absente.' Mais nous sommes au monde. La métaphysique surgit et se maintient dans cet alibi."

explaining all new knowledge as the result of an anamnesis, had already reduced all surprise to a form of memory and interiority.[15] In adhering to the truth as proposed, the searcher is not really shocked, surprised, wounded, or touched by it. The appropriation of the truth reduces it to the immanence of the knower's consciousness. Since Socrates, philosophy has tried to (re)construct and (re)build theoretically the universe of being in the element of lucid intuitions and transparent concepts. The deepest motivation for this project was the wish to be free, at home, in that which at first presented itself as alienation. The roots of Western civilization lie in an attitude that precedes its theory as well as its practice: the human subject affirms itself as a freedom engrossing and reducing to itself all that resists its powers, even if only by the obscurity of its being. Thought's ideal is the integration of everything in the immanence of a total knowing. Freedom and immanence! The reduction of all alterity to the reflexive identity of a supreme consciousness is the ideal of *autonomy*, the legislation of the *Same*.

With the formula "man's conquest of being through history," Levinas alludes to the neo-Hegelian language that, in the 1950s, was the koine of Parisian intellectual circles. With Hegel, one can read the history of humanity as a grand voyage toward the discovery of the auto(de)monstration of the universe of beings. We will see that the formula, with an important but not radical distinction, can also be applied to the thought of Being by which Heidegger attempts to surpass the traditional theory of the "whole of all beings" (*das Ganze des Seienden*). Even in Heidegger's view, the horizon of all understanding is the light of Being illuminating itself within the openness that constitutes human *Dasein.*

The reference to Hegel's philosophy of history passes on to a formula that summarizes the whole of Western philosophy: freedom is *the reduction of all Otherness to the Same* (*la réduction de l'Autre au Même*). Here one should reread the *Sophist* in the light of the epistemological combat between those who defend autonomy and those who defend heteronomy. It is not by chance that Levinas recalls at this point—as he also does at the beginning of *Totality and Infinity*—the dialogue cited by Heidegger on the first page of *Sein und Zeit* to orient the reader toward the question of the meaning of Being (cf. *Sophist* 244a), which is for Heidegger the ultimate and first and, indeed, the unique question of philosophy. Levinas quite agrees that Western philosophy,

---

15 Cf. *Meno* 80d–82e; *Phaedo* 72e ff.; *Phaedrus* 249bc.

since Parmenides, has been a "gigantomachy in relation to being" (*Sophist* 246a, cf. *Sein und Zeit,* beginning of part 1), but
he also makes it understood, alluding to other pages of the same
dialogue, that it is not the conceptual pair of *on* and *me on* but
rather that of *tauton* and *heteron* that is the most radical.[16] By
stressing the fact that the *Same* and the *Other* are "mixed" with
the other "supreme genera" (Being, Resting, Movement) while
remaining, themselves, "without mixture" (*Sophist* 254e), one
could make a case that *they* are the ultimate and absolutely first
categories. For Levinas, as for Heidegger, all of this is concerned
with "first philosophy" or with that which is the most "fundamental." But rather than an ontology or thought of being, first
philosophy should be a thought of the irreducible relation between the other and the same, a relation that cannot be absorbed
in the totality of a supreme being or of universal Being integrating all alterity as a moment of itself.

The questions of *philosophia prima* cannot be separated from
the question of man. The reduction of all phenomena to the Same
is the fact of a subject that denies the alterity of all otherness
as it reveals itself in the subject's experience. The monism of
Parmenides, having survived all attempts at parricide, has
shown its true face in the modern celebration of the human ego.
The project of autoaffirmation, clearly represented by the various
forms of idealism, grounds at one and the same time a theory
of categorical structures of reality and an anthropology where
the I figures as the point of convergence and center of reality.
The ego, conquering being and identifying it with itself through
a history of (re)productive negations, is the source and end of
all that is. Thus Western thought can be characterized as an
"egology" in a sense much more critical than the one in which
Husserl employed the term.[17]

It is important to realize that the freedom which inspires
the "Western project" precedes both theoretical and practical
expressions. Moreover, the search for truth is never limited to
scientific or philosophical activity alone; as Heidegger has shown,
it is a way of being or existing in the verbal and transitive sense
that the words "to be" and "to exist" received in his meditations.

---

16 Cf. also *Timaeus* 35ab and *Theaetetus* 185cd.
17 *EDHH* 168. Cf. Husserl, *Ideen* 2:110; *Erste Philosophie,* 172–73
and 176; *Die Krisis der europäischen Menschheit und die Philosophie,*
258. Levinas quotes from the *Krisis* in the article "M. Buber, G. Marcel
et la philosophie," *Revue Internationale de Philosophie* 32 (1978): 509.

Truth comes to the fore—"*se produit,*" as *Totality and Infinity* puts it—in many ways, among which there are many practical and affective ones. The "level" on which the most radical intention of philosophy should be defined precedes the schism between theory and practice.[18] The diagnosis given is thus one of Greek and Western existence as such.

It may seem rash to undertake the apology of a certain heteronomy against an ideal of autonomy extolled by philosophy from the beginning. Has not the struggle for emancipation against all forms of alienation been at the very heart of the philosophical enterprise, beginning with the Socratic and Platonic struggles against tyranny and the rhetorical violence of the Sophists, against the appearances of truth paraded about by public opinion? In the ninth book of the *Republic,* Plato describes at length the sickness and enslavement of the soul that results from an absolute faith in *doxa.* Levinas cites the words that Valéry puts into the mouth of "Monsieur Teste" (who is a symbol for the thoughts in the Cartesian head or *tête*) with which the character explains the existence of other captive souls: "Only for others are we *beautiful, extraordinary! They* are eaten by the others."[19] Still, we will see that there is another way of "being-for-the-others," a way that neither falls into slavery, nor becomes a tyranny using disguises and other forms of hidden violence.

A soul that abandons itself to opinion and conforms to the thoughts and wishes of "the others" resembles the way of being described by Heidegger in *Sein und Zeit* §27 as the existence of the impersonal everyman with its common sense. A Platonic explication diagnoses this as a function of the difference between the realm of *doxa* here-below and the realm discovered by looking and searching up-there. Levinas adds that abandonment to the domination of public opinion (and all its radio and television apparatus) presupposes that it is possible to lose oneself in a human collectivity, as if an unbridgeable separation did not exist between human individuals. Such a loss of self (*ipséité*) was found in the mythical and magical existence of primitive cultures as described by Lévy-Bruhl.

---

18 Cf. *TI* xvii/25: "The traditional opposition between theory and practice will disappear in light of the metaphysical transcendence by which a relation with the absolutely other, or truth, is established. . . . At the risk of appearing to confuse theory and practice, we will treat both as modes of metaphysical transcendence." Cf. also *TI* 85/113.

19 Valéry, *Œuvres,* Editions de la Pléiade (Paris: Gallimard), 2:20. Cf. also *AE* 85^{13}/*OB* 61^{32}.

As early as his first book, *From Existence to Existent,* and at greater length in the article "Lévy-Bruhl et la philosophie contemporaine,"[20] Levinas had interpreted the participation described by the French ethnologist as a fusion with being's "there is" (*il y a*) wherein one loses all ipseity. In texts dealing more directly with religious topics, found for the most part in *Difficile Liberté,* Levinas contrasts, on the one hand, enthusiasm for a mystical world full of divine elements with, on the other hand, the sober and ethical religion defended by the prophets of Israel against the idols of a magical sacralization. The fusion of the earthly and the divine degrades the latter and deprives humans of their freedom. The background to all philosophies of participation, from Neoplatonism to Louis Lavelle, remains tarnished with a pagan enthusiasm. True religion presupposes a humanity separated from God; their relation is not a mystical union: "The separated being maintains itself in existence all by itself, without participating in the Being from which it is separated" (*TI* 29/58). Without such a separation, there is respect neither for man nor God; it can be called "atheism."

"Faith purged of myths, the monotheist faith itself implies metaphysical atheism. Revelation is discourse; in order to welcome revelation a being apt for this role of interlocutor, a separated being, is required. Atheism conditions a veritable relationship with a true God $\varkappa \alpha \theta$' $\alpha \dot{\upsilon} \tau \acute{o}$."[21]

Levinas's review of Lavelle's philosophy as contained in *Dialectique de l'Eternel Présent* (1920) and *La Présence Totale* (1934) can be found as early as 1934–35 in *Recherches Philosophiques* 4 (1934–35): 392–95. It does not criticize Lavelle's attempt to renew the "ancient and obscure notion" of a "participation in total being ... through recourse to a living experience" and states that a "rehabilitation of presence" is "the only means to break the tragic game of the present" Heideggerian times. Still, this rehabilitation must not be accomplished as a wandering outside of time, toward eternity (394–95). Later, in criticizing Simone Weil and Heidegger, Levinas is, however, much more severe with the idea of "participation."[22]

---

20 *EE* 98–100 (60–61) and *Revue philosophique de la France et de l'Etranger* 147 (1957): 556–59.

21 *TI* $50^8/77^3$. Cf. *TI* 29–31, 49–50, 61, 66, 121, 156, 191/58–60, 77–78, 88–89, 93, 147–48, 181, 216.

22 Cf. *DL* 133–37, 178–88, 299–303. More technical criticism can be found in *TI* 29–30, 32, 52, 61, 66, 91, 155, 169, 193, 207, 269, 231, 293/58–59, 61, 79, 88, 93, 118–19, 180, 195, 217, 231, 293.

Plato and the other great philosophers thought that a truly human existence required a break with "participation." The existence of the individual, "the soul," can only be human if it is separated from God as well as from other human individuals. In the name of the humanity of the human being and of the transcendence brought to light above, the insurmountable distance between "separate souls" must be maintained. It is necessary "to maintain the separation of beings, not to founder in participation against which the philosophy of the Same has the immortal merit to have protested" (*EDHH* 172 / *CPP* 54). Nevertheless, the error of this philosophy was to identify the separate existence with the existence of an egological I (*un Moi égologique*) integrating all beings as subordinate moments of the Same. If we want to do justice to alterity and transcendence, as opposed to the magical and violent cultures our century has seen more than one attempt to regenerate, we do not need a new rooting of philosophy in native soil but a new exodus. We are in the process of uncovering a heteronomy that does not abolish the freedom of the ego but rather provides it with its most authentic meaning.

The Primacy of the Same, or Narcissism

The structure of this section is clear:

1. Paragraphs 1–5 show, through several major examples, how Western thought has been a philosophy of the Same and that its inspiration rests in a fundamental narcissism of an ego which takes itself to be the center and the all.

2. Paragraphs 6 and 7 then pose the decisive critical question: Can this philosophy do justice to the truth of human being? Can humanity as it constitutes itself be recognized in this vision?

3. Paragraphs 8–14 show that Heideggerian thought, no less than classical philosophy, is a celebration of the Same and deserves the same radical criticism.

Narcissism and Western Thought (paragraphs 1–5)

In privileging the Same, philosophy presents itself as autonomous thought: freedom is affirmed as its principle. Is this principle justified, or is its affirmation arbitrary? The response of the moderns would be that the principle is self-evident and that it is justified by the exposition and development of the philosophical autoaffirmation; in ridding itself of all alienation, thinking shows that it can (re)produce all truth starting from its own immanence.

As examples of those elements of the universe that autonomous thought tries to integrate, Levinas names the earth, the sky, nature, things (e.g., tools), and people. To a freedom that wants to appropriate them, all of these elements present themselves like obstacles resisting the design of integration. Nevertheless, even if the ego does not overcome them through the violence of enslavement and possession, it subordinates them by giving them to itself in the self-evidence of their truth. To understand this interpretation of the inspiration that animates the theoretical enterprise as it has been developed in the West, one must take note that Levinas here makes use of Husserlian language in order to characterize the fundamental desire of the entire tradition. If, according to Husserl, truth consists of that which reality gives "in flesh and bone" (*leibhaftige Gegebenheit*), so that the intention of the one who looks for truth is "filled" (*erfüllt*) and "accomplished in the evidence" of the given, we again find at this level of the theory the project of a free subject who reduces all that is other to an element of its own immanence. Consciousness encompasses the universe, and transcendence is the possibility of the absorption of all things. The fact that things can be "comprehended by me"—and here one can already hear an allusion to Heidegger's *Verstehen*, which is translated by Levinas as "*compréhension*"[23]—shows that their resistance is not absolute. Nevertheless, if there are absolutely other beings, this sort of understanding reveals a form of violence, be it in a provisional, postponed, or hidden way.

The second paragraph of this section interprets the history of philosophy from the basic perspective of the Cartesian and idealistic project, which can also be found in the Platonic definition of philosophy. If Plato in the *Sophist* (263e, 264a) calls philosophy a dialogue of the soul with itself, and if he explains the discovery of new truths by the (re)membering of that which already existed in the depths of the soul,[24] truth does not transport the soul toward an outside; its interior dialogue is only a narcissistic form of monologue. All things, and history itself, thus come down to the ideas of an overall consciousness that has no means of transcending itself. The height of narcissism was reached when Hegel deduced, by the logic of the Universal, the very essence

---

23 Cf., e.g., *EDHH* 68.
24 *Meno* 80 d–e, *Theaetetus* 150a–151d, *Phaedo* 72e ff.

and existence of that being which Aristotle had defined as "an animal possessing reason."

The last sentence of the second paragraph refers to the third of Descartes's *Meditations,* where he explains that one cannot be sure that the ideas of exterior things (bodies, angels, animals, and even other men similar to me) are not the products of the "I think," which makes me an incorporeal substance.[25]

"The essence of truth," with which the third paragraph begins, translates the Heideggerian expression *"das Wesen der Wahrheit,"* and it is possible that "the already known" (which it is necessary to discover ... freely in oneself) refers to the "pre-understanding" (*Vorverständnis*) of Being affirmed in *Sein und Zeit.* In this case, Heidegger would here be placed in the same group as Socrates, whose maieutical teaching also presupposes that the subject of the search contains "always already" (*je schon,* as Heidegger likes to say) the knowledge that must be acquired.

The manner in which Descartes explains the power of reason is different from Plato's and Heidegger's explanations because he tries to show, in his fourth *Meditation* (AT, 9:45ff.), that affirmation depends, in the last analysis, on the power of the will; but this theory shows, even more clearly than theirs, that the meaning of truth lies in freedom.

In any case, the project of Western philosophy has excluded the possibility of ego's transcending itself toward a God who would be absolutely other and irreducible to any element or to the whole of the universe. Under the name of God, the philosophers, as did the theologians, built many idols, as for example Logos, *Esse ipsum,* Substance, Nature, or Spirit, but a God neither known or preknown, nor concealed in the unconscious or preconscious memory of conscience, a God who must *reveal* in order to be accepted—such a God is impossible within the traditional framework. Despite appearances, the thinking West was always without religion (that is to say, without any relation to any absolutely Other) and was thus atheistic, as the beginning of section three shows. In giving this diagnosis of philosophical atheism, Levinas is thinking especially of its neo-Hegelian (including Marxian) and Heideggerian versions.

The rejection of all heteronomy excludes not only the alterity of God but also all individual alterity, thus establishing the

---

25 AT (*Œuvres de Descartes,* edited by Ch. Adam and P. Tannery in 11 volumes [Paris: Cerf, 1897–1909]), 9:31. Cf. also the beginning of the fifth *Meditation,* AT, 9:50.

typical anonymity of a philosophy that abolishes the uniqueness inherent to individuals. The thematization of the singular reduces all individuality to being a case or instance of a nameless universal; the individual is recognized only insofar as it illustrates, as an example, the conceptual structures by which it is enclosed. The individual as such does not count and cannot even appear; as Aristotle said, science is not concerned with it.[26]

In the neo-Hegelian climate in which "Philosophy and the Idea of the Infinite" was written, references to *mediation* and *dialectic* were almost obligatory. Levinas sees their secret in the triumph of the universal qua nonindividual, anonymous, and neutral (cf. *TI* 12–14, 60/42–44, 87–88). The cunning of reason consists of capturing the object studied in a logical network, i.e., in the fundamental structure of an a priori "knowledge" that nothing can elude.

The first part of section 2 ends by identifying as the source of this philosophy a possessive and domineering attitude, which is also the secret of Western civilization in its entirety. The quest for wealth, its colonial and imperial capitalism, and the project of a totalitarian theory all manifest a single will to power. If the proposed diagnosis is true, it follows that a proposed redress of the faults committed by our culture could not be brought about by a refinement of the sciences or an extension of emancipations but only by a radical reversal that changes our civilization's fundamental intention.

The Other As the Calling into Question of Freedom (paragraphs 6–7)

It may be that things allow themselves to be treated as elements subordinated to a global and hierarchical system, but do people not somehow resist this? Does their resistance not refute the claims of freedom?

In speaking of human freedom, social philosophers from Hobbes and Rousseau to Hegel and Marx tried to defeat the necessary conflict resulting from a multiplicity of wills by integrating them through contracts into a truer and collective freedom of which they were a part. The idea of freedom as the final

---

26 *Metaphysics* 999a25–b5; cf. the scholastic dictum: *individuum est ineffabile* and what Levinas says in "Le moi et la totalité," 303; *CPP* 36: "the ego is ineffable."

foundation was not shaken by the repetition of wars. Just as a Platonic ascension toward things up-there required a return (*epistrophè*), so the orientation that can justify freedom requires a radical change of human attitude. In turning toward the alterity of the Other, I discover that my freedom is called into question; the Other's appearance reveals the injustice of my monopoly. If, by the shock of this encounter, the I seeking domination discovers itself to be unjust, this discovery is not a quality added to the preliminary existence of an innocent and neutral freedom but rather the beginning of a new way of existing and being conscious of myself and the world. The original state is not that of an ego enjoying its isolation before it would meet others; from the beginning, and without escape, the Same sees itself related and linked to the Other from which it is separated, and it is unable to escape from this relationship. Thus the principle (*archè*) no longer is the sameness of the selfsame (if it is necessary at all to speak again of principle and not, rather, of the emergence of the "an-archic") but the relation of the Same to Otherness, a relation that can be neither avoided nor reduced to a more original union.

Heideggerian Ontology As a Philosophy of the Same (paragraphs 8–14)

Do the two traits of the Same, as described in paragraphs 1–4, also characterize the thought of Being as presented by Heidegger? Despite Heidegger's critique of the traditional onto-theology, Levinas's response is affirmative. While admitting the discovery of the verbal and transitive sense of Being and the radical importance of the ontological difference, Levinas also recognizes in Heidegger the structures described above. Although Being is neither a universal nor a supreme or foundational being, it illuminates and dominates thought as a Neutral which, nevertheless, does not abolish but affirms the central position of *Dasein*, which replaced the transcendental I of modern philosophy. The supremacy of reason, by which the human subject, according to Plato, feels at home in understanding the world as a realization of ideas,[27] is replaced by another relation between *Dasein* and Being, but still *Dasein* stays shut up in its relation to the phosphorescent Anonymous enabling all beings to present themselves to it, without ever producing a true alterity. The truth of

27 *Phaedo* 76 d–e, 100b.

Dasein is that the being which is "always mine" (*jemeinig*) is also a being for which its own being is *the* issue.[28] This is why Levinas, without denying the plan formulated in section 6 of *Sein und Zeit*, can say that Heidegger "does not destroy" but "summarizes an entire current of Western philosophy." The "obscure clarity," by which Levinas depicts the clear-obscure of Heideggerian being, refers to Corneille's *Le Cid*,[29] while the "mystery" of being could be an allusion to the *"Geheimnis"* that Heidegger speaks of in *Holzwege* and elsewhere.[30] Even death, which seems to be the enemy of all ipseity, is interpreted in *Sein und Zeit* as something that can be owned. Despite the expected impossibility, proceeding-toward-death is still a possibility: the "possibility of no longer being able-to-be there" (*die Möglichkeit des Nicht-mehr-dasein-könnens*) or "the possibility of the absolute impossibility of being there" (*die Möglichkeit der schlechthinnigen Daseinsunmöglichkeit*).[31] Authentic existence can assume its being-toward-death, thus realizing a "freedom certain of itself and anguished for death" (*die ihr selbst gewisse und sich ängstende Freiheit zum Tode*), which no longer refers to help or concern of others.[32]

The absence of otherness is also marked by the absence of any essential relation to the infinite. The finitude of *Dasein* is not discovered in the distance that separates Descartes's infinity from the limited existence of human beings[33] but rather in *Dasein*'s limited existence, mortality tending to inauthenticity. Since *Dasein*, in this framework, is closed on itself, it can have no other lack than that of a failure in regard to itself. The idea of a debt or guilt toward others than the self is excluded from this thought. By the absence of a true alterity that could question and accuse *Dasein*'s freedom, that is, by the absence of an ethical "principle," the Heideggerian perspective belongs to a tradition the barbarous depths of which were shown by Nazism. When Heidegger criticizes the essence of technology,[34] he forgets that

---

28 *SuZ*, 142, 191ff.
29 Cf. Corneille, *Le Cid*, 4.3.
30 *Holzwege*, 244; *Wegmarken*, 89–94; *Unterwegs zur Sprache*, 140, 148–49.
31 *SuZ*, 250ff.
32 *SuZ*, 266 and §62; cf. also Levinas's commentary in *EDHH* 85–87.
33 Cf. Descartes's *Meditations*, AT, 9:36 and 41, and Plato's *Republic* 508a, 509b, 517b, 518d.
34 Cf. "Die Frage nach der Technik," VA, 1: 5–36/QCT, 3–35.

the source of modern evil, such as it was manifested in Nazism, is found at a depth that lies deeper than the realm of technology. Alluding to certain expressions found in Heidegger's later works, Levinas sketches the portrait of a pagan existence rooted in mother earth and prone to exploitation—very different from the sober existence of availability for the needs of others. The individuals are immersed in the *physis* that encompasses them like elements of its unfolding. The intoxication of a polytheistic enthusiasm renewed by Heidegger through his interpretations of Hölderlin and the Presocratics shows by exaggeration what inspiration is hidden at the bottom of the "lucid sobriety" of philosophers.[35]

In the Western tradition, freedom precedes and surpasses justice; the Same encompasses and envelops the Other;[36] monism wins out over the pluralism of existent beings.

I The Idea of the Infinite

The reversal proposed by Levinas is not a simple reversal of terms, as if the Same, Being, Freedom, Power, Conscience, Greece, and Western culture should be swallowed and absorbed by Otherness, Justice, and Judaism. In retrieving the prophetic Jewish tradition, which is "at least as ancient" as the Socratic and Presocratic Greek traditions, it is a matter of doing justice to the Other and, by this, to the relation of the Other to the Same, which thereby receives its true significance.

The call to the tradition of Israel in no way seeks to replace philosophical thought with an appeal to faith. The defense of the Other against the monopoly of the Same can be at least as philosophical as Heidegger's commentaries on a poem of Parmenides or the aphorisms of Heraclitus. It must be possible to formulate and justify the essential points of another tradition in a philosophical and "Greek" language that can be understood by contemporary humanity without necessarily appealing to a particular faith or conviction.

---

35 Cf. *Republic* 501d2, 563a5, 537d8; *Symposium* 218e7. Cf. also the articles "Le lieu et l'utopie," "Simone Weil contre la Bible," "Heidegger, Gagarine et nous," gathered in *DL* 133–37, 178–88, 299–303.

36 Cf. Plato, *Timaeus* 35ab: the circle of the Same encompasses the circle of the Other; and Levinas, "Philosophie et positivité," in *Savoir, faire, espérer: les limites de la raison* (Brussells: Facultés Universitaires Saint-Louis, 1976), 194–206.

Levinas takes up some elements of Western philosophy by which it opens itself to the second way described in section 1, even though the results have not been developed in the course of Western philosophy. These features are, above all, Plato's affirmation that the goal of the philosophical ascension is found, *beyond being*, in *the Good*, his thesis that real discourse (conceived of elsewhere as an interior dialogue) is a discourse with the gods[37] and Descartes's analysis of the idea of the infinite, such as can be found in his third *Meditation*. One could find other hints of true heteronomy at the interior of Western philosophy. Thus, Levinas speaks elsewhere of Aristotle's "from the outside" (*thurathen*),[38] of the Platonic and Plotinian One,[39] and of Kant's practical philosophy.[40] The texts most frequently referred to are, however, those of Plato on the Good[41] and those of Descartes on the idea of the infinite.[42] In the essay considered here, it is the latter text that receives all the attention.

The method by which Levinas proceeds includes two steps: the first phase distinguishes in Descartes the analysis of a fundamental structure that Levinas will separate from its concretization by the relation of the person to God (§3). The formal structure can be called "the idea of the infinite," although Descartes in the third *Metaphysical Meditation* makes no distinction between "the idea of God" and "the notion of the infinite." After this, Levinas asks how a formal structure thus uncovered can concretize itself, or which experience "fills" the intention that this structure represents (§4). The answer will be that only the Other, i.e., any other human, can respond to such an intention.

In order to follow Levinas's interpretation, one must recall some elements of the argument developed in the third Cartesian *Meditation*.[43] Wondering how he can be sure of the truth of his idea and judgments (29), Descartes begins with a list of ideas found in his consciousness: "In addition to the idea that represents me to myself," there is also found an idea "that represents

---

37 *Republic* 517b and 518d; *Phaedrus* 273e–274a.
38 MT 367/*CPP* 39; *TI* 22/51 Cf. Aristotle, *De generatione animalium* 736b 28; and Husserl, *Formale und transzendentale Logik*, 208.
39 *EDHH* 197, 189, 201
40 *AE* 166/*OB* 129; Transc. Int. 19–20.
41 E.g., *TI* 76, 235/102–3, 257–58; *EDHH* 189; and Plato, *Republic* 508e, 509b, 517b, 518d.
42 *TI* 18–20/48–50, 185–87/210–12; TH 94, 105; the article "Infini" in the *Encyclopedia Universalis* 8:991–94; Transc. Int. 25–29.
43 AT, 9:27–42.

to me a God, other ideas that represent animals, and still others representing people similar to me" (34). Of all these ideas, however, excepting those of God and me, "I see no reason why they could not be produced by me and why I cannot be the author of them," or, at least, why they would not be "contained in me eminently" (35). "Thus there remains only [apart from the idea of me] the sole idea of God of which it must be considered if there is something in it which could not have come from myself."

Descartes describes this idea as the idea of "an infinite, eternal, immutable, independent, all-knowing, all-powerful substance, by which I myself, and all the other things that are (if indeed it is true that there are things that exist) were created and produced." Thus it is the idea of God of traditional metaphysics. Levinas's purpose is not the saving of this tradition, but he admires in this text the affirmation of the irreducible originality of this idea, an affirmation that remains true when it is stripped of its elaboration by the "natural theology" of the scholastic tradition. The irreducibility is expressed by Descartes's pointing out that the idea of God must necessarily have been "placed in me" by something exterior and transcendent to me "because, although the idea of substance is in me, from the very fact that I am only a finite substance, I could never have the idea of an infinite substance, if this idea had not been placed in me by some substance that is truly infinite."[44]

For Descartes, the idea of the infinite cannot be the result of a negation of something finite "because, on the contrary, it is manifestly clear to me that there is more reality found in the infinite substance than in the finite substance and thus that I have the notion of the infinite in some way before that of the finite."

How would it be possible to know my own finitude (which is manifested, for example, in my doubts and other wants) "if I did not have in me any idea of a being more perfect than my being in comparison to which I could know the defaults of my own nature?" The idea of this "sovereignly perfect and infinite being," which is thus the first of all my notions, cannot be false because it is "very clear and very distinct" and "there is no other

---

44 AT, 9:36. Cf. also 38: "The idea that I have of a being more perfect than my own being must necessarily have been placed in me by a being which is indeed more perfect"; and 48: "And certainly one must not think it strange that God, in creating me, has placed in me this idea as the mark of the craftsman stamped on his work; and it is not as necessary that this mark be something different from this very work."

notion that by itself is more true."[45] "And this remains true, although I do not understand the infinite . . . , for it belongs to the nature of the infinite that my nature, which is finite and limited, cannot understand it" (37).

Thus, even for Descartes, the understanding is not the way in which the finite being of the ego is acquainted with the infinite, which has marked it with its imprint. And yet, knowledge of the self includes knowledge of this noncomprehensive relationship:

> When I reflect on myself, I know not only that I am an imperfect and incomplete thing depending on other people, as well as desiring and striving continually for something better and greater than I am, but at the same time I know also that he on whom I depend possesses in himself all the great things towards which I am striving and whose ideas I find in myself. He does not only possess them in an indefinite way and potentially only, but he enjoys them in fact, actually and infinitely, and thus he is God (41).

And as if to attempt an intention that goes further than the intention to understand, Descartes ends his *Meditation* on a "contemplation" of this all-perfect God, who causes him to "consider, admire and adore the incomparable beauty of this immense light, at least to the extent that the strength of my mind, which is in some sense blinded by it, can allow" (41).

The text that I have just quoted and paraphrased retrieves in a modern way the Neoplatonic and Christian tradition about the presence of the supreme One in the depth (the "heart," "thought," "consciousness," "mind," or "spirit") of the human essence. Although theologians such as Augustine and Anselm thematized the perfection of this ultimate being in terms of knowledge and—like Descartes, who followed them—tried to present it as the result of so-called "proofs for the existence of God," they always knew and stated that this God could not really be reached by a purely theoretical attitude but by some *other* way, that is, by a deeper and more radical attitude which precedes the distinction between theory and practice: the attitude of adoration and gratitude.

The idea of the infinite, which constitutes the formal design of the Cartesian idea of God, is an "intention" and a "thought" whose "noema" does not fulfill the "noesis" of which it is the correlate because this "thought" (which is neither a concept, nor a conception, nor a mode of understanding) can in no way contain

---

45 AT, 9:36. Cf. section 2 on the difference between the knowledge of the finite according to Descartes and according to Heidegger.

or grasp within its "content." Here the *ideatum* surpasses the idea. The idea of the infinite *thinks more than it thinks*. In this manner, the infinite shows its exteriority, its transcendence, and its radical highness. Thus it is not the grandeur, the universality, or the all-encompassing and unlimited character that defines the positive infinitude of the infinite but rather its absolute alterity.[46] By refuting the possibility of applying the fundamental concepts of Husserlian phenomenology (such as intentionality, truth as fulfilling, adequation, evidence, the self-given "in flesh and bones," etc.), Levinas shows that the idea of the infinite is an exceptional relationship that cannot be described in terms of container and contained. If consciousness cannot contain the infinite, neither can it be exact to reverse the terms. The infinite does not contain the I that is in relation to it. Their relation cannot be transformed in any sort of fusion or union. If their relation did not imply an unbridgeable separation that no mystical or theoretical mediation can abolish, neither the finite nor the infinite would retain its own nature. The idea of the infinite escapes from the soul's possibility of accounting for its own content, a possibility that Descartes had affirmed in reference to ideas of finite things.[47] The argument repeated so often by Hegel—according to which an absolute separation between the finite and the infinite would rob the latter of its infinity because the opposition of the infinite to something else would limit it—presupposes that the infinite must surpass all limits and encompass all finite beings. It identifies the infinite, thus, in some manner, with the universe of all that can be. The finite becomes a moment of the infinite (something that "participates" in the life of the infinite), while the infinite is degraded by becoming the totality of all moments.

Thus interpreted, the Cartesian "idea of the infinite" corresponds to that which, in the first section of Levinas's essay, was indicated as a specific trait of that toward which all experience (in the full sense of the word) transports us. The infinite is the absolutely other, the exterior that reveals itself over-there and up-there, the transcendent that surpasses all of our powers of appropriation. Radical alterity, transcendence, or highness "constitute[s] the first mark of its infinitude."

---

46 *TI* 11–12/40–42 and 170–71/196–97.

47 AT, 9:35: "Je ne vois point de raison pourquoi elles ne puissent être produites par moi-même" ("I do not see any reason why they could not be produced by myself").

By this unique relation with complete otherness, the I is more than it would be were it only an ego with the power to integrate, to anticipate, or to project all things, acts, and thoughts within the horizon of a narcissistic universe. One way of thematizing such an ego is found in the Heideggerian and Sartrean interpretations of the human essence as a project (*Entwurf*) or projection by which all novelty would only be the result of an autonomous deployment giving to existence its own sense.[48] *The more in the less* that constitutes the Same in its linkage to the Other cannot be deduced from the consciousness or autoconsciousness of an ego but is produced like the initial *mise-en-scène* by which all existence discovers itself already oriented before all initiative of its own.

By his interpretation of the third *Meditation,* Levinas gave a new sense to the ontological argument that "the idea of absolute perfection, coming from St. Anselm and Descartes, expresses the relation to the infinite upon which depends all sense and all truth."[49] Levinas's interpretation thus recalls the statute of the "idea" of the Platonic Good (which is not an idea but rather the source and the light that gives existence to all ideas) or of the Plotinian One. By showing that the "idea" of the infinite does not fall under the same kind of knowledge as other ideas, Levinas retrieves, in a very original way, the old debate on the two main types of knowledge previously placed in opposition to each other: "discursive" knowledge and "intuitive" knowledge, *ratio* and *intellectus, Verstand* and *Vernunft, Erkennen* and *Fürwahrhalten.* With the great philosophers, as with the mystics, there has always been the certitude that ultimate realities do not reveal themselves to a thinking that wants to *understand,* i.e., that wants to seize its object by circumscribing it at the interior of a horizon. A thinking that thinks without knowing seems to be a contradiction: how can one affirm the truth of a "thing" of which one knows neither the essence nor the quiddity? And yet, how could one affirm a radical relation with someone or something that comes from elsewhere and "from on high" if one can understand all reality as a part, or as the ensemble, of the totality of definable things? Even a rationalist like

---

48 Cf. J.-P. Sartre, *L'être et le néant* (Paris: Gallimard, 1943), 588–91; Heidegger, *SuZ,* 144 and §§31 and 65; Levinas, *TI* 172–73/197–99.
49 *TI* 11–12/40–42.

Descartes understood that, though we are completely unable to understand the infinite, we must nevertheless affirm, with complete certitude, the truth of the relation that links us to it. The first truth is that the I perceives itself in relation to that which surpasses its understanding.

In a contribution to a book entitled *The Passion of Reason,*[50] Levinas continued his meditation on Descartes's third *Meditation.* He remained faithful to his first effort but stressed more the affective character of the relation: it is "*an affecting of the finite by the infinite*" (50). "This affectivity of adoration and this passivity of bewilderment (*éblouissement*)" are the result of the reasoning to which Descartes abandons himself at the end of his *Meditation.* True thinking "does better than to think" (51) because, more than a love of wisdom, thinking finds itself in a "wisdom of desire" that reveals itself to be a "wisdom of love."[51]

| The Idea of the Infinite and | the Face of the Other

Having designed, with Descartes, the necessary formal structure of what he still called, at this stage of his thinking, an exceptional "experience," Levinas asks in which concrete experience this structure can realize itself. His response is no longer simply the traditional one of the Greeks or Christian theologians, who identify the absolutely Other with the unique God above finite beings, but the other human. This is not to say that God is suppressed or abolished. The absoluteness and infinitude of the human other can never be disavowed, but the relationship between this Other and the completely other Otherness of God is a question that still must be answered. The initial ambiguity of "the Other" with which I am in relation is expressed in a passage of *Totality and Infinity* where the alterity is said to be "understood as the alterity of the human Other (*Autrui*) *and* as that of

---

50 Paris, 1983, 49–52. This text was reprinted as the final part of *Transcendance et Intelligibilité,* 25–29.

51 *AE* 195/*OB* 153 and *AE* 205-7/*OB* 161-62. However, in *TI* 187/211–12 already Levinas quoted the end of Descartes's third *Meditation* as the "expression of the transformation of the idea of the infinite, as contained in knowledge, into majesty approached as face."

the Most-High."[52] Thus, right from the very beginning, "the idea of the infinite is the social relationship."

To determine the specific characteristics of this relationship with a concrete infinity, one must avoid the automatisms of a conceptual network developed in relation to finite objects and beings. One must ask, and Levinas does so later, whether thematization as such (and is philosophy not always an attempt at thematization?) betrays the foreign "object" or "theme" that is the Other. Within the traditional conceptualization, all otherness is either converted into a possession or resists such conversion as a force that starts a war. Prey or predator, master or slave, depreciated object or subject dominating everything from its all-encompassing point of view, these are the possible alternatives if we stay within the context of the social philosophy of our tradition. The alterity of the other can, however, show its value only if we manage to transform its metaphysical presuppositions from top to bottom. Even the word *phenomenon* is not adequate for rendering the otherness of the other met by me. The hesitation that can be noticed in Levinas's formulations in this essay shows that the search for another, less ontological language has already begun. "The exteriority of the infinite *manifests itself* in the absolute resistance which—through its *appearance*, its *epiphany*—it opposes to all my powers."[53] This search will lead to a distinction between the phenomenon and another way of coming to the fore[54] and to a radical critique of all monopolistic phenomenology. It will be followed by a critique of all thematization (which, nevertheless, will remain inevitable for philosophy) and lead to the distinction between the Said (*le Dit*) of the text and the Saying (*le Dire*), which can neither be reduced to a theme nor can be grasped by description or analysis.[55]

The apparition of a phenomenon is the emergence of a form into the light of a certain space-time; it is one with the *aisthesis* or *noesis* of a subject open for it. The encounter with the human other, however, is not the union of an act by which two potential beings identify with one another in the transparency of a perception or a concept but rather a shock which, by its (non)apparition, refutes the pretension of the I, which appropriates everything that stands in its way. The other "shows itself" in a different

52 *TI* 4/34.
53 *EDHH* 173/*CPP* 55; my italics.
54 "Se produire." Cf. *EDHH* 203-16/*CPP* 61-74.
55 *AE* 167ff./*OB* 131ff.

manner; his/her way of "being" is other; it "is" in another way than the being of phenomena. That is why Levinas can say in *Totality and Infinity* that the Other is neither given nor visible and that there can be no idea of it.[56] The truly other Other is invisible (51/78–79): "To be unable to enter into a theme," "to be unable to appear—invisibility itself."[57] In *Otherwise Than Being*, the rejection of the ontological language, which still prevails in *Totality and Infinity*, results even in the thesis that it is inexact to say that the Other's mode of being is completely other than that of all (other) phenomena, since the Other as such cannot be called "a being." Transcendence is "passing over to being's *other*, otherwise than being. Not *to be otherwise*, but *otherwise than being*."[58]

How could all these negative expressions be replaced by a positive discourse? How must we characterize the *logos* of a discourse that is not indifferent to the excellence of the infinite in relation to everything else? The response to this question cannot be given without recourse to ethical language. The answer to the ontological or metaphysical questions, "Who is the other?" and "What is the 'principle' or 'archè,' the first 'truth' and the 'base' of all philosophy?" cannot be given by an objectifying theory in which all otherness ultimately is lost in thematization, but only by the language of commandment: "Thou shalt not kill!" The other *"is"* the one that we *ought* not (that we do not have the right to) kill.

This answer means neither that we must simply reverse the traditional dependence between theoretical and practical philosophy by making human practice the foundation of all theory, nor that it is necessary to promote moral philosophy as a fundamental discipline upon which one can construct the rest of philosophy. The ethical point of view (or the "moral sense") is an indispensable perspective for the discovery of how the Other differs from all other reality. The look that raises itself to the Other's "highness" perceives that she does not manifest herself as a phenomenon but reveals herself as an epiphany of the infinite, of absolute otherness. In this way, the I awakens to the impossibility of behaving or interpreting itself in terms of autonomous power. "I can" (*Ich kann*) can no longer sum up human existence, and the

---

56 *TI* 4/34.

57 *EDHH* 224/*CPP* 115–16.

58 *AE* 3/*OB* 3. This is also programmatically stated by the title "Otherwise Than Being" (and not "Being otherwise").

"able-to-be" of possibility (*Seinkönnen*) is not the most radical human "essence."[59] The power of this possibility is nothing bad in itself; on the contrary, it is a necessary moment of the constitution of the I—which itself is not abolished but rather demanded and confirmed by the infinite to which it is related. However, the Other's existence subordinates ego's spontaneous capacity of being to an imperative that ego has neither invented, nor chosen, nor freely accepted: it forbids the ruthless accomplishment of ego's tendency to imperial totalization.

The Other is not a moment within a dialectical order of mutually opposed forces. This is shown by the fact that the "no" against the powerful possibilities of the I does not have the form of a great force or violence but rather of an essential weakness that *forbids* me to continue my project of universal domination. If the Other started a fight against me, thus becoming a warrior, he would be only (like me) an element of a human universe: a country, a realm, a church, or a world, dialectically constructed by means of human sacrifices. The Other, rather, shows his infinity as the most naked, poor, and vulnerable of all weaknesses. A human *face* has no defense.

"Face" is the word Levinas chooses to indicate the alterity of the Other forbidding me to exercise my narcissistic violence. "Language" is another expression of the same nucleus of meaning if it is understood as spoken language or discourse and not as a text detached from its author. The Other regards me and speaks to me; you are my interlocutor; "the face speaks." This is the concrete way in which I am in relation with the infinite.

With an allusion to the *Phaedrus*,[60] Levinas characterizes the authority and the height of the look and the word through which the other turns toward me. In his apology for the excellence of the spoken word, Plato writes that it is only the living and animated *logos*, as opposed to the written text, that is capable of bringing help to itself.[61] The Other even replaces, in some way, the "pure act (*energeia*)" in which Aristotle saw the unmoved mover, which brings all other beings in motion by the *eros* that orients them.[62]

This proximity of the Other as the Highest makes itself felt when my conscience recognizes that the other's existence forbids

---

59 Cf. Husserl, *Ideen* 2:257ff.; Heidegger, GA 20 (summer 1925): 421; *SuZ*, 191–94.
60 *Phaedrus* 274b–277a.
61 *Phaedrus* 275e, 276a, c, e; cf. *TI* 45, 69, 71/73, 96, 98.
62 *Metaph.* 1071b–1073a.

me to hoard certain realities which I need and imposes upon me heavier and more pressing duties than those I have toward myself. While I can sacrifice myself for the other, to require the same of another with regard to me would be the equivalent of murder. "We are all guilty of everything before everyone, and I more so than the rest."[63]

| The Idea of the Infinite As Desire

"Philosophy and the Idea of the Infinite" began with the metaphysical and epistemological question: How can one arrive at the truth? The analysis of experience brought us to the discovery of a relationship more fundamental than knowledge if we understand "knowledge" in the sense of the Greek and modern tradition: a theoretical relation that would be the foundation as well as the perfection of all contact with beings in their being. The more fundamental structure that shows itself in the encounter with the Other has an ethical and imperative character; it is simultaneously the revelation of a *fact* and the source of all *obligations* and *prohibitions*. Thus ethics cannot be understood as a secondary discipline based on a theoretical philosophy, an ontology, or epistemology that would precede any command or normativity. The ethical relation is not a "superstructure" but rather the foundation of all knowledge, and the analysis of this relation constitutes a "first philosophy."[64] If one uses the words "cognitive" and "objective" to indicate a reality and a truth more originary and radical than those of *theoria*, one could say that the relation which, in the experience of the other, links me to the infinite is "more cognitive than knowledge itself," and that "all objectivity must participate in that relation."

In the second of his *Conversations on Metaphysics and Religion*, Malebranche states:

> Note especially that God or the infinite is not visible by means of an idea that represents him. The infinite is its own idea for itself. It has no archetype. . . . Everything finite can be seen in the infinite which includes the intelligible ideas of that thing. But the infinite can be seen only in itself. If one thinks of God, it is necessary that he exists. It is possible that this or that being, notwithstanding its being known, does not exist. We can see its essence apart from its existence,

---

63 A sentence from Dostojevski's *The Brothers Karamazow* often quoted by Levinas. Cf., e.g., *EI* 105.
64 TH 99.

its idea without itself. But we cannot see the essence of the infinite apart from its existence, the idea of its being without its being.[65]

Malebranche shows clearly that all knowledge of finite things is in reference to the idea of the infinite, which serves as their foundation, and that this "ultimate knowledge" is of a different structure and quality. If all knowledge were essentially a way to objectify and thematize the known, there would be no knowledge of the infinite because the Other is never an object or a theme and can never be reduced to such. One cannot place the Other in front of oneself, nor could one embrace it by measuring its horizon. There are no demarcations, there is no definition of the infinite.

While for Malebranche all knowledge and thematization derives from the fundamental relation between the knowing subject and the infinite, Descartes adheres to two theses that are not easy to reconcile. On the one hand, he admits that, from the beginning, the *cogito* is oriented and dominated by the idea of God; on the other hand, the recognition of God's existence as infinite still depends upon a decision of the will of the conscious subject. The second thesis follows from his general theory of the truth as it was propounded in the fourth *Meditation*. If clear and distinct evidence present to the understanding is not enough for a true judgment because it needs also a correct use of the will (whereas error is the result when the will does not remain within the limits of understanding), all knowledge depends on the freedom of the finite subject.[66] When one does not distinguish a radical difference between knowledge of finite beings and the idea of the infinite, the latter is also subordinated to the exercise of human freedom. Thus, one inevitably returns to the framework of autonomy.

After having given a response, in the fourth section, to the question of which "noema" might correspond to the formal structure found in the third section, Levinas returns to the question of the specific characteristics of this structure by asking in which "noesis" or "intention" the structure manifests itself concretely. If the relation of the I to the absolute Other is not a kind of knowledge or contemplation, is it perhaps *eros* itself, evoked in

---

65 Malebranche, *Œuvres complètes,* ed. A. Robinet (Paris: Vrin, 1965), 12:53–54.

66 AT, 9:45–49.

the second sentence of the essay? Let us first agree upon the sense of *eros* as a tendency toward the infinite. If one sees here a profound *need* making us desire that which we do not have, one falls again into an explication by the Same. The I is then seen as an ensemble of privations, and its original tendency would consist of the nostalgia for a satisfaction that could procure plenitude. The paradigm of all human orientations would then be hunger, and the meaning of life would be found in an appeasement of that hunger.

The preceding analyses indicate a different relation than that of the need by which the subject sees beings as prey that it can appropriate and enjoy. Without denying the necessity and value of enjoyment, and without belittling it—on the contrary, enjoyment is necessary for the constitution of the subject as an independent ego that can have a relationship with alterity—the fundamental structure can be characterized as *eros* only if one thereby means a *desire* completely different from need. Far from being a hunger that disappears as soon as it is satisfied, true desire *grows* the more one tries to satisfy it. The desire of the Other can never be satisfied because the closer one comes to the desired, the more one is confronted with the profound distance and separation that belongs to the essence of its alterity. To illustrate the truth of this experience, in which proximity and distance grow with the same intensity, there are not only mystical texts concerning union with a God who remains infinitely foreign and distant; the experience is also felt in more "mundane" experiences, as in the struggle for justice or the experience of erotic love, even though the latter is mixed with a union where the Other and the I are united by a reciprocal love.[67]

By recalling what Plato, in the *Symposium,* writes on *Eros* as the son of *Poros* ("competence" but also "he who abounds") and *Penia* ("destitution" or "poverty") and on Aristophanes' myth of the hermaphrodite,[68] Levinas asks whether Plato has not had an inkling of the difference between the Greek conception of life as an odyssey that ends at the Ithaca from whence it began and the adventure of a subject such as Abraham or Moses, who began their journeys in order to lose their country and the treasures

---

67 Cf. the analysis of *need* and *desire* in *TI* 3–5, 34–35, 74–78, 87, 89–92, 275/33–35, 62–64, 101–5, 114–15, 117–20, 299 and of *eros* in *TI* 232ff./254ff.

68 *Symposium* 203b, 189–193d, 205d–206a; and *TI* 34/63, 87/114–15.

in which they rejoiced. The attitude of the good person is not the nostalgia of a return to an existence one has always lived but the "rectitude" of someone "who does not lack anything."[69] The exodus of the just is different from the odyssey of a hero; it leads toward a land promised rather than possessed.[70]

As we already said, "Philosophy and the Idea of the Infinite" proceeds in the same manner as the summary cited above of *Totality and Infinity*, with one exception: the order in which *the face* and *desire* are presented is reversed. *Before* describing the concrete "experience" of the encounter with the Other (*TI* 9ff./39ff.), the book opens with an analysis of the "desire of the absolute" as primary and original "intention" that replaces the *cogito* and the freedom of the moderns (*TI* 3–5/33–35). Thus, it shows that the nucleus of the Cartesian idea of the infinite (section 3 of the essay) is only the negative side of the desire (section 5) and that both sections are ways of expressing the radical relation of human beings to the absolute Other. Section 4 cuts the description of this relation in two, and the order followed by the book seems simpler and better.

The Idea of the Infinite and Conscience

The primacy of the will, the Cartesian version of which was depicted in the previous section, threatens the alterity of the face. If the concept of freedom is the supreme concept, the Other will succumb to the philosophical domination of the Same. The I will then have the comfortable consciousness that the Other is but a thought that belongs to it as a subordinate moment of its own universe. The I must be awakened by the presence, or rather by the word, of the face that uncovers the wickedness of its egocentrism. An autonomous ego is not innocent; its free spontaneity is violence. The Other's emergence puts the freedom of the ego into question.

By will and freedom, neither Descartes nor Kant nor Hegel nor Levinas mean the power to choose freely among different possibilities. Classical philosophy has always insisted on the difference between freedom of choice (or, as Kant puts it, *Willkür*) and the true freedom that obeys reason and reasonable laws.

---

69 Cf. Psalm 23:1.
70 *TI* 75/102; *EDHH* 188.

Even thus, as completely rooted in the law and order of universal reason, freedom is still in solidarity with the Same because its ultimate foundation is found in a supreme reason, a transcendental consciousness, a first substance, or a universal spirit, all of which are conceived according to the model of free identity of the spirit with itself.

Modern philosophy, from Hobbes to Marx and beyond, saw that the arbitrariness of the free will had to be subdued in the name of an ideal higher than freedom, but it did not call into question the postulates of the Same from which it started. The tension between true freedom and the power of choice required a foundation in the name of which the spontaneity of inclinations and passions influencing that choosing power is limited. The dialectics of freedom unfolded the opposition between the power of an absolute freedom and the limited power of human choices oriented by a natural and spontaneous expansion. There could be no other evil than the limitation or finitude of freedom. Of course, the ideal of freedom requires that one accept certain limits at subordinate levels, as was known in the traditional view of autodetermination as autolimitation. According to this tradition, pain is meaningful to the extent that it stimulates reason and produces a knowledge that enlarges our autonomy. But all of these limitations had to serve a larger freedom. Radical evil consisted in the ultimate impossibility of being free, in affirming oneself as center and source, in choosing oneself as an autonomous instant.

Most anthropological, sociopolitical, and ethical theories of the modern epoch begin with the same principle: freedom is the source, the end, and the ideal of the Being of beings. The Same triumphs in autonomy, suppressing all radical alterity. Instead of limiting the fight against violence to an attack on the arbitrary in the name of a superior autonomy, one must wake up to a more primordial dimension than that of freedom: the dimension of a measure by which the "fact" of the Other imposes on me the respect of the Other's highness and accuses me in as much as I am "a force that goes," as Victor Hugo puts it in his *Hernani*.[71]

The discovery of the Other's respectability is at the same time a feeling of shame with regard to myself insofar as I am

---

71 Levinas quotes this phrase rather often; cf., e.g., *TI* 146 and 280/ 171 and 303; TH 100; *DL* 21, 326; it is taken from V. Hugo, *Hernani*, 3.4; cf. V. Hugo, *Théâtre Complet* (Paris: Gallimard), 1:1227: "Je suis une force qui va."

a tendency toward a murderous imperialism and egoism. The seizure of land, a wife, friends, colleagues, associates, and so on treats them as prey and converts me into a murderer. The idea of "creation" implies, at the least, that the meaning which I find in them cannot be reduced to their being possessed or enjoyed by me. The Other is a gift, not only in the sense of a positivistic or phenomenological given but as the irreducible who surprises me unexpectedly, requiring that I place my powers at his/her disposition.

Without in the least devaluing or abolishing it, Levinas discovers in freedom a much deeper meaning than the one it holds in philosophies that place it at the summit of all beings. The Same in the shape of a spontaneous and free ego who appropriates the world in order to be at home in a worldwide realm is a constitutive principle of the primordial relationship and not a fault of which one must be cured or a radical evil making all existence tragic. Without autonomy and a certain egoism, the separation between the Same and the Other would be impossible: the two poles of the relationship would inevitably fuse. However, the autonomy of the I must be submitted to the primordial relation and discover its true significance by respecting the highness of the Other, which gives it its task. With an image borrowed from the feudal world, Levinas calls this "an investiture of freedom."[72]

A freedom (or autonomy) invested by the Other, *this* is the heteronomous moment that was indicated in the first section of this essay. The rectitude of a just being is the meaning of freedom ordained by such rectitude. Such a being does not concentrate on its own happiness or even on the sublime form in which this happiness can present itself within the framework of a belief in human immortality or soul. It gives less attention to Kant's third question ("What can I hope for?") and more to the second question ("What must I do?") because it has turned from egoistical injustice in order to dedicate itself to the service of the Other.[73] As we have already said, this conversion is not the transformation of egoism into altruism but the reversal of the order that relates the one to the Other by henceforth reorienting the being-who-is-at-home and its enjoyment. The Other gives it an ultimate significance that does not abolish the existence of an ego searching for truth but makes its ultimate meaning possible.

---

72 *TI* 57ff./84ff.
73 Cf. *Kritik der reinen Vernunft* A 805; B 833.

Heteronomy or investiture justifies freedom by making it responsible for the Other before a judgment that is chosen neither by the Other nor by me, who finds myself submitted to it. This responsibility grows as one tries to take it. The requirements of justice can never be satisfied; it remains a desire that empties itself in giving what it possesses without end. It is disinterested goodness.[74]

The subordination of freedom to the law of the Other, the heteronomy that links freedom and justice, avoids the impasses of an absolutized autonomy and avoids falling into one of the opposite traps. It does not violate free will but rather gives it direction in giving it a task and a meaning. The subordination protects free will from the confusion of a magical union by maintaining the separation between the Other and me; it avoids the negations of freedom that submit it to a cosmic determinism or a supreme and irresistible *moira*.

By implicitly criticizing the fifth of Husserl's *Cartesian Meditations*, Levinas refutes the traditional approach of the problem of intersubjectivity. He notes that the project of a proof for the existence of other human beings presupposes that the starting point would lie in the isolated existence of an ego conscious of itself. In *Sein und Zeit* (§§27–29), Heidegger had already shown that such a solipsistic ego does not exist because "being-with" (-others) is an existential that, together with other existentials, constitutes the being of *Dasein*. Being-for-the-other or the investiture of ego's freedom has not, however, the same structure as the Heideggerian *Mitsein*, for the latter belongs to a realm of autonomy, while investiture puts ego into question and subordinates its freedom to a higher meaning. Levinas agrees that the relation of ego to the Other precedes the proof for the existence of the Other, and he goes further than Heidegger in affirming that this relation also precedes all knowledge (and thus all modes of *understanding* that can be interpreted as comprehension or knowledge). The reason for this is that all knowledge is a form of appropriation and domination and thus of autonomy. The dimension of knowing is the dimension of a solitary I trying to subdue everything else to the mastery of its thought.

For Husserl, the proof for the existence of other minds was a condition for the possibility of an intersubjective and objective knowledge. But Levinas shows that all knowledge and all certitude are forms of autonomy. If it is true that autonomy discovers

---

74 *TI* 4/35.

itself as always already invested, there can be no autonomy or certitude preceding the transcendence that orients the one toward the Other. The dimension of certitude and incertitude, or of knowledge in general, can arise only on the foundation of the primordial relation that supports them.[75] In Husserlian language, it is not possible that a transcendental ego "constitutes" from an unengaged point of view a noema called "face," "word," or "apparition of the other." Rather, one must say that the consciousness of ego finds itself constituted as already related to the Other before any possibility of getting ahold of itself or of identifying itself with itself as consciousness. Nor would it be exact to say that the I "knows" the Other by an "anticipated comprehension" (*Vorverständnis*), as Heidegger thinks. The face (or the word, or the Other) is the most immediate revelation there is. By piercing any sort of concept and perception, it is finally this revelation that procures for us the experience in the strong sense of the word, whose structure this essay has been concerned with from the beginning.

While the essay began with the experience of truth, it ends with the evocation of God. In effect, it is in the commandment that requires ego's freedom to dedicate itself to others that the unique God is revealed, a God that absents itself from all confusion or magical participation. If the search for truth is a voyage toward the *archai*, as Aristotle taught, the principle of principles, the first *archè* preceding all principles, will be the face of the Other awakening me to the meaning of my life (the "an-archic" nature of which will be highlighted in all Levinas's later works). If we define philosophy, with Kant, as a critical enterprise with regard to everything we opine, say, construct, or believe, the measure of any critique reveals itself in moral consciousness, which is not a special genre of "human consciousness" but the supreme criterion upon which all justice and truth depend.

---

75 *TI* 142–49/168–74.

| "La philosophie
| et l'idée de l'Infini"

| *I.—Autonomie et Hétéronomie.*

Toute philosophie recherche la vérité. Les sciences, elles aussi
peuvent se définir par cette recherche, car elles tiennent de
l'*eros* philosophique, vivant ou sommeillant en elles, leur noble passion. Mais si la définition semble trop générale et
quelque peu vide, elle permet de distinguer deux voies où
s'engage l'esprit philosophique et qui en éclairent la physio-
nomie. Ces voies se croisent dans l'idée même de vérité.

1° Vérité implique expérience. Le penseur entretient dans
la vérité un rapport avec une réalité distincte de lui, *autre*
que lui. «Absolument autre», selon l'expression reprise par
Jankélévitch. Car l'expérience ne mérite son nom que si elle
nous transporte au delà de ce qui reste notre nature. La
vraie expérience doit même nous conduire au delà de la Nature qui nous entoure, laquelle n'est pas jalouse des merveil-
leux secrets qu'elle garde, se plie, de connivence avec les
hommes, à leurs raisons et inventions. En elle aussi les hommes se sentent chez eux. La vérité indiquerait ainsi l'aboutissement d'un mouvement partant d'un monde intime et
familier—même si nous ne l'avons pas encore entièrement
exploré—vers l'étranger, vers un *là-bas,* Platon l'a dit. La
vérité impliquerait mieux qu'une extériorité, la transcendance. La philosophie s'occuperait de l'absolument autre, elle
serait l'hétéronomie elle-même. Avançons encore de quelques
pas. La distance seule ne suffit pas pour distinguer transcendance et extériorité. Fille de l'expérience, la vérité pré-
tend très haut. Elle s'ouvre sur la dimension même de
l'idéal. Et c'est ainsi que philosophie signifie métaphysique et
que la métaphysique s'interroge sur le divin.

2° Mais vérité signifie aussi adhésion libre à une proposition, aboutissement d'une libre recherche. La liberté du chercheur, du penseur, sur laquelle ne pèse aucune contrainte, s'exprime dans la vérité. Qu'est cette liberté sinon un refus pour l'être pensant, de s'aliéner dans l'adhésion, sinon la conservation de sa nature, de son identité, sinon le fait de rester le Même malgré les terres inconnues où semble mener la pensée? Vue de ce biais, la philosophie s'emploierait à réduire au Même tout ce qui s'oppose à elle comme *autre*. Elle marcherait vers une *auto-nomie*, vers un stade où rien d'irréductible ne viendrait plus limiter la pensée et où, par conséquent, non limitée, la pensée serait libre. La philosophie équivaudrait ainsi à la conquête de l'être par l'homme à travers l'histoire.

La conquête de l'être par l'homme à travers l'histoire—voilà la formule à laquelle se ramène la liberté, l'autonomie, la *réduction de l'Autre au Même*. Celle-ci ne représente pas un je ne sais quel schéma abstrait, mais le Moi humain. L'existence d'un Moi se déroule comme identification du divers. Tant d'événements lui arrivent, tant d'années le vieillissent et le Moi demeure le Même! Le Moi, le Soi-même, l'ipséité comme on le dit de nos jours, ne reste pas invariable au milieu du changement comme un rocher attaqué par les flots. Le rocher attaqué par des flots n'est rien moins qu'invariable. Le Moi reste le Même en faisant des événements disparates et divers une histoire, c'est-à-dire son histoire. Et c'est cela le fait originel de l'identification du Même, antérieur à l'identité du rocher et condition de cette identité.

Autonomie ou hétéronomie? Le choix de la philosophie occidentale a penché le plus souvent du côté de la liberté et du Même. La philosophie ne naquit-elle pas sur la terre grecque pour détrôner l'opinion où toutes les tyrannies menacent et guettent? A travers l'opinion filtre dans l'âme le poison le plus subtil et le plus perfide qui l'altère dans ses tréfonds, qui en fait un autre. L'âme «mangée par les autres» comme le dirait M. Teste, ne sent pas sa propre altération et s'expose dès lors à toutes les violences. Mais cette pénétration et ce prestige de l'opinion supposent un stade mythique de l'être où les âmes participent les unes des autres au sens de Lévy-Bruhl. Contre cette participation troublante et trouble que l'opinion suppose, la philosophie a voulu les âmes séparées et, en un sens, impénétrables. L'idée du Même, l'idée de liberté, semblaient offrir la garantie la plus sûre d'une telle séparation.

Aussi la pensée occidentale parut-elle très souvent exclure le transcendant, englober dans le Même tout Autre et proclamer le droit d'aînesse philosophique de l'autonomie.

II.—Le primat du Même ou le narcissisme.

L'autonomie—la philosophie qui tend à assurer la liberté ou l'identité des êtres—suppose que la liberté elle-même est sûre de son droit, se justifie sans recours à rien d'autre, se complait comme Narcisse, en elle-même. Quand dans la vie philosophique qui réalise cette liberté surgit un terme étranger à cette vie, un terme autre—la terre qui nous supporte et qui trompe nos efforts, le ciel qui nous élève et nous ignore, les forces de la nature qui nous tuent et nous aident, les choses qui nous encombrent ou qui nous servent, les hommes qui nous aiment et nous asservissent—il fait obstacle. Il faut le surmonter et l'intégrer à cette vie. Or, la vérité est précisément cette victoire et cette intégration. La violence de la rencontre avec le non-moi, s'amortit dans l'évidence. De sorte que le commerce avec la vérité extérieure, tel qu'il se joue dans la connaissance vraie, ne s'oppose pas à la liberté, mais coïncide avec elle. La recherche de la vérité devient ainsi la respiration même d'un être libre, exposé aux réalités extérieures qui abritent, mais qui menacent aussi cette liberté. Grâce à la vérité, ces réalités dont je risque d'être le jouet, sont comprises par moi.

Le «je pense», la pensée à la première personne, l'âme conversant avec elle-même, ou retrouvant comme réminiscence les enseignements qu'elle reçoit, promeuvent ainsi la liberté. Elle triomphera quand le monologue de l'âme sera arrivé à l'universalité, aura englobé la totalité de l'être et jusqu'à l'individu animal qui logeait cette pensée. Toute expérience du monde—les éléments et les objets—se prêtent à cette dialectique de l'âme conversant avec elle-même, y entrent, y appartiennent. Les choses seront idées, et au cours d'une histoire économique et politique où cette pensée se sera déroulée, elles seront conquises, dominées, possédées. Et c'est pour cela sans doute que Descartes dira que l'âme pourrait être l'origine des idées relatives aux choses extérieures et rendre compte du réel.

L'essence de la vérité ne serait donc pas dans le rapport hétéronome avec un Dieu inconnu, mais dans le déjà-connu qu'il s'agit de découvrir ou d'inventer librement en soi, et où tout inconnu se coule. Elle s'oppose foncièrement à un Dieu révélateur. La philosophie est athéisme ou plutôt irreligion, négation d'un Dieu se révélant, mettant des vérités en nous. C'est la leçon de Socrate, qui ne laisse au maître que l'exercice de la maïeutique: tout enseignement introduit dans l'âme y fut déjà. L'identification du Moi,—la merveilleuse autarcie du moi—est le creuset naturel de cette transmutation de l'Autre en Même. Toute philosophie est une égologie pour employer un néologisme husserlien. Et lorsque Descartes distinguera l'acquiescement de la volonté dans la vérité la plus raisonnable, il n'expliquera pas seulement la possibilité de l'erreur, mais posera la raison comme un moi, et la vérité comme dépendant d'un mouvement libre et, par là-même, souverain et justifié.

Cette identification exige la médiation. D'où un deuxième trait de la philosophie du Même: son recours aux Neutres. Pour comprendre le non-moi, il faut trouver un accès à travers une entité, à travers une essence abstraite qui est et n'est pas. Là se dissout l'*altérité* de l'autre. L'être étranger, au lieu de se maintenir dans l'inexpugnable forteresse de sa singularité, au lieu de faire face—devient thème et objet. Il se range déjà sous un concept ou se dissout en relations. Il tombe dans le réseau d'idées *a priori*, que j'apporte pour le capter. Connaître, c'est surprendre dans l'individu affronté, dans cette pierre qui blesse, dans ce pin qui s'élance, dans ce lion qui rugit, ce par quoi il n'est pas cet individu-ci, cet étranger-ci, mais ce par quoi, se trahissant déjà, il donne prise à la volonté libre frémissant dans toute certitude, se saisit et se conçoit, entre dans un concept. La connaissance consiste à saisir l'individu qui seul existe, non pas dans sa singularité qui ne compte pas, mais dans sa généralité, la seule dont il y a science.

Et là commence toute puissance. La reddition des choses extérieures à la liberté humaine à travers leur généralité ne signifie pas seulement, en toute innocence, leur compréhension, mais aussi leur prise en main, leur domestication, leur possession. Dans la possession seulement, le moi achève l'identification du divers. Posséder c'est maintenir certes la réalité de cet autre qu'on possède, mais en suspendant précisément son indépendance. Dans une civilisation réflétée par la philosophie du Même, la liberté s'accomplit comme richesse. La raison qui réduit l'autre est une appropriation et un pouvoir.

Mais si les choses ne résistent pas aux ruses de la pensée et confirment la philosophie du Même, sans jamais mettre en question la liberté du moi, qu'en est-il des hommes? Se rendent-ils à moi comme les choses? Ne mettent-ils pas en question ma liberté?

Ils peuvent d'abord la mettre en échec en lui opposant plus que leur force, en lui opposant leurs libertés. Ils font la guerre. La guerre n'est pas une pure opposition de forces. La guerre se définit peut-être comme rapport où la force n'entre pas seule en ligne de compte, car comptent aussi les imprévus de la liberté: adresse, courage et invention. Mais, dans la guerre la libre volonté peut échouer sans, pour autant, se mettre en question, sans renoncer à son bon droit et à la revanche. La liberté ne se trouve mise en question par Autrui et ne se révèle injustifiée que quand elle se sait injuste. Se savoir injuste,—cela ne vient pas s'ajouter à la conscience spontanée et libre qui serait présente à soi, et se saurait *de plus* coupable. Une situation nouvelle se crée. La présence à soi de la conscience change de façon. Les positions s'effondrent. Pour le dire d'une façon toute formelle, le Même n'y retrouve pas sa priorité sur l'autre, le Même ne repose pas en toute paix sur soi, n'est plus principe. Nous tâcherons de préciser ces formules. Mais, si le Même ne repose pas en toute paix sur soi, la philosophie ne semble pas indissolublement liée à l'aventure qui englobe tout Autre dans le Même.

Nous y reviendrons dans un instant. Précisons pour le moment que cette suprématie du Même sur l'Autre nous semble intégralement maintenue dans la philosophie de Heidegger, celle qui, de nos jours, connaît le succès le plus éclatant. Quand il trace la voie d'accès à chaque singularité réelle à travers l'Etre, qui n'est pas un être particulier ni un genre où entreraient tous les particuliers, mais en quelque façon l'acte même d'être qu'exprime le verbe être et non pas le substantif (et que nous écrivons comme M. de Waelhens, Etre avec *E* majuscule), il nous conduit vers la singularité à travers un Neutre qui éclaire et commande la pensée et rend intelligible. Quand il voit l'homme possédé par la liberté plutôt qu'un homme qui la possède, il met au-dessus de l'homme un Neutre qui éclaire la liberté sans la mettre en question—et ainsi, il ne détruit pas, il résume tout un courant de la philosophie occidentale.

Le Dasein que Heidegger met à la place de l'âme, de la conscience, du Moi, conserve la structure du Même. L'indépendance,—l'autarcie—venait à l'âme platonicienne (et à toutes ses contrefaçons) de sa patrie, du monde des Idées auxquelles, d'après le Phédon, elle s'apparente; et par conséquent dans ce monde, elle ne pouvait rencontrer rien de véritablement étranger. La raison, la faculté de se maintenir, identique, au-dessus des variations du devenir, formait l'âme de cette âme. Heidegger conteste à l'homme cette position dominante, mais il laisse le Dasein dans le Même, comme mortel. La possibilité de s'anéantir est précisément constitutive du Dasein, et maintient ainsi son ipséité. Ce néant est une mort, c'est-à-dire ma mort, ma possibilité (de l'impossibilité), mon pouvoir. Personne ne peut se substituer à moi pour mourir. L'instant suprême de la résolution est solitaire et personnel.

Certes, pour Heidegger, la liberté de l'homme dépend de la lumière de l'Etre et, par conséquent, ne semble pas principe. Mais il en fut ainsi dans l'idéalisme classique où le libre-arbitre passait pour la forme la plus basse de la liberté, et où la vraie liberté obéissait à l'universelle raison. La liberté hei-deggerienne est obéissante, mais l'obéissance la fait jaillir sans la mettre en question, sans révéler son injustice. L'Etre qui équivaut à l'indépendance et à l'extranéité des réalités, équi-vaut à la phosphorescence, à la lumière. Il se convertit en in-telligibilité. Le «mystère», essentiel à cette «obscure clarté», est un mode de cette conversion. L'indépendance s'en va en rayon-nement. *Sein und Zeit*, l'œuvre première et principale d'Heideg-ger, n'a peut-être jamais soutenu qu'une seule thèse: l'Etre est inséparable de la compréhension de l'être, l'Etre est déjà invo-cation de la subjectivité. Mais l'Etre *n'est pas* un étant. C'est un Neutre qui ordonne pensées et êtres, mais qui durcit la vo-lonté au lieu de lui faire honte. La conscience de sa finitude ne vient pas à l'homme de l'idée de l'infini, c'est-à-dire ne se révèle pas comme une imperfection, ne se réfère pas au Bien, ne se sait pas méchante. La philosophie heideggerienne marque précisément l'apogée d'une pensée où le fini ne se réfère pas à l'infini (prolongeant certaines tendances de la philosophie kantienne: séparation entre entendement et raison, divers thèmes de la dialectique transcendantale), où toute déficience n'est que faiblesse et toute faute, commise à l'égard de soi,— aboutissement d'une longue tradition de fierté d'héroïsme, de domination et de cruauté.

L'ontologie heideggerienne subordonne le rapport avec l'Autre à la relation avec le Neutre qu'est l'Etre et, par là, elle continue à exalter la volonté de la puissance dont Autrui seul peut ébranler la légitimité et troubler la bonne conscience.

Quand Heidegger signale l'oubli de l'Etre voilé par les diverses réalités qu'il éclaire, oubli dont se rendrait coupable la philosophie issue de Socrate, lorsqu'il déplore l'orientation de l'intelligence vers la technique, il maintient un régime de puissance plus inhumain que le machinisme et qui n'a peut-être pas la même source que lui. (Il n'est pas sûr que le national-socialisme provienne de la réification mécaniste des hommes et qu'il ne repose pas sur un enracinement paysan et une adoration féodale des hommes asservis pour les maîtres et seigneurs qui les commandent). Il s'agit d'une existence qui s'accepte comme naturelle, pour qui sa place au soleil, son sol, son *lieu* orientent toute signification. Il s'agit d'un *exister* payen. L'Etre l'ordonne bâtisseur et cultivateur, au sein d'un paysage familier, sur une terre maternelle. Anonyme, Neutre, il l'ordonne éthiquement indifférent et comme une liberté héroïque, étrangère à toute culpabilité à l'égard d'Autrui.

Cette maternité de la terre détermine en effet toute la civilisation occidentale de propriété, d'exploitation, de tyrannie politique et de guerre. Heidegger ne discute pas le pouvoir pré-technique de la possession qui s'accomplit précisément dans l'enracinement de la perception et que personne d'ailleurs n'a décrit d'une façon aussi géniale que lui. Perception où l'espace géométrique le plus abstrait se loge en fin de compte, mais perception qui ne peut trouver de place dans tout l'infini de l'étendue mathématique. Les analyses heideggeriennes du monde qui, dans *Sein und Zeit,* partaient de l'attirail des choses fabriquées, sont, dans sa dernière philosophie, portées par la vision des hauts paysages de la Nature, impersonnelle fécondité, matrice des êtres particuliers, matière inépuisable des choses.

Heidegger ne résume pas seulement toute une évolution de la philosophie occidentale. Il l'exalte en montrant de la façon la plus pathétique son essence anti-religieuse devenue une religion à rebours. La sobriété lucide de ceux qui se disent amis de la vérité et ennemis de l'opinion, aurait donc un prolongement mystérieux! Avec Heidegger, l'athéisme est paganisme, les textes pré-socratiques—des anti-Écritures. Heidegger montre dans quelle ivresse baigne la sobriété lucide des philosophes.

En somme, les thèses connues de la philosophie heideggerienne: la précellence de l'Etre par rapport à l'étant, de l'ontologie par rapport à la métaphysique, achèvent d'affirmer une tradition où le Même domine l'Autre, où la liberté—fût-elle identique à la raison—précède la justice. Celle-ci ne consiste-t-elle pas à mettre avant les obligations à l'égard de soi, l'obligation à l'égard de l'Autre—à mettre l'Autre avant le Même?

| III.—L'idée de l'Infini.

En renversant les termes, nous pensons suivre une tradition au moins aussi antique—celle qui ne lit pas le droit dans le pouvoir et qui ne réduit pas *tout autre* au Même. Contre les heideggeriens et les néo-hegeliens pour qui la philosophie commence par l'athéisme, il faut dire que la tradition de l'Autre n'est pas nécessairement religieuse, qu'elle est philosophique. Platon se tient en elle quand il met le Bien au-dessus de l'être, et, dans Phèdre, définit le vrai discours comme un discours avec des dieux. Mais c'est l'analyse cartésienne de l'idée de l'infini qui, de la manière la plus caractéristique, esquisse une structure dont nous voulons retenir d'ailleurs uniquement le *dessin formel*.

Chez Descartes, le moi qui pense entretient avec l'Infini une relation. Cette relation n'est ni celle qui rattache le contenant au contenu—puisque le moi ne peut contenir l'Infini; ni celle qui rattache le contenu au contenant puisque le moi est séparé de l'Infini. Cette relation décrite aussi négativement—est l'idée de l'Infini en nous.

Certes, des choses aussi nous avons des idées; mais l'idée de l'infini a ceci d'exceptionnel que son *idéatum* dépasse son idée. La distance entre idée et idéatum n'équivaut pas, pour l'idée de l'infini, à la distance qui sépare dans les autres représentations, l'acte mental de son objet. L'abîme qui sépare l'acte mental de son objet n'est pas assez profond pour que Descartes ne dise pas que l'âme peut rendre compte par elle-même des idées des choses finies. L'intentionalité qui anime l'idée de l'infini ne se compare à aucune autre: elle vise ce qu'elle ne peut embrasser et dans ce sens, précisément, l'Infini. Pour prendre le contrepied des formules dont nous avons usé plus haut—l'altérité de l'infini ne s'annule pas, ne s'amortit pas dans la pensée qui le pense. En pensant l'infini—le moi d'emblée *pense plus qu'il ne pense*. L'infini ne rentre pas dans l'*idée* de l'infini, n'est pas saisi; cette idée n'est pas un concept. L'infini, c'est le radicalement, l'absolument autre. La transcendance de l'infini par rapport au moi qui en est séparé et qui le pense, constitue la première marque de son infinitude.

L'idée de l'infini n'est donc pas[1] la seule qui apprenne ce qu'on ignore. Elle a été *mise* en nous. Elle n'est pas une réminiscence. Voilà l'expérience au seul sens radical de ce terme: une relation avec l'extérieur, avec l'Autre, sans que cette extériorité puisse s'intégrer au Même. Le penseur qui a l'idée de l'infini est *plus que lui-même,* et ce gonflement, ce surplus, ne vient pas de dedans, comme dans le fameux *projet* des philosophes modernes, où le sujet se dépasse en créant.

Comment une telle structure peut-elle demeurer philosophique? Quel est le rapport qui, tout en demeurant *le plus dans le moins,* ne se transforme pas en relation où, selon les mystiques, le papillon attiré par le feu se consume dans le feu. Comment maintenir les êtres séparés, ne pas sombrer dans la participation, contre laquelle la philosophie du Même aura l'immortel mérite d'avoir protesté?

IV.—L'idée de l'infini et le visage d'Autrui.

L'expérience, l'idée de l'infini, se tient dans le rapport avec Autrui. L'idée de l'infini est le rapport social.

Ce rapport consiste à aborder un être absolument extérieur. L'infini de cet être qu'on ne peut pour cela même contenir, garantit et constitue cette extériorité. Elle n'équivaut pas à la distance entre sujet et objet. L'objet, nous le savons s'intègre à l'identité du Même. Le Moi en fait son thème, et, dès lors, sa propriété, son butin ou sa proie ou sa victime. L'extériorité de l'être infini se manifeste dans la résistance absolue que, de par son apparition—de par son épiphanie—il oppose à tous mes pouvoirs. Son épiphanie n'est pas simplement l'apparition d'une forme dans la lumière, sensible ou intelligible, mais déjà ce *non* lancé aux pouvoirs. Son *logos* est: «Tu ne tueras point.»

Certes, Autrui s'offre à tous mes pouvoirs, succombe à toutes mes ruses, à tous mes crimes. Ou me résiste de toute sa force et de toutes les ressources imprévisibles de sa propre liberté. Je me mesure avec lui. Mais il peut aussi—et c'est là qu'il me présente sa face—s'opposer à moi, par-delà toute mesure—par le découvert total et la totale nudité de ses yeux sans défense, par la droiture, par la franchise absolue de son regard. L'inquiétude solipsiste de la conscience se voyant,

---

1 See page 107, note 50 below.

dans toutes ses aventures, captive de Soi, prend fin ici: la vraie extériorité est dans ce regard qui m'interdit toute conquête. Non pas que la conquête défie mes pouvoirs trop faibles, mais je ne *peux plus pouvoir:* la structure de ma liberté, nous le verrons plus loin, se renverse totalement. Ici s'établit une relation non pas avec une résistance très grande, mais avec l'absolument Autre—avec la résistance de ce qui n'a pas de résistance—avec la résistance éthique. C'est elle qui ouvre la dimension même de l'infini—de ce qui arrête l'impérialisme irrésistible du Même et du Moi. Nous appelons *visage* l'épiphanie de ce qui peut se présenter aussi directement à un Moi et, par là-même, aussi extérieurement.

Le visage ne ressemble point à la forme plastique, toujours déjà désertée, trahie par l'être qu'elle révèle, comme le marbre dont, déjà, les dieux qu'il manifeste, s'absentent. Elle diffère de la face animale où l'être ne se rejoint pas encore dans sa stupidité de brute. Dans le visage l'exprimé *assiste* à l'expression, exprime son expression même—reste toujours maître du sens qu'il livre. «Acte pur» à sa manière, il se refuse à l'identification, ne rentre pas dans du déjà connu, porte, comme dit Platon, secours à lui-même, parle. L'épiphanie du visage est tout entière langage.

La résistance éthique est la présence de l'infini. Si la résistance au meurtre, inscrite sur le visage, n'était pas éthique mais réelle—nous aurions accès à une réalité très faible ou très forte. Elle mettrait, peut-être, en échec notre volonté. La volonté se jugerait déraisonnable et arbitraire. Mais nous n'aurions pas accès à l'être extérieur, à ce qu'absolument, on ne peut ni englober, ni posséder, où notre liberté renonce à son impérialisme du moi, où elle ne se trouve pas seulement arbitraire, mais injuste. Mais, dès lors, Autrui n'est pas simplement une liberté autre; pour me donner le savoir de l'injustice, il faut que son regard me vienne d'une dimension de l'idéal. Il faut qu'Autrui soit plus près de Dieu que Moi. Ce qui n'est certainement pas une invention de philosophe, mais la première donnée de la conscience morale que l'on pourrait définir comme conscience du privilège d'Autrui par rapport à moi. La justice bien ordonnée commence par Autrui.

| V.—*L'idée de l'infini comme désir.*

Le rapport éthique ne se greffe pas sur un rapport préalable de connaissance. Il est fondement et non pas superstructure.

Le distinguer de la connaissance, ce n'est pas le réduire à un sentiment subjectif. Seule l'idée de l'infini où l'être déborde l'idée, où l'Autre déborde le Même rompt avec les jeux internes de l'âme et mérite le nom d'expérience, de relation avec l'extérieur. Elle est, dès lors, plus *cognitive* que la connaissance elle-même et toute objectivité doit y participer.

La vision en Dieu (du 2ᵉ Entretien Métaphysique) de Malebranche, exprime à la fois cette référence de toute connaissance à l'idée de l'infini et le fait que l'idée de l'infini n'est pas comme les connaissances qui se réfèrent à elle. On ne peut, en effet, soutenir que cette idée elle-même soit une thématisation ou une objectivation sans la réduire à la présence de l'Autre dans le Même, présence sur laquelle précisément elle tranche. Chez Descartes, une certaine ambiguïté reste sur ce point, le cogito reposant sur Dieu, fonde par ailleurs l'existence de Dieu: la priorité de l'Infini se subordonne à l'adhésion libre de la volonté, initialement maîtresse d'elle-même.

Que le mouvement de l'âme qui est plus cognitif que la connaissance, puisse avoir une structure différente de la contemplation—voilà le point sur lequel nous nous séparons de la lettre du cartésianisme. L'infini n'est pas objet d'une contemplation, c'est-à-dire n'est pas à la mesure de la pensée qui le pense. L'idée de l'infini est une pensée qui à tout *instant pense plus qu'elle ne pense*. Une pensée qui pense plus qu'elle ne pense est Désir. Le Désir «mesure» l'infinité de l'infini.

Le terme que nous avons choisi pour marquer la propulsion, le gonflement de ce dépassement, s'oppose à l'affectivité de l'amour et à l'indigence du besoin. En dehors de la faim qu'on satisfait, de la soif qu'on étanche et des sens qu'on apaise, existe l'Autre, absolument autre que l'on désire par-delà ces satisfactions, sans que le corps connaisse aucun geste pour apaiser le Désir, sans qu'il soit possible d'inventer aucune caresse nouvelle. Désir inassouvissable non pas parce qu'il répond à une faim infinie, mais parce qu'il n'appelle pas de nourriture. Désir sans satisfaction qui, par là-même, prend acte de l'altérité d'Autrui. Il la situe dans la dimension de hauteur et d'idéal qu'il ouvre précisément dans l'être.

Les désirs que l'on peut satisfaire ne ressemblent au Désir que par intermittence: dans les déceptions de la satisfaction ou dans les accroissements du vide qui scandent leur volupté. Ils passent pour l'essence du désir à tort. Le vrai Désir est celui que le Désiré ne comble pas, mais creuse. Il est bonté. Il ne se réfère pas à une patrie ou à une plénitude perdues, il n'est pas le mal du retour—il n'est pas nostalgie. Il est le manque dans l'être qui *est* complètement et à qui rien ne manque. Le mythe platonicien de l'amour, fils de l'abondance et de la pauvreté, peut-il s'interpréter aussi comme attestant, dans le Désir, l'indigence d'une richesse, l'insuffisance de ce qui se suffit? Platon en rejetant dans le Banquet le mythe de l'androgyne n'a-t-il pas affirmé la nature non-nostalgique du Désir, la plénitude et la joie de l'être qui l'éprouve?

VI.—*L'idée de l'infini et la conscience morale.*

Comment le visage échappe-t-il au pouvoir discrétionnaire de la volonté qui dispose de l'évidence? Connaître le visage n'est-ce pas en *prendre* conscience et prendre conscience n'est-ce pas adhérer *librement*? L'idée de l'infini, comme *idée,* ne ramène-t-elle pas inévitablement au schéma du Même englobant l'Autre? A moins que l'idée de l'infini ne signifie l'effondrement de la bonne conscience du Même. Tout se passe en effet comme si la présence du visage—l'idée de l'infini en Moi—était la mise en question de ma liberté.

Que le libre-arbitre soit arbitraire et qu'il faille sortir de ce stade élémentaire—voilà une vieille certitude des philosophes. Mais l'arbitraire renvoie, pour tous, à un fondement rationnel, justification de la liberté par elle-même. Le fondement rationnel de la liberté est encore la prééminence du Même.

La nécessité de justifier l'arbitraire ne tient d'ailleurs qu'à l'échec subi par le pouvoir arbitraire. *La spontanéité même de la liberté ne se met pas en question*—telle semble être la tradition dominante de la philosophie occidentale. Seule la limitation de la liberté serait tragique ou ferait scandale. La liberté pose un problème uniquement parce qu'elle ne s'est pas choisie. L'échec de ma spontanéité éveillerait la raison et la théorie. Il y aurait une douleur qui serait mère de la sagesse. L'échec m'amènerait à mettre frein à ma violence et introduirait de l'ordre dans les relations humaines, car tout est permis sauf l'impossible. Surtout les théories politiques modernes depuis Hobbes déduisent l'ordre social de la légitimité, du droit incontestable de la liberté.

Le visage d'Autrui—n'est pas la révélation de l'arbitraire de la volonté, mais de son injustice. La conscience de mon injustice se produit quand je m'incline non pas devant le fait, mais devant Autrui. Autrui m'apparaît dans son visage non pas comme un obstacle, ni comme menace que j'évalue, mais comme ce qui me mesure. Il faut, pour me sentir injuste, que je me mesure à l'infini. Il faut avoir l'idée de l'infini, qui est aussi l'idée du parfait comme le sait Descartes, pour connaître ma propre imperfection. L'infini ne m'arrête pas comme une force mettant la mienne en échec, elle met en question le droit naïf de mes pouvoirs, ma glorieuse spontanéité de vivant, de «force qui va».

Mais cette façon de se mesurer à la perfection de l'infini, n'est pas une considération théorétique à son tour où la liberté reprendrait spontanément ses droits. C'est une *honte* qu'a d'elle-même la liberté qui se découvre meurtrière et usurpatrice dans son exercice même. Un exégète du deuxième siècle, plus soucieux de ce qu'il devait faire que de ce qu'il avait à espérer ne comprenait pas que la Bible commençât par le récit de la création au lieu de nous placer d'emblée devant les premiers commandements de l'Exode. C'est à grand'peine qu'il convint que le récit de la création était tout de même nécessaire à la vie du juste: si la terre n'avait pas été *donnée* à l'homme, mais simplement *prise* par lui, il ne l'aurait possédée que comme brigand. La possession spontanée et naïve ne peut se justifier par la vertu de sa propre spontanéité.

L'existence n'est pas condamnée à la liberté, mais jugée et investie comme liberté. La liberté ne saurait se présenter toute nue. Cette investiture de la liberté constitue la vie morale elle-même. Elle est de part en part hétéronomie.

La volonté qui dans la rencontre d'Autrui est jugée, n'assume pas le jugement qu'elle accueille. Ce serait encore le retour du Même décidant en dernier ressort de l'Autre, l'hétéronomie absorbée dans l'autonomie. La structure de la volonté libre devenant *bonté* ne ressemble plus à la spontanéité glorieuse et suffisante du Moi et du bonheur et qui serait l'ultime mouvement de l'être. Elle en est comme l'inversion. La vie de la liberté se découvrant injuste, la vie de la liberté dans l'hétéronomie, consiste pour la liberté en un mouvement infini de se mettre toujours davantage en question. Et ainsi se creuse la profondeur même de l'intériorité. L'accroissement d'exigence, que j'ai à l'égard de moi-même aggrave le jugement qui se porte sur moi, c'est-à-dire ma responsabilité. Et l'aggravation de ma responsabilité accroît ces exigences. Dans ce mouvement, ma liberté n'a pas le dernier mot, je ne retrouve jamais ma solitude, ou, si l'on veut, la conscience morale est essentiellement insatisfaite, ou si l'on veut encore, toujours Désir.

L'insatisfaction de la conscience morale n'est pas seulement la douleur des âmes délicates et scrupuleuses, mais la contraction, le creux, le retrait en soi et la systole même de la conscience tout court; et la conscience éthique elle-même n'est pas invoquée dans tout cet exposé comme une variété «particulièrement recommandable» de la conscience, mais comme la forme concrète que revêt un mouvement plus fondamental que la liberté, l'idée de l'infini. Forme concrète de ce qui précède la liberté et qui, cependant, ne nous ramène ni à la violence, ni à la confusion de ce qui est séparé, ni à la nécessité, ni à la fatalité.

Voilà, enfin, la situation par excellence où l'on n'est pas seul. Mais si cette situation ne livre pas la preuve de l'existence d'Autrui, c'est que la preuve suppose déjà le mouvement et l'adhésion d'une libre volonté, une certitude. De sorte que la situation où la libre volonté s'investit, précède la preuve. Toute certitude, en effet, est l'œuvre d'une liberté solitaire. Accueil du réel dans mes idées *a priori*, adhésion de ma libre volonté—le dernier geste de la connaissance est liberté. Le face à face où cette liberté se met en question comme injuste, où elle se trouve un maître et un juge, s'accomplit avant la certitude, mais aussi avant l'incertitude.

La situation est, au plus fort sens de ce terme, une expérience: contact d'une réalité qui ne se coule en aucune idée *a priori*, qui les déborde toutes—et c'est pour cela précisément que nous avons pu parler d'infini. Aucun mouvement de liberté ne saurait s'approprier le visage ni avoir l'air de le «constituer». Le visage a déjà été là quand on l'anticipait ou le constituait—il y collaborait, il parlait. Le visage est expérience pure, expérience sans concept. La conception par laquelle les données de nos sens s'agrègent au Moi, finit—devant Autrui—par la dé-ception par le désaisissement qui caractérise toutes nos tentatives d'embrasser ce réel. Mais il faut distinguer l'incompréhension purement négative d'Autrui qui dépend de notre mauvaise volonté—et l'incompréhension essentielle de l'Infini qui a une face positive—est conscience morale et Désir.

L'insatisfaction de la conscience morale, la dé-ception devant autrui coïncident avec le Désir. C'est l'un des points essentiels de tout cet exposé. Le Désir de l'infini n'a pas la complaisance sentimentale de l'amour, mais la rigueur de l'exigence morale. Et la rigueur de l'exigence morale—ne s'impose pas brutalement—mais est Désir, par l'attraction et l'infinie hauteur de l'être même, au bénéfice de qui s'exerce la bonté. Dieu ne commande que par les hommes pour qui il faut agir.

La conscience,—la présence de soi à soi, passe pour le thème ultime de la réflexion. La conscience morale, variation sur ce thème, variété de conscience y joindrait le souci de valeurs et de normes. Nous avons à ce sujet posé quelques questions: le soi peut-il se présenter à soi, avec tant de naturelle complaisance? Peut-il sans honte apparaître à ses propres yeux? Le narcissisme est-il possible?[2] La conscience morale n'est-elle pas la critique et le principe de la présence de soi à soi? Dès lors, si l'essence de la philosophie consiste à remonter en deçà de toutes les certitudes vers le principe, si elle vit de critique, le visage d'Autrui serait le commencement même de la philosophie. Thèse d'hétéronomie qui rompt avec une tradition très vénérable. En revanche, la situation où l'on n'est pas seul ne se réduit pas à l'heureuse rencontre d'âmes fraternelles qui se saluent et qui conversent. Cette situation est conscience morale—exposition de ma liberté au jugement de l'Autre. Dénivellement qui nous a autorisé d'entrevoir dans le regard de celui à qui justice est due, la dimension de la hauteur et de l'idéal.

---

2 Nous avons traité les divers thèmes qui s'y rapportent dans trois articles publiés dans la *Revue de Métaphysique et de Morale:* L'ontologie est-elle fondamentale? (Janvier-Mars 1951), Liberté et Commandement (Juillet-Septembre 1953), Le Moi et la totalité (Octobre-Décembre 1954).

| Text and Commentary

| "Philosophy and the Idea
| of the Infinite"

| 1. Autonomy and Heteronomy

Every philosophy seeks truth. Sciences, too, can be defined by this search, for from the philosophic *eros*,[1] alive or dormant in them, they derive their noble passion. If this definition seems too general and rather empty, it will, however, permit us to distinguish two directions the philosophical spirit takes, and this will clarify its physiognomy. These directions interact in the idea of truth.

1. Truth implies experience.[2] In the truth, a thinker maintains a relationship with a reality distinct from him, other than

---

The following pages reprint—with a few changes—Alfonso Lingis's translation (in Levinas, *Collected Philosophical Papers*, Phaenomenologica, vol. 100 [Dordrecht: M. Nijhoff, 1987]: 47–59) of Levinas's article "La philosophie et l'idée de l'Infini," which was published in the *Revue de Métaphysique et de Morale* 62 (1957): 241–53 and reprinted in Levinas's *En découvrant l'existence avec Husserl et Heidegger*, 2nd ed. (Paris: Vrin, 1967), 165–78. Most of my notes explain Levinas's text or its background; there are also references added to the essay's publication in *CPP*. The question as to whether *"l'Infini"* in the title is rendered better by "Infinity" (as in *CPP*) or by "the Infinite" (as translated here) will be discussed in note 53.

1 As Désir (desire), the Platonic notion of *eros* opens also *Totality and Infinity* (*TI* 3–5). The analysis there given is anticipated in section 5 of this article. However, Levinas's analysis of desire is also inspired by Plato's *Philebus* (50b ff.).

2 "Experience" or "genuine experience" is used here and also in *TI* (cf., for example, *TI* 20^{34}, 22^{22}, $46^{1,2}$, 170^{19}, $194^{29,31,34}/50^3$ 51^{23}, $73^{23,30}$, 196^{16}, $219^{9,10,12}$) to indicate the nonidealistic, transcendent moment of all knowledge. Afterwards, however (cf. already *TI* xiii^{33}/25^{21}), "experience" is seen as belonging to the constellation of ontological words (such as "evidence," "phenomenon," "living presence," "consciousness," "be-

him—"absolutely other," according to the expression taken up again by Jankélévitch.[3] For experience deserves its name only if it transports us beyond what constitutes our nature.[4] Genuine experience must even lead us beyond the Nature that surrounds us, which is not jealous of the marvelous secrets it harbors, and, in complicity with men, submits to their reason and inventions; in it men also feel themselves to be at home. Truth would thus designate the outcome of a movement that leaves a world that is intimate and familiar, even if we have not yet explored it completely, and goes toward another region,[5] toward a *beyond*, as Plato puts it.[6] Truth would imply more than exteriority: transcendence.[7] Philosophy would be concerned with the absolutely

---

ing," and even "truth") that constitutes the realm of Being to be transcended toward a beyond.

3 *Philosophie première: Introduction à une philosophie du "presque"* (Paris: PUF, 1954), 120–22; Jankélévitch uses the expression to indicate the neoplatonic One.

4 The word "nature" is ambiguous. Besides "human nature" and the nature that surrounds us, it might here also point to *physis* as interpreted by Heidegger in his commentary on Aristotle's *Physics* B 1: "Vom Wesen und Begriff der Φύσις: Aristoteles Physik B,1" (*Wegmarken,* GA 9, 239–302), according to which interpretation it is the overall process of self-unfolding and appearance ("das aufgehende Anwesen" des "Seienden als solches im Ganzen"). Cf. also "Vom Wesen der Wahrheit" §4 in *Wegmarken,* GA 9, 189–91; *Basic Writings,* 126–30.

5 The French expression "vers l'étranger" is intentionally ambiguous. It expresses at the same time a foreign country, that which is abroad—namely the realm of the unknown (compare Plato's image of another, far away, higher, more divine and truly real region)—and the stranger who knocks on my door asking for hospitality, as defended by the prophetic tradition of the Bible. (Lingis's translation "goes toward the stranger" privileges this second meaning.) In opposition to our "being at home" mentioned in the former sentence, the orientation toward the strangeness of the "étranger" expresses the heteronomous side of all experience opposed to its "homely" or autonomous side.

6 Cf. *Phaedo* 61de. Both dying and philosophizing are a journey abroad (literally, "out there"). Cf. also *Phaedo* 66bc and 117c ("a change of dwelling-place from here to yonder"); *Symposium* 211d–212a (a noble life presupposes that one looks "out there," where "the beautiful itself" is to be seen); and *Republic* 484c.

7 "Exteriority" is taken here as a qualification of a reality that, at first met outside consciousness (for example as matter or "nature"), can, however, be assimilated and integrated in the form of a representation or concept. In the subtitle of *Totality and Infinity* and elsewhere, "exteriority" means, on the contrary, the transcendent, which cannot be engulfed by consciousness.

other; it would be heteronomy[8] itself. Let us go yet further. Distance alone does not suffice to distinguish transcendence from exteriority. Truth, the daughter of experience, has very lofty pretensions; it opens upon the very dimension of the ideal. In this way, philosophy means metaphysics, and metaphysics inquires about the divine.[9]

2. But truth also means the free adherence to a proposition, the outcome of a free research. The freedom[10] of the investigator,

---

8 "Heteronomy" summarizes here the following moments: (a) experience implies otherness; (b) otherness is not simple exteriority (which could be assimilated by the subject of experience); (c) transcendence, not sufficiently qualified by the metaphor of distance or farness.

9 The transcendent (a) is radically different; (b) it comes from "on high" (this "height" is expressed in the phrase "la vérité pretend très haut," rendered as "has very lofty pretensions"); (c) it imposes a law; and (d) it is therefore "ideal." The last determination is ambiguous. First, it points to Plato's ideas, to which all phenomena point as the essence of their being and splendor as well as the ideal of this perfection; second, it points through them toward the source of the ideality of all ideas: ("the idea" of) the Good, which is the giving source of all beingness and truth. As beyond the ideas, the Good itself is not an idea or essence but "beyond essence." Plato calls it "divine" (theion). By Christian, Arab, and Jewish theologians "the Good" has been understood as a name or pseudonym of the God represented in the Bible and the Koran. In Totality and Infinity, Levinas prefers to call "the beyond" the infinite. The adjective "divine" is dangerous insofar as the transcendent—according to TI 4/34—is both the other human being and "the Most High." "Metaphysics" as the passage of thinking from "Nature" and Being toward the Beyond is here opposed to "ontology" as a thought that remains within the horizon of Being (cf. also the end of section 2). This opposition is maintained in and after TI, but the word "metaphysics" is given up in later works.

10 Freedom is here understood as a being-at-home through a full possession of the world. Hegel's "being-at-home-in-the-world" (zu Hause sein in der Welt) is a good concretization of this mastership. On the theoretical level, it takes the form of a knowledge in which all a posteriori elements are (re)produced by a complete deduction from a priori principles, and ultimately from one all-encompassing Principle, which includes the totality of beings as well as all knowledge and is their germinal and final unity. Truth, then, is the transparent integration and possession of the universe of beings by a conceptual insight that could have created them if it had not only their concepts but also the power to make them exist. Philosophy is then no longer research, journey, hospitality with regard to the surprises of experience but the restful possession of a safe property and enjoyment of the truth. The intimate coincidence of freedom and truth expressed in this sentence might be a hint at Heidegger's meditation on their unity in his essay "On the Essence of Truth" (1943), but Levinas's description of philosophical autonomy fits much better into Hegel's explicit identification of freedom with reason and truth.

the thinker on whom no constraint weighs, is expressed in truth. What else is this freedom but the thinking being's refusal to be alienated in the adherence, the preserving of his nature, his identity, the feat of remaining the same despite the unknown lands into which thought seems to lead?[11] Perceived in this way, philosophy would be engaged in reducing to the Same all that is opposed to it as *other*.[12] It would be moving toward *auto-nomy*, a stage in which nothing irreducible would limit thought any longer, in which, consequently, thought, nonlimited, would be free. Philosophy would thus be tantamount to the conquest of being by man over the course of history.[13]

Freedom, autonomy, the *reduction of the Other to the Same*, lead to this formula: the conquest of being by man over the course of history.[14] This reduction does not represent some abstract

---

11 Although it recognizes to a certain extent that philosophy is a journey abroad or "from here to there" (*"vers l'étranger"*), on which one is surprised by strange and unsuspected events, the interpretation of philosophy as the conquest of autonomous knowledge sees it as an odyssey: by the integration of all his adventures, the traveler comes back to his point of departure. He has enriched himself but has not changed radically. The truth he found was already there from the outset. In opposition to Abraham, who went out to "unknown lands," Ulysses remained the same. By the interpretation of freedom as self-possession and (theoretical as well as practical) mastership over all beings, Levinas prepares his identification of "auto-nomy"—i.e., the being ruled by the law (*nomos*) of oneself (*autos*)—as realm of "the same" (*tauton*). As "preserving of" human "nature," this active self-identification will later on be equated with Spinoza's *conatus essendi.*

12 The set of concepts Same (*tauton*) and Other (*to heteron*) is taken from Plato's *Sophist* (254b–256b), where they figure as highest categories of being. Cf. also *Timaeus* 35ab and *Theaetetus* 185cd. In "La pensée de l'Etre et la question de l'Autre," first published in 1978, Levinas refers to the circle of the Same encompassing the circle of the Other, as stated in the *Timaeus* (*DDVI* 176).

13 This is a clear allusion to the (neo-)Hegelian interpretation of history as the conquest of the universe by technical, economical, and political practice and above all by the theoretical understanding in the forms of art, religion, science, and philosophy. The limitations that presented themselves as obstacles to humankind's historical search for self-possession and self-knowledge are not abolished but integrated and thus no longer felt as obstacles. As limitations by which the spirit liberates itself from indeterminateness and thus concretizes itself in the form of a human world, they form the inner structure of its historical unfolding and actual existence.

14 The secret of Western philosophy (and of Western civilization as a whole) is not, as Heidegger thought, a fundamental stand with regard to the relation between Being and beings, but its nonrecognition of the

schema; it is man's Ego. The existence of an Ego takes place as an identification of the diverse.[15] So many events happen to it, so many years age it, and yet the Ego remains the Same! The Ego, the Self, the ipseity (as it is called in our time), does not remain invariable in the midst of change like a rock assailed by the waves (which is anything but invariable); the Ego remains the Same by making of disparate and diverse events a history—its history. And this is the original event of the identification of the Same, prior to the identity of a rock, and a condition of that identity.[16]

Autonomy or heteronomy? The choice of Western philosophy has most often been on the side of freedom and the Same. Was not philosophy born, on Greek soil, to dethrone opinion, in which all tyrannies lurk and threaten?[17] With opinion, the most subtle and treacherous poison seeps into the soul, altering it in its

---

radical difference of the Same (*tauton*) and the Other (*to heteron*), as expressed in its reduction of all heteronomy to absolute autonomy. Both Heidegger and Levinas, in their search for a renewal of "first philosophy," retrieve the central question of Plato's *Sophist.* Whereas Heidegger begins *Sein und Zeit* by quoting the gigantic fight about the sense of Being (*to on*), Levinas takes the categories of the Same and the Other, as pure in themselves but mixed with the other highest categories (being, movement, and rest), to be more "fundamental" than Being (cf. *Sophist* 254b–256b, especially 254e). The reduction of all otherness to the Same of Being, with which Parmenides started the Western history of philosophy, remained its leading thread, including Hegel's philosophy of history and even Heidegger's philosophy of Being if—as Levinas claims—this, too, must be understood as a gigantic "tautology."

15 Heidegger's renewal of Husserlian phenomenology has shown that human existence as such and in all its ways—like hammering, signifying, being anxious or angry, loving, enjoying, etc.—is an active practicing and understanding of the world and its phenomena. Levinas characterizes the way in which this praxis and understanding were performed and interpreted in Western civilization as an assimilation of all otherness to the all-embracing identity of an ego-centered universe. The active identification of beings by which the ego posits itself as world center constitutes its very selfhood.

16 The identity of the ego, for and by whom the universe of beings opens and unfolds itself as a panoramic world, is not a static substance surrounded by things and only accidentally touched by lived events but rather an active process by which its own being is changed as much as the world of things and events in which it is involved. The process of identification is the ego's (and humanity's) being a history; its having an identity—and possessing a world—is built up through this sort of history.

17 Cf. Plato's discussion, in book 10 of the *Republic,* of the affinities between a life governed by *doxa* (opinion) and the varieties of violence characteristic of tyranny, and Levinas's analyses of the opposition between freedom and violence in "Freedom and Command" (*CPP* 15–23).

depths, making of it an other. The soul "eaten up by others," as Mr. Teste would say,[18] does not feel its alteration, and is hence exposed to all violences. But this penetration and this prestige of opinion presuppose a mythical stage of being in which souls participate in one another, in the sense Lévy-Bruhl has given to the term.[19] Against the turbid and disturbing participation opinion presupposes, philosophy willed souls that are separate and in a sense impenetrable. The idea of the Same, the idea of freedom, seemed to offer the most firm guarantee of such a separation.[20]

Thus Western thought very often seemed to exclude the transcendent, encompass every Other in the Same, and proclaim the philosophical birthright of autonomy.

---

18 Monsieur Teste, Valéry's retrieval of Descartes, spoke of another captivated soul when at the opera he whispered: "On n'est beau, on n'est extraordinaire que pour les autres! Ils sont mangés par les autres!" (*Œuvres* [Paris: Gallimard, 1960], 2:20: "One is beautiful and extraordinary only for the others! They are devoured by the others!").

19 This is explained in Levinas's article "Lévy-Bruhl et la philosophie contemporaine," *Revue Philosophique de la France et de l'Etranger* 147 (1957): 556–69.

20 Attempts to overcome all kinds of intellectual slavery belong to the greatness of the Western tradition, as expressed from the outset by Parmenides and Plato. Opinion is still the most treacherous and effective weapon by which Machiavellian dictators deprive their subjects of their capacity to judge and will by themselves. The philosophical and scientific fight against opinion seems therefore to be a fight for emancipation, selfhood, liberty. By freeing us from a nonchosen and violently extracted agreement with tyrants, it seems to grant us independence. The lack of freedom caused by credulity and fought against by the Greek philosophers was the expression of the immersion in a world of myths and magic, in which "participation" is the rule. As his article "Lévy-Bruhl and Contemporary Philosophy" (see note 19) shows, and as he indicated already in *De l'existence à l'existant* (98–100), Levinas has been impressed by the similarities between the description of mythical cultures as cultures of monistic immersion and certain features of Western civilization. The emergence of Greek philosophy is here interpreted as an attempt to escape from a prephilosophical world of participation by conquering individual freedom and responsibility. Freedom is not possible unless the human individuals ("souls" or *psychai*) have become separated from the totality of which they were elements; by this separation, they are then also separated from one another. The way in which Greek (and Western) philosophy tried to emancipate individuals from mythical monism introduced, however, another form of monism: the philosophical reduction of all otherness to the Same of Being. The task of philosophy as pursued by Levinas is to find a way of thinking of individual separateness and responsibility without either justifying any form of slavery or falling back into mythical or "mystical participation." This task coincides with the task of discovering a nonalienating sense of heteronomy.

2. Narcissism, or the Primacy of the Same

Autonomy, the philosophy which aims to ensure the freedom, or the identity of beings, presupposes that freedom itself is sure of its right, is justified without recourse to anything further, is complacent in itself, like Narcissus.[21] When, in the philosophical life that realizes this freedom, there arises a term foreign to the philosophical life, other—the land that supports us and disappoints our efforts, the sky that elevates us and ignores us, the forces of nature that aid us and kill us, things that encumber us or serve us, men who love us and enslave us—it becomes an obstacle; it has to be surmounted and integrated into this life. But truth is just this victory and this integration. In evidence the violence of the encounter with the non-I is deadened. The commerce with exterior truth as enacted in true cognition is thus not opposed to freedom but coincides with it. The search for truth becomes the very respiration of a free being, exposed to exterior realities that shelter, but also threaten, its freedom. Thanks to truth, these realities, whose plaything I am in danger of becoming, are understood by me.[22]

The "I think," thought in the first person, the soul conversing with itself or, qua reminiscence, rediscovering the teachings it receives, thus promote freedom.[23] Freedom will triumph

---

21 The characterization of autonomy as given here has ethical overtones insofar as it hints at a lack of "bad conscience" (*mauvaise conscience*) that belongs to the normal experience of human existence as a whole. Cf., for instance, Levinas's essays "De la déficience sans souci au sens nouveau," *Concilium*, no. 113 (1976) and "La mauvaise conscience et l'inexorable," *DDVI* 258–65. However faithful to the primary question of first philosophy, Levinas's purpose is not to found philosophy, ontology, or metaphysics on ethics but to reach the point or the dimension where the theoretical and the practical still coincide.

22 Having enumerated a few examples of experiences that seem to support a realistic epistemology, Levinas argues that understanding and truth not only cope with the "violence" of surprising events and appearances but also reduce it to a harmless element of a spiritual property that testifies to our freedom. In the evidence of a theory, all obstacles have been conquered and all exteriority interiorized. Truth is integration.

23 Descartes's cogito is here equated with Plato's dialogue of the soul with itself (*Sophist* 263e4 and 264a9), in which it rediscovers, by reminiscence (*anamnesis*), the truth that was hidden in its own depth. In the Platonic model of discovery, which prevailed in Western philosophy, the role of the teacher is reduced to the help I need in order to remember what I always already (*je schon*) knew. Once I know, I no

when the soul's monologue will have reached universality, will have encompassed the totality of being, encompassing even the animal individual which lodged this thought.[24] Every experience of the world, of the elements and objects, lends itself to this dialectic of the soul conversing with itself, enters into it, belongs to it. The things will be ideas, and will be conquered, dominated, possessed in the course of an economic and political history in which this thought will be unfolded. It is doubtless for this reason that Descartes will say that the soul might

---

longer need a guide. Cf. Plato, *Theatetus* 150a–151d; *Meno* 80d ff., *Phaedo* 72e ff.; *Phaedrus* 249bc.

Another model of thought is found in other traditions in which all thinking is seen as essentially supported by instruction. Here teachers cannot be replaced by the knowledge of their pupils. They remain unique, and their death cannot be compensated for. The only "compensation" for which they can hope is the emergence of other teachers— maybe their former pupils—in order to continue a traditional as well as absolutely new and unique instruction (*enseignement*). Cf. *TI* 70, 38, 62, 64–65/97, 67, 89, 92. Since Heidegger's philosophy is always at the background of Levinas's thought, it might be helpful, notwithstanding the enormous differences between Plato and Heidegger, to compare Plato's interpretation of philosophy as *anamnesis* with the summary of Heidegger's "method" given by T. Sheehan at the end of his excellent article "Heidegger's Topic: Excess, Recess, Access," *Tijdschrift voor Filosofie* 41 (1979): 615–35: "Therefore there is no method which could show us for the first time the topic of philosophy or lead us to the place of thought. For we are already there. The point is not to be led to the topic/*topos* but rather to remember what we already know and to become what we already are. In the words of the poet [T.S. Eliot],

> We shall not cease from exploration
> And the end of all our exploring
> Will be to arrive where we started
> And know the place for the first time."

Compare also this conception of space, place (*topos*), and traveling with what has been said above about the going "*vers l'étranger*" and the radical difference between Ulysses and Abraham.

24 By the phrase "jusqu'à l'individu animal qui logeait cette pensée," Levinas alludes to Aristotle's definition of the human being as an "animal" (or better, "a living being") "having logos" ("*zooion logikon*" or "*zooion logon echon*") in *Politics* 1253a10 (cf. 1332b4) and *Nic. Ethics*, 1102a330 and 1139a5. Logos is interpreted here as the overwhelming ability to transform everything into an idea of the soul. With allusions to Hegelian dialectics, the following two phrases present the practical aspects of human existence as the unfolding of a more fundamental idealism at the roots of our civilization. Cf. *Transcendance et Hauteur*, 89, 91–93.

be the origin of the ideas that relate to exterior things, and thus *account* for the real.[25]

The essence of truth will then not be in the heteronomous relationship with an unknown God, but in the already-known which has to be uncovered or freely invented in oneself, and in which everything unknown is comprised. It is fundamentally opposed to a God that reveals.[26] Philosophy is atheism, or rather unreligion, negation of a God that reveals himself and puts truths into us. This is Socrates' teaching when he leaves to the master only the exercise of maieutics: every lesson introduced into the soul was already in it. The I's identification, its marvelous autarchy,[27] is the natural crucible of this transmutation of the Other

---

25 Cf. Descartes, third *Meditation*, AT, 9:31 (translation by Laurence J. Lafleur: *Meditation on First Philosophy* [Indianapolis, Ind.: Bobbs-Merrill, 1960], 36).

26 "The essence of truth" seems to be a translation of *"das Wesen der Wahrheit"* (Cf. *Wegmarken*, GA 9:177–202; *Basic Writings*, 113–41), by which Heidegger evokes the realm of interaction between the truth's disclosing and withdrawing itself and the openness of *Dasein*. If Levinas aims here indeed at Heidegger's conception of truth, he suggests that it is the direct continuation of Socrates' teaching insofar as this sees thinking as the explanation of a prephilosophical familiarity with the ultimate horizon of Truth, within which eventually—at a later stage of the search— "the gods" or "the God" might appear as beings who owe their being to Truth of Being itself. Levinas's suggestion that a certain "relationship of heteronomy with regard to an unknown God" (who might or might not reveal himself) would be more radical than the essence of truth as understood in Western philosophy can be taken seriously only if such a relationship does not presuppose the slavery of authoritarian opinions, i.e., if there are ways of being in touch with the transcendent that are neither opinions nor philosophical concepts. As excluding all transcendence (see the end of §1) and nonrecuperable instruction, the philosophy of absolute autonomy excludes all truth that cannot be reproduced by one's own free thinking and, consequently, all revelation. It excludes a *revealing* God. Western philosophy is essentially atheistic (or polytheistic or pantheistic—all of which are ultimately the same if only a revealing God is (a) true God). The exclusion of *all* sorts of heteronomy implies a sharp separation not only between philosophy and faith but equally between ontology and theology. The "god" of the so-called "onto-theo-logy" is nothing more than a being among and above other beings and, thus, a mere idea within the horizon of the human soul. Levinas's rejection of Western theology is, however, inspired by a motive very different from the average atheism of our time: traditional theology is too philosophical if "philosophy" is the name for the Western tradition; it is not philosophical enough if true philosophy is a thinking in the trace of radical transcendence.

27 Besides the normal meaning of *autarchy* ("independent being in command"), this word alludes also to the fact that the ego for which philosophy must find a foundation or "principle" (*archè*), in the Western tradi-

into the Same. Every philosophy is—to use Husserl's neologism—
an egology. And when Descartes comes to discern an acquies-
cence of the will in even the most rational truth, he not only
explains the possibility of error but sets up reason as an ego and
truth as dependent on a movement that is free, and thus sovereign and justified.[28]

This identification requires mediation. Whence a second characteristic of the philosophy of the same: its recourse to Neuters.
To understand the non-I, access must be found through an entity,
an abstract essence which is and is not. In it is dissolved the
other's *alterity*. The foreign being, instead of maintaining itself
in the impregnable fortress of its singularity, instead of facing,
becomes a theme and an object. It fits under a concept already
or dissolves into relations. It falls into the network of a priori
ideas, which I bring to bear so as to capture it. To know is to
surprise in the individual confronted, in this wounding stone,
this upward plunging pine, this roaring lion, that by which it is
not this very individual, this foreigner, that by which it is already
betrayed and by which it gives the free will, vibrant in all certainty, hold over it, is grasped and conceived, enters into a concept. Cognition consists in grasping the individual, which alone
exists, not in its singularity which does not count, but in its
generality, of which alone there is science.[29]

And here every power begins. The surrender of exterior
things to human freedom through their generality does not

---

tion is identified with the ground or foundation itself: ego itself (*autos*)
is its own ground (*archè*). As philosophizing subject, it is an active
tautology; and since the whole of truth is enclosed within its horizon,
philosophy is an "egology." Cf. Husserl, *Ideen* 2:110; *Die Krisis der
europäischen Wissenschaften,* 258 (*The Crisis of European Sciences and
Transcendental Phenomenology,* trans. David Carr [Evanston, Ill.:
Northwestern University Press 1970], 255); *Erste Philosophie* 2:172–73,
176.

28 Cf. Descartes, Fourth *Meditation,* AT, 9:45 (translation Lafleur,
55) on the rule of the will in the affirmation of the truth.

29 The integration of all surprising and strange phenomena by the
ego is a sort of alchemy in which various techniques are used to change
them into ego's property. These techniques have in common that they
make use of something intermediate to deprive the phenomena of that
"element" which makes them precisely independent, real, and other.
This "element" is their singularity. The intermediate has two main
characteristics: it is neutral or—as it will be said below—anonymous;
and it is universal. Aristotle is often quoted as an authority for the
axiom that the singularity of beings cannot enter into the horizon of
science and philosophy (*de individuis non est scientia,* cf. *Metaphysics*

only mean, in all innocence, their comprehension, but also their being taken in hand, their domestication, their possession. Only in possession does the I complete the identification of the diverse. To possess is, to be sure, to maintain the reality of this other one possessed, but to do so while suspending its independence. In a civilization which the philosophy of the Same reflects, freedom is realized as a wealth. Reason, which reduces the other, is appropriation and power.

But if things do not resist the ruses of thought, and confirm the philosophy of the Same, without ever putting into question the freedom of the I, is this also true of men? Are they given to me as things are? Do they not put into question my freedom?[30]

They can, to begin with, block it by opposing it with more than their force—their freedoms. They wage war. War is not a pure confrontation of forces; it can perhaps be defined as a relationship in which force does not alone enter into account, for

---

999a25–b25). As the attempt to integrate all (singular) beings (and their totality), thought prevents them from facing me by treating them as *themes.* It captures them in a network of universal concepts (categories, genera, or species, etc.). Making abstraction from that by which a being is "this-now-here," philosophy and science see it as a concrete universal, leaving the rest as something unimportant to the opinions and manipulations of everyday life. Universalization, the secret weapon of Western thought, thus turns out to be the source of all betrayals and overpowering of reality as it is. Autonomy without heteronomy and the universalism of an anonymous reason are the guiding principles of Western civilization, which is also the civilization of exploitation and imperialism. Western philosophy is inspired by a spirit that is also the spirit of appropriation and capitalistic colonization.

30 The mediating instance whereby the identification of knowledge was made possible was described as *neutral* and *universal.* Whereas universality is contrasted with singularity, neutrality is here the opposite of personality. This is a prelude to the second part of §2: after having reflected upon the possibility of reducing inanimate and nonhuman phenomena to instances of the ego's ideas, the following will concentrate on the question whether humans, too, can be reduced to mere elements of universal concepts or totalities. The difference between human and nonhuman beings was already hinted at when Levinas, some twenty-five lines earlier, wrote: "instead of facing, becomes a theme." The opposition between the face and a theme, central in *TI,* will be developed later on (especially in *AE*) into the difference between the Saying (*le Dire*) and the Said (*le Dit*). Whereas the Said can be treated as a theme or topic of an "objective" treatment, the Saying essentially resists all thematizing. "To put into question my freedom" is a summary of all Levinas's descriptions of the other's face or speech insofar as they resist and forbid the ruthless deployment of my autonomy into a monopolistic appropriation of the universe of beings.

the unforeseeable contingencies of freedom—skill, courage, and invention—count too. But in war the free will may fail without being put into question, without renouncing its rights and its revenge.[31] Freedom is put into question by the Other, and is revealed to be unjustified, only when it knows itself to be unjust. Its knowing itself to be unjust is not something added on to spontaneous and free consciousness, which would be present to itself and know itself to be, *in addition*, guilty. A new situation is created; consciousness's presence to itself acquires a different modality; its positions collapse.[32] To put it just in formal terms, the Same does not find again its priority over the other, it does not rest peaceably on itself, is no longer the principle. We shall endeavor to make these formulas more clear. And if the Same does not peaceably rest on itself, philosophy does not seem to be indissolubly bound up with the adventure that includes every Other in the Same.[33]

We shall return to this shortly; let us first observe that this supremacy of the Same over the Other seems to be integrally

---

31 The social problem of Greek and modern social philosophy has always been how autonomous beings could peacefully unite in one community. The tensions caused by their confrontation result in war unless every singular freedom poses limits on its own egocentric self-satisfaction. As long as the principle of autonomy is maintained, its limitations or subjections by others or by the ego itself are justified in the name of freedom, and social philosophy remains faithful to the project of a universal egology. The ego's autonomy as such is not questioned and does not feel guilty of monopolizing as much as possible, on the condition that every ego has the right to be equally egocentric.

32 The "principle" itself of social philosophy becomes another one—and this is the radical turn—when the consciousness of a free ego discovers the injustice of its monopoly confronting the existence of another (*Autrui*). This discovery does not simply add an accidental surplus to an essentially innocent consciousness; it also reveals a certain duplicity in the heart of the subject: spontaneously inclined to a universal conquest, it is at the same time aware that, since there are others, the world and I belong (also) to them.

33 The Same (which is simultaneously a formal category and the concrete self-realization of a monopolistic ego) is no longer the absolute coincidence with itself of the "egonomic" subject; its peaceful enjoyment has been disturbed by the claims of the Other (the formal *Autre*, which is at the same time concrete *Autrui*) and thus becomes aware of the guilt contained in its "egonomy." By this "turn," philosophy changes radically. If the Other is taken seriously, the inclusion of its circle within the circle of the Same, which according to Plato's *Timaeus* (35ab) constitutes the ultimate horizon of the cosmos, is undone and the ultimate meaning of all things and humans has been changed.

maintained in the philosophy of Heidegger, the most renowned of our time.[34] When Heidegger traces the way of access to each real singularity through Being, which is not a particular being nor a genus in which all the particulars would enter, but is rather the very act of being which the verb to be, and not the substantive, expresses (and which, with M. De Waelhens, we

---

34 The rest of §2 is a summary of Levinas's interpretation and criticism of Heidegger's philosophy. By applying the general characterization of Western philosophy, as given above, to Heidegger's ontology, Levinas wants to prove that—notwithstanding the depth and greatness of its renewal—it remains faithful to the traditional inspiration. This first extensive statement of Levinas's criticism is contained in his important article "L'ontologie est-elle fondamentale?" *Revue de Métaphysique et de Morale* 56 (1951): 88–98; its development from 1929 until 1951 has been outlined in my "Phenomenology—Ontology—Metaphysics: Levinas' Perspective on Husserl and Heidegger," *Man and World* 16 (1983): 113–27.

The argumentation given here can be summed up by the following points: "Being" as Heidegger, according to Levinas, understands it, must be heard as a verb and not as a substantive. It is the active (and—as Levinas says elsewhere—"transitive") deployment and bringing into the open to which all beings owe their being and appearing (cf., for example, Levinas's remarks in Jean Wahl, *Esquisse pour une histoire de l'existentialisme* [Paris: L'Arche, 1949], 95–96). As such, it is "the very act of being" (*l'acte même d'être*); the later Heidegger would call this, rather, *"Seiendheit,"* but Levinas does not distinguish this here clearly from the *Wesen, Walten,* and *Gewähren* of Heidegger's "Being itself" (*das Sein selbst*). Singular beings (or phenomena) are known thanks to the light and under the rule of Being. In this structure, as thematized by Heidegger's analysis of *Dasein*'s understanding, we recognize the structure of the traditional mediation: the knowledge of the singularity of existing beings is due to the intelligibility granted to them by a neuter that has also the character of a universal. A more concrete form of this ruling and enlightenment is found in Heidegger's elucidation of the relation between a human being and its freedom. If freedom as essence of *Dasein* possesses the singular humans, it is *again* a neuter that commands the singular beings that owe their most proper being to it.

Although Heidegger's thought has deeply changed the traditional meaning of human independence, autarchy, and autonomy, as can be illustrated by a comparison of *Sein und Zeit* with Plato's view on the profound affinity of the soul with the ideas (cf. *Phaedo* 76de, 100b), the same fundamental structure shows itself in Heidegger's analysis of *Dasein* as a finite variety of possibilities on the basis of an ultimate possibility: the possibility of its impossibility by death, which can and must be accepted beforehand by resolve. This mortal and finite being constitutes itself as a concentrated, solitary identity, and its sameness is in the end not challenged by any genuine otherness. Cf. *SuZ*, §§52–53 and Levinas's commentary in *EDHH* 85–87.

write with a capital "B"), he leads us to the singularity across a Neuter which illuminates and commands thought and renders intelligible. When he sees man possessed by freedom rather than possessing freedom, he puts over man a Neuter which illuminates freedom without putting it in question. And thus he is not destroying but summing up a whole current of Western philosophy.

The principle of a nonheteronomous autonomy is not betrayed by Heidegger's submitting human freedom to Being—classical idealism defined genuine freedom by a similar obedience—for autonomy is not really challenged if it is not met by genuine otherness, and this cannot be found in Being(ness). The "independence" and pseudo-otherness of Being (as act of being) shows its unity with *Dasein* by approaching it as the radiating mystery that grants intelligibility to all beings.

The *clair-obscur* of Heidegger's *Alètheia*, its mysteriousness, is a special mode of its belonging to *Dasein* as the neutral horizon within which *Dasein* "always already" is at home. (Cf. Heidegger, "Vom Wesen der Wahrheit" and "Brief über den Humanismus," especially GA 9: 187–93; "On the Essence of Truth" and "Letter on Humanism" in *Basic Writings,* 113–41, 189–242.) Being and its understanding by an illuminated subject form a union without separation. In bringing *noein* and *einai* together, the neutrality of Being confirms the central position of a quiet subject.

That Being is not different enough to be truly other shows itself most clearly in the fact that *Dasein,* according to Heidegger's description of mortality and conscience (*Gewissen*), experiences its finitude as pure deficiency but not as an imperfection or as guilt (cf. *SuZ,* §§58–60). Heidegger departs from the classical thesis that the finiteness of beings cannot be known unless in contrast with the prior notion of the infinite. (Through a note—note 1 of the original publication and of *EDHH* 170—Levinas refers the reader to his commentary on Heidegger's analysis of *Dasein*'s finitude in *EDHH* 102, whereas—further on, in §3—Levinas himself will retrieve Descartes's version of that classical insight.) The experience of the contrast between the finite and the infinite, as revealed in the face of another, is not simply the discovery of a privation but the awakening to one's own profound indebtedness and bad conscience. The infinite reveals itself as the Good (cf. Plato, *Republic* 50de, 509b, 577b, 518d), in the "light" of which the position of a monopolistic ego "appears" as the usurpation of a tyrannical, "hard," and "cruel" will. (Cf. also the texts already cited: "De la déficience sans souci au sens nouveau," *Concilium* (1976), n. 113; and "La mauvaise conscience et l'inexorable," *DDVI* 258–65). If the assurance of egocentrism can only be troubled by real otherness, i.e., by the immediate encounter with another being, the relationship of *Dasein* with neutral Being cannot unsettle its good conscience. Since the relationship with the Other in Heidegger's analyses—insofar as they do not simply ignore it—is subordinated to the former relation, which is considered more important, *Dasein* remains free to understand and will itself as the absolute center of its world. Behind its understanding of Being and its own relation to Being lurks the self-affirmation of a will to power capable of all violence and cruelties in order to maintain its domination.

The *Dasein* Heidegger puts in place of the soul, consciousness, or the Ego retains the structure of the Same. Independence—autarchy—came to the Platonic soul (and to all its counterfeit versions) from its homeland, the world of Ideas; according to the *Phaedo*, the soul is related to that world and consequently cannot encounter anything really foreign in it. Reason, the power to maintain oneself identical above the variations of becoming, formed the soul of this soul. Heidegger contests this dominant position for man, but leaves *Dasein* in the Same, qua mortal. The possibility of being annihilated is in fact constitutive of *Dasein*, and thus maintains its ipseity. This nothingness is a death, is my death, my possibility (or impossibility), my power. No one can substitute himself for me to die. The supreme moment of resoluteness is solitary and personal.

To be sure, for Heidegger man's freedom depends on the light of Being, and thus does not seem to be a principle. But that was also the case in classical idealism, where free will was considered the lowest form of freedom, and true freedom obeyed universal reason. The Heideggerian freedom is obedient, but obedience makes it arise and does not put it into question, does not reveal its injustice. Being, equivalent to the independence and extraneousness of realities, is equivalent to phosphorescence, light. It converts into intelligibility.[35] The "mystery" essential to this "dark light" is a modality of this conversion. Independence ends in radiation. *Being and Time*, Heidegger's first and principal work, perhaps always maintained but one thesis: Being is inseparable from the comprehension of Being; Being already invokes subjectivity. But Being *is not* a being. It is a Neuter which orders thought and beings, but which hardens the will instead of making it ashamed. The consciousness of his finitude does not come to man from the idea of infinity, that is, is not revealed as an imperfection, does not refer to the Good, does not know itself to be wicked. Heideggerian philosophy precisely marks the apogee of a thought in which the finite does not refer to the infinite[36] (prolonging certain tendencies of Kantian philosophy: the separation between the understanding and reason, diverse themes of transcendental dialectics), in which every deficiency is but weakness and every fault committed

---

35 The expression *"obscure clarté,"* taken from Corneille's *Le Cid* (4.3), characterizes here the ambiguity of Heidegger's A*lètheia*, which—as *Geheimnis*—withdraws itself while suggesting itself in enlightening beings.

36 Cf. below section 3 [Levinas's note].

against oneself—the outcome of a long tradition of pride, heroism, domination, and cruelty.

Heideggerian ontology subordinates the relation with the other to the relation with the Neuter, Being, and it thus continues to exalt the will to power, whose legitimacy the Other (*Autrui*) alone can unsettle, troubling good conscience. When Heidegger calls attention to the forgetting of Being, veiled by the diverse realities it illuminates, a forgetting for which the philosophy developed from Socrates on would be guilty, when he deplores the orientation of the intellect toward technology, he maintains a regime of power more inhuman than mechanism and which perhaps does not have the same source as it.[37] (It is not sure that National Socialism arises from the mechanist reification of men, and that it does not rest on peasant enrooted-

---

[37] The argumentation has reached the point where Levinas—in agreement with Heidegger's own remark on the ontic and existenti*ell* source of any existenti*al* analysis (cf. *Sein und Zeit*) undertakes to interpret Heidegger's philosophical position as the theoretical expression of a specific way of existence. Whereas Heidegger interprets the radical crisis of Western thought as a forgetting of Being due to its replacement by the totality of beings and sees the adoration of technology as the expression of a reduction of beingness to its objective or *vorhanden* mode of being (cf. *SuZ*, §§1, 6, 68 etc.), Levinas sees this diagnosis and the orientation of Heidegger's own thought as expressions of a peculiar mode of human existence that—far from being true—sins above all by its lack of ethical concern. Alluding to many different essays of the later Heidegger, such as "Die Frage nach der Technik" ("The Question Concerning Technology"), "Die Ursprung des Kunstwerkes" ("The Origin of the Work of Art") and "Bauen—Wohnen—Denken" ("Building—Dwelling—Thinking"), Levinas draws the portrait of a spontaneous and thus "natural" existence rooted in a natal soil ("Blut und Boden!") resistant to any derangement by strangers and not disposed to any exodus, the existence of a peasantry attached to its familiar spaces and places (allusion to Heidegger's later topology of *"Ort"* and *"Er-örterung"*) and to the fixed hierarchy of its masters and servants. The realm of anonymous Being, to which this existence owes its capacity of cultivating, building, and dwelling, also rules thinking. Its secret is the self-assured maintenance of an amoral heroism ready for all sorts of war and exploitation in the name of drama and power. Thus Heidegger's brilliant descriptions of the world would reveal and hide the same pagan existence of nonethical enrootedness as that which lies at the basis of National Socialism. Similar characterizations of Heidegger's perspective are given in less technical essays, such as "Heidegger, Gagarine et nous" and "Le lieu et l'utopie" ("Site and Utopia") in *Difficile Liberté*, 229–303. Cf. also one of the epigraphs of *AE* taken from Pascal: " 'That is my place in the sun.' That is how the usurpation of the whole world began" (*Pensées*, Edition Brunschvicg, n. 112).

ness and a feudal adoration of subjugated men for the masters and lords who command them).[38] This is an existence which takes itself to be natural, for whom its place in the sun, its ground, its *site*, orient all signification—a pagan *existing*. Being directs it building and cultivating, in the midst of a familiar landscape, on a maternal earth. Anonymous, neuter, it directs it, ethically indifferent, as a heroic freedom, foreign to all guilt with regard to the Other.

Indeed this earth-maternity determines the whole Western civilization of property, exploitation, political tyranny, and war. Heidegger does not discuss the pretechnological power of possession effected in the enrootedness of perception (which no one has described so brilliantly as he), in which the most abstract geometrical space is in the last analysis embedded, but which cannot find any place in the whole infinity of mathematical extension. The Heideggerian analyses of the world which in *Being and Time* were based on gear or fabricated things are in his later philosophy borne by the vision of the lofty landscapes of nature, an impersonal fecundity, matrix of particular beings, inexhaustible matter of things.

Heidegger not only sums up a whole evolution of Western philosophy. He exalts it by showing in the most dramatic way its anti-religious essence become a religion in reverse.[39] The lucid sobriety of those who call themselves friends of truth and enemies of opinion would thus have a mysterious prolongation! In Heidegger atheism is a paganism, the pre-Socratic text anti-Scriptures. Heidegger shows in what intoxication the lucid sobriety of philosophers is steeped.[40]

---

38 Probably Levinas alludes here to Heidegger's reference to Nazism with the words "the inner truth and greatness of this movement (namely the encounter of the planetarily determined technology and modern man)"; cf. *Einführung in die Metaphysik* (1952¹), 152 (*Introduction to Metaphysics*, 199). Whereas Heidegger's diagnosis of the technological civilization traces its blindness to truth back to the identification of being as *Vorhandenes*, an ethically less indifferent perspective would show more positive and, especially, important moral features of modern technology.

39 The last step in the argumentation runs parallel with the general characteristic of ontology as described in the beginning of §2: Heidegger's thought of Being is at the same time atheistic (because God cannot enter into the horizon of his ontology) and a dramatic (*pathétique*) form of "religious" paganism full of reverence for sacred sites and gods.

40 The lucid sobriety stressed by Plato as a condition for a thought that is true to being (*Republic* 501d2, 536a5, 537d8 and *Symposium* 218e7) seems to have returned to the mysteries of opinions from which (cf. §1) the philosophers (as "friends of the truth") had delivered thinking. Is this new *enthusiasm* (literally, "being filled by the divine") the

To conclude, the well-known theses of Heideggerian philosophy—the preeminence of Being over beings, of ontology over
metaphysics—end up affirming a tradition in which the Same
dominates the Other, in which freedom, even the freedom that
is identical with reason, precedes justice. Does not justice consist
in putting the obligation with regard to the Other before obligations to oneself, in putting the Other before the Same?[41]

| 3. The Idea of the Infinite

By reversing the terms[42] we believe we are following a tradition at
least as ancient,[43] that which does not read right in might and does

---

true *mania* that Plato's *Phaedrus* (224a–d) sees as identical with that
lucidity? Behind the Plato-Heidegger opposition evoked here, another
opposition can be heard: that between the biblical prophets and the cult
of the Baals (i.e., of Nature, a fecundity and violence), another celebration of "blood and soil."

41 Levinas summarizes the result of his discussion by formulating
it twice: in a (more) metaphysical, and in a (more) ethical statement.
On the level of *"metaphysics,"* he rejects Heidegger's subordination of
beings to Being by announcing his own thesis that the true beginning
of philosophy lies in the recognition of the relation between the Same
and the Other, in which the Other comes before the Same; on the level
of fundamental *ethics,* which is as radical as—but not a replacement of—
metaphysics, he states as the first "axiom" that justice (the relation to
the Other) precedes freedom (the relation of self-possession in the Same).
It is, thus, not Levinas's purpose to reverse the traditional hierarchy
of philosophical disciplines, in which the first and fundamental place is
occupied by metaphysics or ontology, by putting a fundamental ethics
in their place. His concern is to show how the most radical and truly
"first" "principle" is not a traditional *archè* but rather a relation that
precedes the distinction between the theoretical and the ethical. "Metaphysics," unlike ontology, is at the same time a theoretical and practical
philosophy.

42 The entrance to Levinas's metaphysics demands a "turn" of eyes,
heart, and intelligence that is more radical than Heidegger's *Kehre* and
at least as radical as Plato's *epistrophè* from opinion to the truth of the
Good, but it is not the simple reversal of the traditional scheme. Instead
of abolishing the inclusion of the Other in the Same by enclosing the
Same in the Other, Levinas replaces their union by the unbreakable
relation between them as separate *and* connected terms.

43 The prophetic tradition to which Levinas appeals is "at least
as ancient" as the pre-Socratic philosophers. It is quoted not as an
authoritarian doxa or conviction but as an expression of genuine "experiences" having at least as much of a right to exist within philosophy as
the evocations and descriptions of Parmenides, Heraclitus, Hölderlin, or
Rilke. Resonances of the tradition to which Levinas appeals here are
found in other ancient traditions, such as those of Hesiod and Plato.

not reduce *every other* to the Same.[44] Against the Heideggerians and
neo-Hegelians for whom philosophy begins with atheism, we have to
say that the tradition of the Other is not necessarily religious, that
it is philosophical.[45] Plato stands in this tradition when he situates
the Good above Being, and, in the *Phaedrus*, defines true discourse
as a discourse with gods.[46] But what we find most distinctive is the
Cartesian analysis of the idea of the infinite, although we shall retain
only the *formal design* of the structure it outlines.[47]

In Descartes the I that thinks maintains a relationship with
the Infinite.[48] This relationship is not that which connects a
container to a content, since the I cannot contain the Infinite,

---

44 In opposition to the tradition described in section 2, the other
tradition does not base itself on the will to power, but it confronts the
exuberance of ego's spontaneity with the other's rights. Levinas does
not claim here that *all* other beings (*tout autre*, "every other") resist
assimilation, but he insists on the irreducibility of any other *human*
being.

45 Against the general trend of contemporary thought (in which
Hegel and Heidegger have become closer to each other than each of
them would be willing to concede) but with the whole tradition from
"Moses" *and Plato* to Hegel (and Nietzsche?), Levinas claims that the
"transcendent," the "metaphysical," the "infinite," the "beyond of being," the "Other," and "God" belong essentially to the core concepts of
philosophical thought.

46 Plato defined philosophy not only as "conversation of the soul
with itself" (see note 23), but also as a "talk with gods" (*Phaedrus* 273e–
274a). For the (idea of the) Good above Being, see *Republic* 517b and
518d and innumerable quotations by Levinas, e.g., *TI* 76/102–3 and
EDHH 189.

47 Not only here but as a fundamental device of his method, Levinas
distinguishes between a formal structure and its concrete existence. Cf., for
example, *TI* 21/50, and the way in which the beginning of *TI* analyzes the
relation of the Same and the Other as a relation between abstract ("logical")
categories, which relation only afterwards is concretized as a human face-to-
face encounter and conversation (*TI* 9, 18, 21/39, 47, 50–51).

48 Presupposing that we can separate the formal structure of Descartes's "idea of the Infinite" from its more concrete content, which is the
connection between consciousness and God, Levinas recognizes the basic
structure of the relation he is looking for in that "idea." "The idea of the
Infinite" is, thus, not a representation, a concept, or a normal idea but
rather the primordial relation relating the self-sameness of the ego to the
irreducibility of the Other. All the allusions here are to the third of Descartes's *Metaphysical Meditations on First Philosophy* (AT, 9:29–42; English
translation by Lafleur, especially 43–46, 49). In it Descartes argues for the
thesis (1) that the idea of an infinite, eternal, unchangeable and independent, all-knowing, almighty, and all-creating substance is an originary
idea found in ego's consciousness; (2) that this idea cannot be obtained by
any elaboration (simple or double negation, extension, intensification, or

nor that which binds a content to a container, since the I is separated from the Infinite. The relationship which is thus described negatively is the idea of the Infinite in us.

We have of course also ideas of things; the idea of infinity is exceptional in that its ideatum surpasses its idea. In it the distance between idea and ideatum is not equivalent to the distance that separates a mental act from its object in other representations. The abyss that separates a mental act from its object is not deep enough for Descartes not to say that the soul can account for the ideas of finite things by itself.[49] The intentionality that animates the idea of the Infinite is not comparable with any other; it aims at what it cannot embrace and is in this sense the Infinite. To take the converse of the formulas we used above, we can say that the alterity of the infinite is not canceled, is not extinguished in the thought that thinks it. In thinking the infinite, the I from the first *thinks more than it thinks.* The Infinite does not enter into the *idea* of the infinite, is not grasped; this idea is not a concept. The infinite is the radically, absolutely, other. The transcendence of the infinite with respect to the ego that is separated from it and thinks it constitutes the first mark of its infinitude.

The idea of the infinite is then not [?] the only one that teaches what we are ignorant of.[50] It has been *put* into us. It is not a reminiscence. It is experience in the sole radical sense of

---

exaggeration) of any finite idea; and (3) that its presence in consciousness shows not only its precedence with regard to all other ideas but also that it has been "put into me" by that infinite substance (*"Dieu"*) itself. Levinas's reading stresses the critique of intentionality contained in it. The experience or "idea" by which ego is related to the infinite cannot be described by way of the traditional schemes of a representation (or concept, or, in general, a mental act) and its object; it is not the union of a content and its container and thus does not fit into the structure of an intention and its fulfillment by an intentional correlate. The idea of the infinite "thinks" its ideation as something that it cannot contain; it "thinks more than it can think"; it cannot account for the surplus by which it is surpassed from the beginning and without possibility of ever integrating it. The idea of the infinite is the being ruled by an other that cannot be absorbed into union; it is the transcendence of a primordial heteronomy.

49 Descartes, *Méditations,* AT, 9:35.

50 In the first version of the essay (in the *Revue de Métaphysique et de Morale* of 1957), the sentence reads: "The idea of the infinite is then the only one . . ." ("L'idée de l'infini est donc la seule qui apprenne ce qu'on ignore," 247). For the second edition of *EDHH* 172, Levinas added a "not" (*n'est donc pas*), but this does not seem to give a good meaning because the argument stresses our incapability of knowing what, how, or who the infinite is. Since the infinite is not an object or

the term: a relationship with the exterior, with the Other, without this exteriority being able to be integrated into the Same. The thinker who has the idea of the infinite is *more than himself,* and this inflation, this surplus, does not come from within, as in the celebrated *project* of modern philosophers, in which the subject surpasses himself by creating.[51]

How can such a structure be still philosophical? What is the relationship which, while remaining one of *the more in the less,* is not transformed into the relationship in which, according to the mystics, the butterfly drawn by the fire is consumed in the fire? How can separate beings be maintained and not sink into participation, against which the philosophy of the Same will have the immortal merit to have protested?[52]

4. The Idea of the Infinite and the Face of the Other (*Autrui*)

Experience, the idea of the infinite, occurs in the relationship with the Other (*Autrui*). The idea of the infinite is the social relationship.[53]

---

theme, we are and remain ignorant in our relation to it. *This* ignorance does not, however, extend itself to other beings. In the preceding paragraph Levinas alluded even to the passage where Descartes asks himself why it would not be possible to "account for" (*rendre compte*) the ideas of all finite beings by deducing them a priori. The first version of the sentence (without "not") seems therefore to be the correct one, but it must be read as an interpretation of Descartes's discourse. If it were taken as an expression of Levinas's own thought, it would seem to state that all knowledge of the finite is reminiscence, *anamnesis,* ontological, and a priori, as if there were no otherness at all involved in it. By adding his "not," Levinas probably wanted to restate the thesis with which he began his article: *all* true experience somehow is a learning experience made possible by the otherness of an instructive surprise.

51 Cf. Heidegger's analyses of man as a project (*Entwurf*) in *Sein und Zeit,* 145–48, 221–23, 324–27 (*Being and Time,* 184–88, 263–66, 370–75), and Sartre's explanation of *projet* and *pro-jeter* in *Being and Nothingness,* 650–53.

52 Cf. above Levinas's praise for the Greek dethronement of the tyranny exercised by *doxai,* myths, and participation. Expressions such as "the *more* in the *less*" (*le plus dans le moins*), "surplus," and "to think *more* than one thinks" are, of course, metaphors only to indicate the nonquantitative, nonqualitative, and even "nonbeing" separation-in-connection of the one (who is the same) and the other. This relation is, then, absolutely different from the traditional relation.

53 In this section, Levinas analyzes the concrete form (mode of "being" and "appearing") of the abstract structure sketched in the former sections. The structure of experience has revealed itself to be a relation

This relationship consists in approaching an absolutely exterior being. The infinity of this being, which one can therefore not contain, guarantees and constitutes this exteriority. It is not equivalent to the distance between a subject and an object. An object, we know, is integrated into the identity of the Same; the I makes of it its theme, and then its property, its booty, its prey, or its victim. The exteriority of the infinite being is manifested in the absolute resistance which by its apparition, its epiphany, it opposes to all my powers. Its epiphany is not simply the apparition of a form in the light, sensible or intelligible, but already this *no* cast to powers; its logos is: "You shall not kill."[54]

To be sure, the Other (*Autrui*) is exposed to all my powers, succumbs to all my ruses, all my crimes. Or he resists me with all his force and all the unpredictable resources of his own freedom. I measure myself against him. But he can also—and here is where

---

to the other/the infinite. This relation "is" (concretizes itself in, is concrete as) the relation to another (*autrui*). This relation of immediate intersubjectivity (of you and me) is called here "social relationship" (*rapport social*), to be distinguished clearly from the relation you and I have as members and participants of one society. At this point, we may ask whether "infinity" or "the infinite" is the best translation of Levinas's (*l'*)*infini*, which he sometimes also writes with a capital (e.g., in the title of section 3, but not in that of the present section 4). If we presuppose the possibility of separating a completely abstract structure from its concretization in Descartes's *Dieu* or Levinas's *autrui*, we might be inclined to prefer "infinity" because of its categorial overtones, whereas "the infinite" might suggest too quickly that we are talking about a divine and highest being. We must, then, however explain why Levinas himself does not transform Descartes's "infini" into the perfectly correct French expression "infinitude." The disadvantage of the term "infinity," however, is that it seems to suggest the possibility of categorizing from a transcendental perspective through logical determinations God as well as other humans with whom we meet. If we can understand "the infinite" as the pure equivalent of "the other" (and "infinity" as the equivalent of "al-ter*ity*" or "otherness"), the proper translation of *"l'infini"* seems to be "the infinite." The question, however, becomes more complicated when, in other texts, Levinas will state more clearly that the existence of the human other, because of his/her absolute otherness (or infinity), is *the* only possible revelation of God.

54 This most exterior and infinite "being" is not a phenomenon like other phenomena but an "epiphany" or "revelation" (words very often used in *TI*). Its logos ("principle" or "definition") is not—as the whole tradition from Parmenides to Heidegger would defend—an essence that can be confined within the *horismos* of its horizons but a coming to the fore that simultaneously is an imperative. The first law of ethics is also the first law of human thought and language.

he presents me his face—oppose himself to me beyond all measure, with the total uncoveredness and nakedness of his defenseless eyes, the straightforwardness,[55] the absolute frankness of his gaze. The solipsist disquietude of consciousness, seeing itself, in all its adventures, a captive of itself, comes to an end here: true exteriority is in this gaze which forbids me my conquest. Not that conquest is beyond my too weak powers, but I *am no longer able to have power:*[56] the structure of my freedom is, we shall see further, completely reversed. Here is established a relationship not with a very great resistance but with the absolute Other, with the resistance of what has no resistance, with ethical resistance. It opens the very dimension of the infinite, of what puts a stop to the irresistable imperialism of the Same and the I. We call a *face* the epiphany of what can thus present itself directly, and therefore also exteriorly, to an I.

A face is not like a plastic form, which is always already deserted, betrayed, by the being it reveals, such as marble from which the gods it manifests already absent themselves.[57] It differs from an animal's head, in which a being, in its brutish dumbness, is not yet in touch with itself. In a face the expressed *attends* its expression, expresses its very expression, always remains master of the meaning it delivers. A "pure act" in its own way,[58] it

---

55 The word *"droiture,"* which is rendered here by "straightforwardness," contrasts with the mediation analyzed in section 2 and marks the difference between the dimension of egos as free forces confronting one another and the dimension of moral obligation and vulnerability.

56 "Je ne peux plus pouvoir" is a reversal of the conception that the human being ought to be defined as a primordial possibility (capacity or power) of self-realization. Levinas sees this conception expressed in Heidegger's determination of *Dasein* as a *Seinkönnen* (a being possible) in *Sein und Zeit* (§31). See also GA, 20:421, where the equivalence of *Ich bin* (*Dasein*) and *Ich kann* (*Möglichkeit*) is stated. The formula *"Ich kann"* is found already in Husserl's *Ideen zu einer reinen Phänomenologie und phänomenologischen Philosophie*, 2:257ff.

57 If we observe a face in order to check its proportions, color, or shades, we see a phenomenon comparable to other phenomena but will not see the face as facing us; it will not reveal its otherness. The "plastic form" is the "aesthetic" dimension of a visage, not the epiphany of its unobservable and "invisible" enigma. See "Enigma and Phenomenon" in *EDHH* 203–16/*CPP* 61–74.

58 "Pure act" (*actus purus*) is the Aristotelizing scholastic expression used to characterize God as perfect being without any admixture of passivity (cf. Aristotle, *Metaphysics* 1071b–1073a). Just like the word "master" in the preceding sentence, the word "act" tries to describe the

resists identification, does not enter into the already known, brings aid to itself, as Plato puts it,[59] speaks. The epiphany of a face is wholly language.[60]

Ethical resistance is the presence of the infinite. If the resistance to murder, inscribed on a face, were not ethical, but real, we would have access to a reality that is very weak or very strong. It perhaps would block our will. The will would be judged unreasonable and arbitrary.[61] But we would not have access to an exterior being, to what one absolutely can neither take in nor possess, where our freedom renounces its imperialism proper to the ego, where it is found to be not only arbitrary, but unjust. But then the other is not simply another freedom; to give me knowledge of injustice, his gaze must come to me from a dimension of the ideal.[62] The

---

"imposing" aspect of the face by which it cannot be submitted to the dimension of the oppositions between activity and passivity or mastery and slavery. The imperative voiced by the Other's irruption does not condemn me to slavery at all but makes me free and open for authentic transcendence.

59 Here, and already in the phrase "the expressed *attends* its expression" ("l'exprimé assiste à l'expression"), Levinas alludes to an expression repeatedly used in Plato's *Phaedrus* (247b–277a) to show the preeminence of the spoken word over writing. The speaker "assists" and supports the words he/she speaks.

60 "Language" must be understood here as speaking as such, which does not coincide with its content. Just as *facing* differs from the "plastic form," so *speaking* ("language") differs from the spoken. After *TI*, Levinas concentrates much more on this difference between "the Saying" (*le Dire*) and "the Said" (*le Dit*) than on the analysis of the Face.

61 The "presence" or concrete existence of "the infinite" is the facing as powerless, naked, mortal, and vulnerable resistance to my spontaneous wish to appropriate and overpower whatever comes in my way. The two dimensions are here opposed as *"ethical"* (cf. Plato's "truly being," which cannot be isolated from the "idea" of the Good) and *"real"* (the ontological reality of the *physis* in which autonomous and ruthless forces decide the outcome of all oppositions).

62 The Other (*Autrui*) is the concrete presence of the features with which the first page of this essay characterized the heteronomous aspect of all experience: another looking at me (*son regard*) signifies the ideal and the divine. This signification is not only found in sacred books; if it is also found there, the reason is that they, too, formulate an authentic "experience," the repression of which results in a guilty conscience. The awakening to a moral life coincides with the discovery that the other is the *first* to be respected, served, taken care of by me. It is the discovery of my responsibility for the other, a responsibility that is greater than my concern for myself. This is expressed by the final sentence of this section: "La justice bien ordonnée commence par Autrui," in which the "metaphysical turn" is summarized by a reversal of the French dictum:

Other (*Autrui*) must be closer to God than I. This is certainly not a philosopher's invention, but the first given of moral consciousness, which could be defined as the consciousness of the privilege the Other has relative to me. Justice well ordered begins with the Other.

I 5. The Idea of the Infinite Is Desire

The ethical relationship is not grafted on to an antecedent relationship of cognition,[63] it is a foundation and not a superstructure. To distinguish it from cognition is not to reduce it to a subjective sentiment. The idea of the infinite, in which being overflows the idea, in which the Other overflows the Same, breaks with the inward play of the soul and alone deserves the name experience, a relationship with the exterior. It is then more *cognitive* than cognition itself, and all objectivity must participate in it.

Malebranche's vision in God (cf. the Second *Metaphysical Discourse*) expresses both this reference of all cognition to the idea of the infinite and the fact that the idea of the infinite is not like the cognition that refers to it. For one cannot maintain

---

"charité bien ordonnée commence par soi-même" ("Charity well ordered begins with oneself"). The reason why "charity" is replaced by justice is not that Levinas wants to diminish the extension and the intensity of the dedication I owe to any other. On the contrary, the term "charity" is so much used and abused to express the infinity of the demands imposed on me by a face that the word "justice" might be a better name for the imperative that is as old as the "Law of Moses." Later on, Levinas will also use expressions such as *amour du prochain* (love of the nearest) and *proximité* (proximity). In order to evoke the basic experience, Levinas often quotes a line from Dostoyevski's *Brothers Karamazov:* "All of us are guilty of everything and responsible for everyone in the face of everything and I more than the others" (cf., for instance *EI* 105).

63 "Cognition" (*connaissance*) is taken here in its theoretical and traditional sense, which includes identifying freedom as described in section 2. The "ethical relationship" is *not* its contrary but a more radical relation preceding the scission of contemplation and action. This relation is therefore wiser and more "knowledgeable" than (the traditional sort of) cognition. Implicitly Levinas rejects here the conception of the early Husserl, who thought that all noncognitive intentions were based on *doxic* intentions. Moral intentions are not secondary but rather the unfolding of the most basic of all "intentions": the relation of transcendence itself, which is as much ethical as—in a more fundamental and "experimental" sense—cognitive.

that this idea itself is a thematization or an objectification without reducing it to the presence of the Other in the Same, a presence with which it in fact contrasts.[64] In Descartes, a certain ambiguity concerning this point remains, since the cogito which rests on God elsewhere founds the existence of God: the priority of the Infinite is subordinated to the free adhesion of the will, which initially is master of itself.[65]

We separate ourselves from the letter of Cartesianism in affirming that the movement of the soul that is more cognitive than cognition could have a structure different from contemplation. The infinite is not the object of a contemplation, that is, is not proportionate to the thought that thinks it. The idea of the infinite is a thought which at every moment *thinks more than it thinks*. A thought that thinks more than it thinks is Desire. Desire "measures" the infinity of the infinite.[66]

The term we have chosen to mark the propulsion, the inflation, of this going beyond is opposed to the affectivity of love and

---

[64] In his *Conversations on Metaphysics and Religion* (*Entretiens sur la Métaphysique et sur la Religion, Œuvres Complètes* [Paris: Vrin, 1965], 12:53–54), Malebranche shows that all understanding of finite beings refers to the idea of the infinite as to their foundation and that the "knowledge" of this ultimate idea has a quality and structure radically different from all other knowledge. If knowledge essentially were a way of objectification and thematization, there would be no knowledge of the infinite. For the Other is neither an object nor a theme and cannot be reduced to them. We cannot posit the Other in front of us in order to limit and measure it by a circumscription of its horizons. The infinite does not permit us to define it.

[65] Notwithstanding his effort to do justice to the unique transcendence of the infinite, Descartes insists, in the third and fourth of his *Meditations* (AT, 9:35–50), on the role played by human autonomy in all forms of knowledge.

[66] The exceptional character of the primordial ("ethical," "transcendent," heteronomous as well as autonomous) relation is experienced not only as an obligation and a very special sort of cognition but equally as the most primordial desire. "Desire" (*désir*) differs, however, essentially from all varieties of need (*besoin*); indeed, it cannot and does not desire to be satisfied but grows to the extent to which it seems to reach the desired. Since the eros that lies at the root of human existence and philosophy desires the other as Other, it cannot be united or "fulfilled" by her or him. It wants the other to grow in independence and well-being. Desire is a giving of goodness as opposed to the narcissistic urge for union and fusion. Desire does not fill the holes of ego's being (as the satisfactions of one's needs do) but opens up and dedicates. See also the analyses of desire with which *TI* opens, 3–5/33–35.

the indigence of need. Outside of the hunger one satisfies, the thirst one quenches, and the senses one allays exists the Other, absolutely other, desired beyond these satifactions, when the body knows no gesture to slake the Desire, where it is not possible to invent any new caress.

Desire is unquenchable, not because it answers to an infinite hunger, but because it does not call for food. This Desire without satisfaction hence takes cognizance of the alterity of the Other. It situates it in the dimension of height and of the ideal, which it opens up in being.

The desires one can satisfy resemble this Desire only intermittently, in the deceptions of satisfaction or in the increases of emptiness which mark their voluptuousness. They wrongly pass for the essence of desire. The true Desire is that which the Desired does not satisfy, but hollows out. It is goodness. It does not refer to a lost fatherland or plenitude; it is not homesickness, is not nostalgia. It is the lack in a being which *is* completely, and lacks nothing. Can the Platonic myth of love, son of abundance and of poverty, be interpreted as bearing witness to the indigence of a wealth in desire, the insufficiency of what is self-sufficient? Has not Plato, in the *Symposium*, by rejecting the myth of an androgynous being, affirmed the nonnostalgic nature of desire, the plenitude and joy of the being who experiences it?[67]

---

67 This hint at Psalm 23 ("the Lord is my shepherd; I lack nothing") illustrates the difference between Ulysses's nostalgia and the unstillable hunger for justice stemming from another tradition but perhaps recognizable also in Plato's rejection of the androgynous myth told by Aristophanes as an explanation of eros's desires and in his own proposal of another myth (cf. *Symposium* 189d–193d, 205d–2006a, 203b); *CPP* 57 translates "en rejetant" in the last sentence of the section inadvertently by "with."

Desire is neither the need for satisfaction nor "the affectivity of love" in its various forms, friendship, erotic love, parental love, or piety, etc. Levinas does not explain this thesis here, but we may be sure that the reason lies in the fact that the different forms of *"affective"* love are still somehow prolongations or moments of self-love. Cf. toward the end of section 6: "The Desire for the infinite does not have the sentimental complacency of love, but the rigor of moral exigency." In his article "The Ego and Totality" ("Le Moi et la Totalité"), Levinas showed the difference between *amour* and what he there called *socialité*. Later on, e.g., in *Transcendance et Intelligibilité* (Geneva: Labor et Fides, 1984), 25–29, he elucidates the affective aspect of the "idea of the infinite," which he then calls "an affection of the finite for the infinite." Notice

6. The Idea of the Infinite and Conscience

How does a face escape the discretionary power of the will which deals with evidence? Is not knowing a face *acquiring* a consciousness of it, and is not to acquire consciousness to adhere *freely?* Does not the idea of the infinite, qua *idea*, inevitably refer back to the schema of the Same encompassing the Other? Unless the idea of the infinite means the collapse of the good conscience of the Same. For everything comes to pass as though the presence of a face, the idea of the infinite in Me, were the putting of my freedom into question.[68]

That the free will is arbitrary, and that one must leave this elementary stage, is an old certainty of philosophers. But for all of them the arbitrariness refers to a rational foundation, a justification of freedom by itself. The rational foundation of freedom is still preeminence of the Same.

Moreover, the necessity of justifying the arbitrary is due only to the failure suffered by an arbitrary power. *The very spontaneity of freedom is not put into question*—such seems to be the dominant tradition of Western philosophy. Only the limitation of freedom would be tragic or scandalous. Freedom poses a problem only because it has not chosen itself. The failure of my spontaneity is said to awaken reason and theory; a pain is said to be the mother of wisdom. Failure would lead me to put brakes on my violence and introduce order into human relations, for everything is permitted but the impossible. In particular, modern political theories since Hobbes deduce the social order from the legitimacy, the incontestable right, of freedom.[69]

---

the ontological language that is still used in the phrase: "l'être qui *est* complètement et à qui rien ne manque."

68 *Évidence, prendre* (acquire, grasp), and *adhérer librement* (adhere freely) seem—as expressions of autonomy—to bring us back to the realm of the Same. The only way to escape from it and to pass over to the dimension of the infinite is in having my freedom be put into question. For the understanding of this last section, one must be aware of the fact that the French *conscience* can mean both "consciousness" and "conscience" (*conscience morale*).

69 The classical way of questioning freedom is obsessed by its finitude and remains therefore confined to the opposition of the truly free, i.e., rational and reasonable, will and the arbitrary or contingent will. Its hidden wish is to abolish the finitude of the will by making it into a *causa sui*, chosen and created by itself. The philosophy based on this

The Other's face is the revelation not of the arbitrariness of
the will but its injustice. Consciousness of my injustice is produced when I incline myself not before facts, but before the Other.
In his face the Other appears to me not as an obstacle, nor as
a menace I evaluate, but as what measures me. For me to feel
myself to be unjust I must measure myself against the infinite.
One must have the idea of the infinite, which, as Descartes
knows, is also the idea of the perfect, to know my own imperfection. The infinite does not stop me like a force blocking my force;
it puts into question the naive right of my powers, my glorious
spontaneity as a living being, a "force on the move."[70]

This way of measuring oneself against the perfection of the
infinite is not a theoretical consideration in its turn, in which
freedom would spontaneously take up its rights again. It is a
shame freedom has of itself, discovering itself to be murderous
and usurpatory in its very exercise.[71] A second-century exegete,
more concerned with what he had to do than of what he had to
hope for,[72] did not understand why the Bible begins with the
account of creation instead of putting us from the first before the
first commandments of Exodus. Only with great difficulty did he
come to concede that the account of creation was all the same
necessary for the life of the just man: for if the earth had not
been *given* to man but simply *taken* by him, he would have
possessed it only as an outlaw. Spontaneous and naive possession
cannot be justified by virtue of its own spontaneity.

---

problematic tries to show how the arbitrary and the rational will can
be reconciled in a universal will that diversifies itself in the particular
wants of participating individuals. The legitimacy of full freedom—and
of its unlimited autonomy, if this were possible—is not doubted. The
only means to put this freedom and its pretentions into question is the
face, which, in facing me, reveals the injustice of that autonomy. As
long as philosophy ignores or postpones taking into account the ethical
aspects of human existence, it condemns itself to an ontological and
egological perspective for which the root of existence remains hidden.

70 As noted above in Chapter Two (69 n. 71), the expression "une
force qui va," frequently used by Levinas, is taken from Victor Hugo's
Hernani, 3:2.

71 The primordial experience of conscience is the discovery of one's
being guilty of having taken away the other's possibilities of existence;
it is *not* the mere discovery of my being the ground of ontological negativity, as analyzed in Heidegger's chapters on *Gewissen* (*SuZ*, §§54–60).
Cf. the quote from Pascal quoted in note 37 above.

72 Cf. the three basic questions formulated in Kant's *Critique of
Pure Reason* A 805/B 833: (1) What can we know? (2) What ought we
to do? and (3) What may we hope for?

Existence is not condemned to freedom,[73] but judged and invested as a freedom. Freedom could not present itself all naked. This investiture of freedom constitutes moral life itself, which is through and through a heteronomy.

The will that is judged in the meeting with the Other does not assume[74] the judgment it welcomes. That would still be a return of the Same deciding about the Other in the final analysis—heteronomy absorbed in autonomy. The structure of the free will becoming *goodness* is not like the glorious and self-sufficient spontaneity of the I and of happiness, which would be the ultimate movement of being;[75] it is, as it were, its converse. The life of freedom discovering itself to be unjust, the life of freedom in heteronomy, consists in an infinite movement of freedom putting itself ever more into question. This is how the very depth of inwardness is hollowed out. The augmentation of exigency I have in regard to myself aggravates the judgment that is borne on me, that is, my responsibility. And the aggravation of my responsibility increases these exigencies. In this movement my freedom does not have the last word; I never find my solitude again—or, one might say, moral consciousness is essentially unsatisfied, or again, is always Desire.

The unsatisfiedness of conscience is not simply a suffering of delicate and scrupulous souls, but is the very contraction, the

---

73 Against Sartre's famous statement that we are "condemned to freedom" ("condamnés à la liberté"), Levinas elucidates the judgment that we perceive in the experience of shame by way of another metaphor: like a knight who has received an investiture, we do not primarily possess a home and land of our own but first of all have received the task of protecting widows and orphans, the poor, and the stranger, i.e., any other in its nakedness and vulnerability.

74 Since my responsibility is infinite, I cannot get rid of my guilt and shame. Although I accept (*accueille*) the judgment telling me this, I cannot "assume" it, if "assume" is an equivalent of assimilation or integration; by integration the judgment would no longer come from the "outside," the Other, but would become an element of my soul conversing with itself. The judgment that declares me responsible *precedes* any possibility of choice or consent.

75 With "the ultimate movement of being," Levinas alludes to Heidegger's description of the temporal existence (and *kinesis*) of *Dasein* as accorded to it by Being. Its content is not the spontaneous self-realization according to the rules and reasons of an autarchic ego establishing itself in solitary happiness (this sounds rather Aristotelian) but rather its converse: a primordial belonging to the Other, who steals from me my time, possessions, and happy solitude. Goodness is not a satisfied source of abundance but rather the exhaustion of someone who does not possess his/her own life because it is taken away by the other's existence.

hollow, the withdrawal into itself, and the systole of consciousness as such. Ethical consciousness itself is not invoked in this exposition as a "particularly recommendable" variety of consciousness, but as the concrete form of a movement more fundamental than freedom, the idea of the infinite. It is the concrete form of what precedes freedom, but does not lead us back to violence, the confusion of what is separated, necessity, or fatality.[76]

Here above all is the situation in which one is not alone. But if this situation does not yield proof of the existence of the Other (*Autrui*), this is because proof already presupposes the movement and adherence of a free will, a certainty. Thus the situation in which the free will is invested precedes proof. For every certainty is the work of a solitary freedom. As a welcome of the real into my a priori ideas, an adhesion of my free will, the last gesture of cognition is freedom. The face-to-face situation in which this freedom is put into question as unjust, in which it finds it has a master and a judge, is realized prior to certainty, but also prior to uncertainty.[77]

This situation is an experience in the strongest sense of the term: a contact with a reality that does not fit into any a priori idea, which overflows all of them—and it is just for this reason that we have been able to speak of infinity. No movement of freedom could appropriate a face to itself or seem to "constitute" it. The face has already been there when it was anticipated or constituted; it collaborated in that work, it spoke. A face is pure experience, conceptless experience. The conception according to which the data of our

<hr/>

76 Against all philosophies of freedom—from Descartes and Spinoza to Hegel, Marx, Nietzsche, Sartre, and Heidegger—Levinas claims that freedom is secondary vis-à-vis conscience. This is the originary mode of *Dasein* and consciousness that precedes freedom, but not as violence or magical union ("participation" and "confusion"), since its urgency is not a physical constraint or a blackmailing order. It is not a historical or otherwise contingent *Geschick* (fatality), either, because the primordial command precedes and transcends all history. Against the doxa (and dogma) of Parisian neo-Hegelians and Marxists of the fifties declaring that "history judges morality" ("l'histoire juge la morale"), we must have the courage to state that conscience judges history ("la morale juge l'histoire").

77 These are allusions to Husserl's famous fifth meditation of the *Cartesian Meditations*. The way in which the problem is formulated there shows a solitary ego urging itself to reach certainty about the existence of other, similar egos. Levinas's description of the immediate "experience" of the other (as not similar) shows that the ego is *primordially* nonsolitary and in contact with the Other (through an asymmetric relationship). This primordial, "a priori" relation precedes the dimension of thematic and objectifying argumentation in which the opposition of certainty and uncertainty must be located.

senses are put together in the Ego ends, before the Other, with the de-ception, the dispossession which characterizes all our attempts to encompass this real. But the purely negative incomprehension of the Other, which depends on our bad will, must be distinguished from the essential incomprehension of the Infinite, which has a positive side, is conscience and Desire.[78]

The unsatisfiedness of conscience, the de-ception before the other, coincides with Desire—this is one of the essential points of this exposition. The Desire for the infinite does not have the sentimental complacency of love, but the rigor of moral exigency. And the rigor of moral exigency is not bluntly imposed, but is Desire, due to the attraction and infinite height of being itself, for the benefit of which goodness is exercised. God commands only through the men for whom one must act.

Consciousness, the presence of self to self, passes for the ultimate theme of reflection. Conscience, a variation on this theme, a species of consciousness, is taken to add to it the concern for values and norms. We have raised several questions concerning this: can the self present itself to itself with so much natural complacency? Can it appear, shamelessly, in its own eyes? Is narcissism possible?[79]

Is not moral conscience the critique of and the principle of the presence of self to self? Then if the essence of philosophy consists in going back from all certainties toward a principle, if it lives from critique, the face of the Other would be the starting point of philosophy. This is a thesis of heteronomy which breaks with a very venerable tradition. But, on the other hand, the situation in which one is not alone is not reducible to the fortunate meeting of fraternal souls that greet one another and converse. This situation is the moral conscience, the exposedness of my freedom to the judgment of the Other (l'Autre). It is a disalignment which has authorized us to catch sight of the dimension of height and the ideal in the gaze of him to whom justice is due.

---

78 The dimension of conscience, desire, primordial experience precedes and transcends the dimension traditionally considered to be the most fundamental. It can be characterized neither by Descartes's search for *certainty,* nor by Hegel's *concept,* nor by Husserl's *constitution.*

79 At this point, Levinas refers to his articles "L'ontologie est-elle fondamentale?" (1951), "Liberté et Commandement" (1953), and "Le moi et la totalité" (1954), in which he "has dealt with the different themes relevant to this matter" (see, for the last two essays, *CPP* 15–46).

CHAPTER FIVE | A Key to *Totality and Infinity*

The composition of *Totality and Infinity* can be understood as the unfolding of its twofold title. As we will see, through the concept of "totality," the author characterizes the whole of Western philosophy, whereas "the infinite" indicates the transcendence suppressed by that same tradition. Instead of "totality" and "infinity," the first section of the book, however, most often uses the expression "the Same" (*le Même*) and "the Other" (*l'Autre*). Using the conjunction "and" in its title ("the Same and the Other," 1/31), this section establishes a close connection between *the Same* (which concretizes itself in the behavior of a monopolistic ego) and *the totality* of Greek and European philosophy, whereas, on the other hand, *the Other* (which reveals itself in the human face) is closely associated with *the infinite*. The relation between the Same (or the totality) and the Other (and/or the infinite) is the proper "topic" of the book, whose subtitle ("an essay on exteriority") characterizes the Other as a reality that cannot be integrated or "sublated" into any consciousness, spirit, or other form of interiority. Such a relation is not possible unless its two terms are in a very strong sense of the word *exterior* to each other. Their separation from one another must resist all attempts at fusion or totalizing. They are not and cannot become two moments of one union. This implies their independence: the One and the Other have each a being of their own. For the sameness of the ego, in relation to the whole of its world, this means that its existence is not a part or shadow of the infinite; its concrete mode of existence is described in the phenomenological analyses that constitute section 2 of the book (79–158/107–83). Since the Same reveals itself in the form of the self-centered ego, whose wants and autonomy impose their law (*nomos*) on the world in which it is at home (*oikos*), the title of section 2 characterizes it as an "economy" (*oiko-nomia*). The independence on the basis of which this selfsame is capable of having a relation of *exteriority* with its Other, the infinite, is constituted by a primordial and primitive way of being with oneself characterized as "*interiority.*" The title "Interiority and Economy" (*TI* 79/107) thus indicates that section 2 unfolds the formal but essential structure, which is already put forward in the introductory section. It was presented as "the identification of the Same in the I" or—more concretely—as the relation of an ego and its world, and the constellation of its features was there anticipated in a rapid sketch (7–8/37–38).

The third section (159–225/185–247) of the book contains the descriptions of the Other in its concrete emergence as visage and speech revealing to the I the injustice of its self-enclosure in an egocentric world. Since the exteriority of the other's face can neither be perceived nor respected in isolation from the perceiving ego, the exteriority of the face and of its relation to the I— and thus also the exteriority and independence of the I-at-home-in-its-world—form a constellation that is not a totality but neither is a pure dispersion without connections. This strange constellation is the topic of section 3, "Face and Exteriority." The place and function of the fourth section, entitled "Beyond the Face" (227–61/249–85), are not immediately clear. It contains an original description of erotic intimacy—a relation that in many respects differs from the intersubjective relation described in section 3—but its main purpose is the search for a transhistorical perspective from which the injustices of world history could be overcome.

I The Preface

A preface ought to state without detours the meaning of the work undertaken.[1] The preface to *Totality and Infinity* does this, but in a surprising way. Not only does it seem to take many detours but it also concentrates on the question of war and peace. True, the opening question—are we duped by morality? (ix/21)—belongs to the main problematic of *Totality and Infinity*, but it is immediately followed by a bewildering collection of topics, such as the place and function of politics, the relations between faith and thought, history and eschatology, totality and infinity, language

---

1 *TI* xviii/29–30.

and hypocrisy, theory and practice, methodology, ethics, and phe-nomenology. The approach exemplified by this preface is cer-tainly very different from "an overview, an oracle, or [answers given by] wisdom [itself]," but neither is it common among those who dedicate their time and energy to "philosophical research" (xviii/29–30). Yet, a careful study of *Totality and Infinity* will show that its preface does summarize its central "themes" and "thesis," although, in the initial reading, this might be obscured by some peculiarities of Levinas's approach.

When Levinas states here "without ceremonies" (xviii/30) the central topics of his book, this must be understood within the context of a question that remains the point of orientation and the background of all other questions throughout all of its 284 pages. It is the question of how the violence that seems inherent to all politics (and thus also to history) can be overcome by true peace.

A second peculiarity of this preface lies in the fact that the au-thor—although not outrightly criticizing his own work—already takes a certain distance toward it. Not only is he aware of the fact that a difficult text risks being misunderstood as soon as it is aban-doned by its author, and that it needs help to be freed from being caught in "the inevitable ceremonial" of the linguistic, literary, and conceptual constraints of the situation in which it is produced (xviii/30); but he also knows that—as a thematizing and thetical text—it cannot fully express what should be understood. For both reasons, Levinas tries in this preface—which, of course, has been written after the rest of the book—to "say again" (*redire*) what he meant to say and to undo "the said" (*dédire le dit*) insofar as it is inadequate to its own intentions.[2]

Besides (re)stating from the perspective of violence (or war) and peace the main topic of his book, Levinas wants here also to fulfill another of the tasks we may expect from a preface, namely, "to break through the screen stretched between the author and the reader by the book itself" (xviii/30). A philosophical text is neither a spoken word through which the speaker is immediately present to the listener with whom he communicates, nor is it a "word of honor" ("une parole d'honneur") claiming trust or faith. The imme-diate character of its communication creates a distance demanding

---

2 *TI* xiii/30. Thus, this preface announces the development of Levi-nas's distinction between the Saying (*le dire*), the Said (*le dit*), the Unsaying or denial (*dédire*) and the Saying-again (*redire*), which will be one of the central topics in *AE*.

interpretation; abandoned by its author, it is prey to hermeneutical decipherings that inevitably lead to various ways of understanding. A preface might be the last chance of bridging the distance between the reader and the author and of making the screen as transparent as possible. Of course, in doing so, it produces another text, and thus a new screen, but this is the only possible assistance it can give from a distance.

According to the author (xviii/29), the opening sentence of the preface (ix/21) announces "the theme of the work." Morality (or, more precisely, the question as to whether morality is an authentic and original dimension of human existence, and not an illusion) is brought to the fore by opposing it to the dimension(s) of violence, war, and politics. As *Totality and Infinity* will subsequently show, the world of politics is the world in which traditional philosophy is well at home. Without rejecting all forms of politics, Levinas attacks the idolization (or "absolutization") of politics by defending a pre- or trans-political ethics rooted in the primordial relation between human beings. Thus, he does not confine himself to the traditional question of the tensions and relations between ethics and politics; these relations and tensions stem from a more radical dimension—in fact, it is the most radical, ultimate and "first," one: the originary "dimension" of human existence and Being as such. *Totality and Infinity* is an attempt to show that the "perspective" of morality is not a particular perspective—and therefore not an aspect or perspective at all—since it coincides with the transnatural and transworldly or "metaphysical" (non)perspective of "first philosophy."[3]

The most originary "experience" of the most originary "reality" is already ethical, and from the outset metaphysics is determined ethically. However, Levinas does not argue for the reversal of the traditional order by which ethics, as a particular discipline of philosophy, follows the metaphysical or ontological disciplines in which normative, and especially moral, questions are postponed; the ethical does not belong to any particular discipline or perspective at all; it is as originary as the most fundamental moment of theoretical philosophy because it precedes any

---

3 This "thesis" is clearly expressed in the title of the article, "Ethique comme philosophie première," published in G. Hottois (ed.), *Justifications de l'éthique* (Editions de l'Université de Bruxelles, 1984), 41–51, but already announced in *TI* 281/304: "Morality is not a branch of philosophy, but first philosophy."

possible scission between the theoretical and the practical or between description and evaluation (xvii/29). It is, therefore, a mistake to present Levinas's work as an ethics or as a welcome addition to the phenomenological movement. Its aim is much more radical, at least as radical as that of Aristotle's *protè philosophia*, Hegel's *Logic* or Heidegger's *Being and Time*. The "dimension" or "perspective" thematized in *Totality and Infinity* is that of the most originary and primordial, in which practice and theory, metaphysics and ethics, have not yet separated: it is "the common source of activity and theory" (xvi/27), "the metaphysical transcendence" (xvii/29), in which vision and ethics as the source of all morality are still one. In this originary "dimension," "ethics itself is an optics" (xii/23; xvii/29), whereas metaphysics itself is already oriented toward the Good. *Totality and Infinity* may be characterized as an original plea for authentic morality, but this characteristic would become false as soon as it is cut off from the thesis that the moral "point of view" coincides with the ultimate "event" or "fact" or "structure" or "Being."[4]

A few quick reminders about the ideological situation in which *Totality and Infinity* was written might be helpful in order to understand why Levinas introduces his philosophy by the evocation of key political concepts such as war and peace, violence, freedom, etc. The end of World War II did not terminate the search for an answer to the question of how it had been possible that a nation of great thinkers, poets, and musicians, under the leadership of a barbaric killer, had committed the most extensive mass murder of history. Not only was it barely possible to explain that outburst of modern violence, terror, and tyranny, but similar terrors continued to devastate the face of the earth by means of colonial and imperialistic wars or by systematic torture in the name of communist or capitalistic ambitions and ideologies. The conquest of Eastern Europe, China, and other parts of Asia by communist tyrannies found its most fervent defenders among the French intelligentsia. The literary and philosophical climate in which Levinas prepared *Totality and Infinity* can be partly summarized by pointing to the publications in which, for instance,

---

4 In *TI*, "Being" (*l'être*) is still used as the equivalent of the originary and the ultimate, even in the preface, for instance x^4, $xi^{3,4,9,30,39}$, xii^{9-12}, xv^{22-33}, xvi^4. It is only later that Levinas consequently rejects the ontological claim that Being would be the ultimate by opposing the Good, as beyond Being, to it.

Sartre and Merleau-Ponty discussed the contradictions (they preferred the word "dialectics") in which ethics (the "yogi") and politics (the "commissary") were involved. Other, non-Marxist voices could be heard, but they did not dominate the literary scene. Eric Weil, who published his *Philosophie politique* (Paris: Vrin) in 1956 and his *Philosophie morale* (Paris: Vrin) in 1961, is one of them, and he seems to have impressed Levinas.[5] Nietzsche's critique of European culture and moralism might have played some role, although during the fifties it certainly did not have the arrogant and peremptory overtones some French interpreters lent it in the seventies.

The preface of *Totality and Infinity* introduces morality and ethics by opposing them to war, which immediately is connected with the world of politics and history. How are ethics and politics related? Are they necessarily opposed? Does the fight of all against all suspend the validity of all moral devices? Does morality reveal itself under these circumstances to be an illusion? In that case, it would not be anything infinite.

A commonplace view on the relation between ethics and politics maintains that an individual's will is free insofar as it can

---

5 Levinas refers to Weil in TH 103 and in some pages of his books. The very broad sense of the word "violence," as containing everything that is not rational or reasonable, in the French philosophical literature of the sixties, might have originated in the very important book *Logique de la Philosophie* (1950), in which Weil tried to integrate and to "lift up" Hegel's phenomenological and speculative philosophy. In "Ethique et Esprit" (*DL* 19 n.1), Levinas writes: "We owe to Eric Weil's excellent thesis *Logique de la philosophie* (Paris: Vrin, 1951)—whose philosophical importance and logical strength will impose themselves—the systematic and forceful use of the term 'violence' in its opposition to discourse. We give, however, a different meaning to it—as we already did in our essay ['L'ontologie est-elle fondamentale?'] in the *Revue de Métaphysique et de Morale* of February–March 1951." In *Difficile Liberté*, Levinas defines "violence" in fact as "all action by which one acts as if he were the only acting person; as if the rest of the universe existed only for the *reception* of this action," and—as a consequence—as "all action that we undergo without collaborating in all its aspects. Almost all causality is violent in this sense: the fabrication of a thing, the satisfaction of a need, the desire, and even the knowledge of an object; and also fights and wars, wherein the other's weakness is sought as the betrayal of his personality. But there is also a great deal of violence in the poetical frenzy and enthusiasm by which we become a mouthpiece of the Muse who uses it to speak, and in the fear and trembling through which the sacred carries us away; there is violence in passion, be it the passion of a love wounded by a perfidious arrow" (20).

always distance itself from all material or bodily constraints, power structures, torture, hunger, etc. But this view is too cheap because it naively denies the possibility of techniques that break, submit and enslave, or corrupt any or almost any human will. It is against such naiveté that Levinas maintains that the will is essentially unheroic.[6] In the essay "Freedom and Command"— a hermeneutical retrieval of Plato's meditation on tyranny in the *Politeia*—Levinas had already shown that individual liberty not only can be robbed of its autonomy and made obedient to physical violence, but also that hunger, torture, money, and seduction through love or rhetorics are capable of corrupting one's heart and so enslave one's soul that it no longer cares for itself, having lost any choice of its own.[7] Protection against such a loss of freedom can only be found in political institutions that urge and sanction the exercise of individual freedom. By obeying objective laws and commands, human freedom protects its own liberty. Impersonal and general laws must save the human life and liberty of individuals.[8]

"War," as contrasted with the possibility of effective morality, seems to be a *pars pro toto* for all kinds of violence. In a situation of war, harming others, killing, cheating, and lying become "natural" and "normal"; they are even seen as patriotic obligations. The validity of the moral norms is shaken and seems to be suspended. The conflicting interests and forces of any somewhat extended society constitute milder or fiercer forms of war. No one can escape altogether from this violence, which seems to be inherent to the world of modern politics, even if the existing antagonisms have been harmonized by a temporary balance of powers and strivings. In the light of politics, it seems, therefore, impractical, naive, unrealistic, and even ridiculous to believe in the originary force of pure morality.

The classical answer to the question of how we can overcome violence says that reason, as the source of universality in all our behavior, as well as of rules and insights, can justify and found an "objective" organization that preserves and protects the freedom of all individuals by applying to them the same universal law—the law of reason. As coming forth from reason itself, the imposition of these laws on human subjects is nothing other

---

6 *TI* 213/236. Cf. also "Liberté et Commandement," *Revue de Métaphysique et de Morale* 58 (1953): 264–72/*CPP* 15–23.

7 "Liberté et Commandement," 265–66/*CPP* 16–17.

8 266–67/*CPP* 17–18.

than the (re)shaping of their inner and outer life by their own innermost and typically human possibility. Body and psyche are made reasonable, i.e., human, by realizing corporeally one's own true, essential, and practical reason or will. Insofar as it is the universal law of reason that is made powerful by an objective institutionalization, it treats all individuals with justice as individuals having equal rights, etc. By giving up exorbitant claims and by limiting the range of their desires, individuals become members of one whole, whose collective freedom and well-being they share. In exchange for the sacrifice of their egoism, they receive a reasonable satisfaction of their needs. According to this social theory, the peace aimed at by all politics is based on a compromise of interested forces within an encompassing totality under the auspices of universal reason. Its keys are universality, totality, neglect of the individuals' unicity, equal needs and rights, and the conception of sociality and intersubjectivity as constitutive elements of bigger collectivities.

Levinas's search is oriented to another peace: a prepolitical one that does not result from the calculations of a rational or reasonable compromise, destroyed as soon as the balance of powers is shaken, but rather—as an originary peace—one that precedes the emergence of any violence. This peace is inherent to the originary relationship of unique individuals, a relationship that precedes the constitution of any state or totality based on roles and functional definitions of the participating members only. Before politics and world history, there is the original peace of a lost paradise. It is not the dialectical counterpart of war, for such a counterpart would belong to the alternation of violence and nonviolence typical for the dimension of politics; neither is it the kingdom of a golden age somewhere at the beginning or the end of our history. As originary, "true" peace, it is as much a lost memory as the promise of a future *beyond* all history. Instead of "originary peace," it can, therefore, also be called *eschatological* or—in a more biblical terminology—a *messianic* peace. The political peace of "Greek" and European philosophy is, thus, founded in a peace beyond all peace announced and remembered by the prophets of Israel.

Retrieving the biblical opposition between the king and the prophet, Levinas will try to show *from a philosophical perspective* that the only way of taking morality seriously implies another conception of peace—and therewith of politics, ethics, individuality, universality, reason, and philosophy itself—than that of the classical tradition of European civilization. According to

Plato and Aristotle, the art of living an authentic human life consisted in the beauty of a courageous, liberal, prudent, and contemplative praxis in which the ethical concern of self-realization was interwoven with the performance of political tasks. As the two inherent possibilities of social communication, war and peace dominated both politics and ethics (for instance, but not only, in the form of courage). Levinas refers to Heraclitus's aphorisms about *Polemos* as "father" and source, as well as structure, of all things and suggests that Heidegger's evocation of Being's "polemical" character continues the tradition of Western ontology insofar as this conceives of Being as a dialectical totalization of "warring" oppositions.[9]

The prophetic message of an eschatological peace that would be based on a fair judgment about the injustice of political history interrupted the "polemology" of Greek philosophy. A new, unheard-of concept of peace was announced that belonged to a pre- or post-political morality. Insofar as Western civilization accepted it without abandoning its Greek perspective, it became divided in itself and hypocritical.[10] It did not solve the conflict between the "Greek" search for *truth* and the prophetic proclamation of the *Good* (of which Plato, too, had had an inkling). Modern philosophy has tried, with Hegel and Marx, to synthesize both traditions in a secularized eschatology by conceptualizing the image of a history that would compensate for all human sufferings and sacrifices by a future of full freedom and satisfied humanity.

The secret and source of authentic morality, eschatology, and peace is a relation ignored, forgotten, or neglected by Western philosophy. This relation cannot be absorbed or dialectically integrated by any whole, for it resists all synthesis and transcends all possibilities of totalizing. It is, therefore, "beyond" or "before" or "transcendent with regard to" the dimensions of politics,

---

9 Cf. Heidegger, *Einführung in die Metaphysik*, 47–48/61–62.

10 *TI* xii/24: "an essentially hypocritical civilization, that is, attached both to the True and to the Good, henceforth antagonistic . . . attached to both the philosophers and the prophets." In the discussion that followed his paper "Transcendance et Hauteur" (TH 103), Levinas gives the following commentary on this passage: "It is the fundamental contradiction of our situation (and perhaps of our condition), which is called Hypocrisy in my book, that the hierarchy taught by Athens and the *abstract* and somewhat *anarchic* ethical individualism taught by Jerusalem are both necessary to suppress violence." Does Levinas hint here at an unconquerable contradiction—and an unconquerable choice between onesidedness or hypocrisy ("perhaps of our condition") or at the task of discovering a new form of synthesis?

economy, history, and ontology in its classical and modern synthetic or dialectical form. This relation is not a moment of the universe; it is the original *relatedness to the infinite*. This reason of transcendence, with all its consequences for the issues of human existence and philosophy, is the theme or topic of *Totality and Infinity*. Against all philosophies of "totality" (in which Levinas includes not only Hegel and his predecessors but also Marx, Husserl, and Heidegger), Levinas will show how a nontotalitarian transcendence is possible and how its recognition leads to a radical transformation of the very project of philosophy.[11]

In sketching the core constellation that will be unfolded from many sides in the course of *Totality and Infinity*, the preface stresses the peculiar character of the originary relation of transcendence. It relates me, the subject, to the infinite, which overflows my capacity of encompassing it. The infinite is not the adequate correlate of some intention that—in accordance with the Husserlian conception of intentionality—would connect a noema with a noesis by an adequate correspondence; the infinite surprises, shocks, overwhelms, and blinds by confronting me with another human face. The transcendent or "metaphysical" relation with the invisible infinite *is* speaking (*parole*) or a respectful and dedicated looking up to the Other. The infinite reveals itself neither in philosophical theses nor in dogmatic articles of any faith but rather in concrete hospitality and responsibility with regard to another woman, child, or man.

The shock through which the revelation of the infinite conquers my consciousness can also be characterized as a form of "violence," as Levinas does, for instance, in stating that violence "consists in welcoming a being to which it is inadequate" (xiii/25) or that the transitivity of all acts "involves a violence essentially" (xv/27); but this "violence" differs absolutely from the

---

11 In "Freedom and Command" (1953), too, Levinas draws the line between violence and nonviolence differently than those who, like Eric Weil, equate nonviolence with rationality in the broad sense of a reason that includes *Vernunft* as well as *Verstand.* According to Levinas, a rational system like that of Hegel's objective spirit is violent because it would reduce all individuality to an instance of a universal concept. Levinas himself defines violence through its opposition to the basic human relation of transcendence. Violence is, thus, equivalent to narcissism. It does not permit the Other to surprise, to accuse, or to convert me but tries to find out to what extent the Other's freedom can be captured, used, reduced. A violent person avoids looking at the Other's face and seizes persons from the perspective of universality, i.e., from the perspective of the (other) individual's absence.

violence of political war and peace. Whereas the latter is an essential element of Western civilization and ontology, the inadequacy of the infinite opens a space beyond the dimension of politics, civilization, and their history. Without such a space, we would be caught in the reasonable order of a tamed but not conquered violence that, at any moment, could explode again in the terror of a systematic destruction, unrestrained by absolute morality.

| The Same and the Other

In a way comparable to Aristotle's ontology and Hegel's logic, the first section, called "preparatory" at the end of the preface (xviii/29), and the conclusions (263–84/287–307) draw the main lines of the "first philosophy" comprised by the analyses of *Totality and Infinity*. These texts are difficult because they have to introduce a radically new starting point for philosophical thinking, and also because they show the coherence of such a thought by approaching it from many different angles. The first part (A) of this section is especially difficult because its understanding presupposes an acquaintance with several parts of the phenomenology accomplished in the course of the book. Many anticipations are, thus, necessary. If the study of one of Levinas's own summaries[12] is not enough, only a second reading of *Totality and Infinity* can clarify the meaning of its beginning.

The meaning of the qualification "preparatory," as the author calls this section (xviii/29), is not that it can be read as an easy introduction but that it "sketches the *horizon* of all the investigations" of the book. The titles of the section and of its first part (A. "Metaphysics and Transcendence," 3–23/33–52) are programmatic, as is the content of the five subsections of part A. Since Levinas sees the whole Western tradition from Parmenides to Heidegger as a philosophy of the Same, the "and" in the title of the section is polemical. He does not, however, fall into the trap of a contrary opposition. Indeed, he does not defend a philosophy of the Other (and not either—as we will see—a philosophy of dialogue), for without any sameness, unity, and totality, only the dispersion of an extreme atomism would remain, which

---

12 See PhI (with the commentary given here in the second and third chapters above) and TH, which gives the text of the paper Levinas was invited to present at the Société Française de Philosophie on 27 January 1962, together with the discussion that followed it.

would be the end of all philosophy and thought in general. The "and" of the title "Metaphysics and Transcendence" does not express an opposition but announces that transcendence, when taken seriously—namely as the relation from the Same to an irreducible Other—cannot be respected unless by a thought that overcomes the totality of *physis,* and, in this sense, is metaphysical.[13] At the same time, it gives—under the cover of the Aristotelian term "metaphysics"—homage to Plato, whose questions and attempt will be often alluded to in the course of the text.

The division of part A (3–23/33–52) can be explained in the following way: the first subsection ("Desire of the Invisible") states—with allusions to Plato—the basic structure or "principle"; the second one ("The Breach of Totality") contrasts this with the monistic principle of (Western) philosophy; the third ("Transcendence Is Not Negativity") and the fourth ("Metaphysics Precedes Ontology") set it off against Hegelian dialectics and Heidegger's thought of Being, and the fifth subsection ("Transcendence as the Idea of the Infinite") shows that the father of modern philosophy, Descartes, in his *Metaphysical Meditations* has given an account of transcendence that can be retrieved in a promising way.

In my commentary, I will concentrate on the positive aspects of Levinas's thought and leave out what has already been explained in former chapters of this book. For the moment, it may suffice to say that *Totality and Infinity* announces itself as an attempt to write a post-Heideggerian and, therefore, also post-(neo-)Platonic metaphysics.

Without immediately asking critical questions about the possibility and the inner coherence of Levinas's beginning, I simply observe that the first pages state the relation of the Same and the Other (or true transcendence) as the ultimate horizon that should replace the question of Being or the question of Being, beingness, and beings. Levinas's strategy is no longer the reversal of Heidegger's move from beings (and their essence) to Being, as he announced in the title of his early book *From Existence to Existents,* but it is an altogether new start. As most modern philosophers do, he begins with the outline of a sort of (onto-)logic, the "logic of the relation that unites *and separates* the Same and the Other," but neither the word "logic" nor the characteristic of its "theme" as something ontic or ontological is adequate to

---

13 Cf. Chapter Two above.

indicate his concern. Moreover, he does not begin by stating an abstract relationship as more fundamental than any other but by the phenomenological analysis of what he, in this book, still calls an "experience": the experience of desire, which reveals that relationship to be a concrete movement of transcendence. Aside from this *phenomenological* aspect, the beginning has also a *hermeneutical* one because it should be read as a retrieval of Plato's texts on eros and desire in the *Symposium* and the *Philebus,* and it has a *polemical* aspect insofar as it opposes, from the outset, some central convictions of classical and contemporary philosophy.

The first sentences of the opening subsection of part A (3/33), "The Desire for the Invisible," contain the declaration that metaphysics should be reinstated against all post-Hegelian attempts to take away from philosophy its most noble moment by leveling it to a surface without any elevation. These attempts, in fact, bring the hidden spirit of the Western tradition to the light: the "transdescendence" of its antitheism and antihumanism. In order to show the sense in which the old Platonic conception and practice of philosophy must be retaken, Levinas chooses as his point of departure a phenomenological analysis of *desire,* as he did in "Philosophy and the Idea of the Infinite." These allusions to Plato's description of eros in the *Symposium* and the *Phaedrus* were obvious, but another less obvious association refers back to the *Philebus* (50e ff., especially 51b), where "alongside of needs whose satisfaction amounts to filling a void, Plato catches sight also of aspirations that are not preceded by suffering and lack, and in which we recognize the pattern of Desire: the need of someone who lacks nothing, the aspiration of someone who possesses one's being entirely, who goes beyond one's plenitude, who has the idea of the Infinite," as Levinas writes in *TI* 76/103. Probably the Platonic eros still has too many features of a need to be a model for a description of the desire *without lack* that opens up the most radical dimension.

The way Levinas introduces this desire (3/33ff.) confronts us with three voices: that of Rimbaud, whose exclamation "the true life is absent," in expressing the nihilism of our epoch, simultaneously expresses an eternal desire of the human heart;[14] that

---

14 "La vraie vie est absente. Nous ne sommes pas au monde." Cf. A. Rimbaud, *Une saison en enfer,* in *Œuvres Complètes* (Paris: Pléiade, 1963), 229.

of Heidegger, the greatest philosopher of our century, who determined the human mode of existence as "being in the world"; and that of Plato, who formulated the task of philosophy as an ascension toward the truth "yonder" and "up there."[15] "Metaphysics" is the name by which Levinas, in this book, indicates the thinking that, by taking all of these three voices very seriously, occupies the space between the "here-below" in the world (*ici-bas*) and the "elsewhere" (*là-bas*). Its turning to the otherwise and the height of the "elsewhere" is not, however, fleeing away from worldliness. Loyalty to the human world does not imply at all the betrayal of all transcendence or "trans-ascendence" (5/35); the otherness of true life is not an alibi by which we can excuse ourselves for not taking full responsibility for the adventures of our history. On the contrary, it is the absolute condition for a humane world. A total immersion in the factual histories and customs of our "fate" would be the triumph of the Same; an exodus must be given to us, but this will not be possible unless the otherness of a shocking surprise disrupts the coherence of our immanence and autonomy.

Desire is the concrete way of human transcendence to the (truly or absolutely) Other. It must be sharply distinguished from any form of *need*. While the satisfaction of needs stands for the whole economy of the Western way of life and thought, desire is a radically different "principle" that shakes and reorients the customs and reflexes of that economy.

All the features of desire are marked by the exceeding character of the desiring instance and the exteriority, the strangeness, or the otherness of the desired. Needs are always directed to a satisfaction, which indeed can be found, albeit only for a certain time. "Need" is the name for all human orientations toward something that is lacking or makes an achievement incomplete. It is accompanied by a certain pain, the pain of privation. Hunger is a good example, but we are also in need when we have fallen from an agreeable position or chased from some sort of paradise and when we are nostalgically longing for some situation of inner peace. Radically different from need, desire cannot be satisfied because it cannot be fulfilled. Through a need, a human subject lacks certain goods that it can assimilate and make part of its own body, surrounding, or world. Such an integration is not possible for desire. Its transcendence to the exterior is not an anticipation of fulfillment or of a beginning integration. On the

15 Cf. Chapter Two above.

contrary, its "hunger" is intensified to the same extent to which it approaches the desired. The desired is not anything that can become familiar to me; it cannot have a function or place in the economy of the desiring one. The impossibility of being integrated gives the desired not only the character of exteriority but also of height: the Other resists any attempt to convert it or him or her into something that is my own; the Other is not even a theme or a noema that I could "grasp" or encompass by representing or comprehending it. Insofar as all visible realities can be mastered by putting them before me, by presenting them through perception, and by representing them through reflection, the desired is invisible, irrepresentable, and nonconceptual. Desire and desired do not correspond as correlates that "fit" adequately into one another. *Desire does not have the structure of intentionality.* It is, thus, neither the natural tendency that was thematized in Aristotle's ethics as a teleological striving for self-realization nor a nostalgic "eksisting" toward a contentment that—although delayed—could fulfill the longing subject and bring it to its rest.

If the relation between the desiring subject and the desired Other is essentially insatiate and insatiable, the distance that separates them cannot be abolished by any caress or comprehension. Their separation is an essential impossibility of fusion or union. The desired Other resembles in this respect *death*. Both surprise and shock me by their absolute otherness: neither death nor the Other can take a place within the unfolding of my possibilities. The difference between need and desire is that between a self-centered love and the goodness of being—and thus also suffering and ultimately even dying—for the Other.

But, more concretely, what or who is "the Other"? To what or whom does the desire transcend and relate? In a programmatic statement (4/34), Levinas declares that the alterity of the desired is the alterity of *Autrui* (the human other) *and* that of *le Très-Haut* (the Most-High, or God). The "and" of this phrase announces a problem that can be formulated in several ways—for instance, as the problem of the relation between morality and religion. *Totality and Infinity* concentrates on the relation between ego and the *human* Other, who is—in the sense indicated above—the desired invisible and absolute Other, although some of its passages begin to clarify also the relation between this Other (*Autrui*) and God, but it is only later on, especially in "The Trace of the Other" (1963), "God and Philosophy" (1975), and *Otherwise Than Being* (1974) that Levinas thematizes that question extensively.

The double-sidedness of desire as separation *and* relation opens the space for an analysis of human existence as two-dimensional reality: as separated individuals, we are independent and egocentric, centers and masters of an economy that is also an egonomy; as transcending toward the Other, we live in a different dimension, the structure of which is made of transcendence, alterity, and the impossibility of totalization and identification. The difficulty of Levinas's enterprise lies in the task of showing—in the form of a thematic, and thereby necessarily gathering, discourse—that gathering, coherence, and unity do not constitute the ultimate horizon of such a discourse, and that otherness, separation, and transcendence are irreducible to any unity.

In the second subsection, "The Breach of Totality" (5/35ff.), Levinas analyzes the paradoxical structure of the relation that was found in desire. The Other reveals itself as impeding certain ways of approaching him or her. He/she resists and condemns my trying to submit any otherness to the rule of my self-centered economy. This way of meeting me is not equal; it is not even remotely similar to my meeting the Other. The Other and the I reveal themselves as radically different. My relation to the Other (whose "height" was stated in Platonic terminology) is asymmetrical, not symmetrical. My relation to the Other is different from the relation of the Other to me. In this sense, Levinas calls the relation of transcendence (or the "metaphysical relation") "irreversible" and also "nonreciprocal." He does not consider the concept of a double (or reciprocal) asymmetry.

The asymmetrical relation is not a relation between two people that can be observed by a third person from the outside or from "above." Seen from an outside standpoint, the encounter of two or more persons is the relation of two or more equal and similar instances of a universal class or genus of beings. In this perspective, the asymmetry, with all nonrelative otherness and transcendence, has disappeared. By this perception, the observer embraces the people involved and reduces them to similar realizations of the Same. The only concrete way in which the relation of transcendence and nontotalizable alterity can be saved is the position of an I that does not escape from the face-to-face to which it is brought by the Other. I must remain in the position that places me before the surprising Other and not surpass the relation in which I am caught—for instance, by reflecting or talking about it from a higher, nonengaged, and universal standpoint.

But what am I doing when I write such a sentence or a book about transcendence, the Other, and the metaphysical relationship? I am treating them, including myself, as a moment of my face-to-face with the absolutely Other, *as* a moment of a discourse in which all human beings can be "I" or "Other" and in which "the I," "the Other," and their "relation" inevitably acquire universal meanings. This contradiction between the concrete relation of me(-now-here) to you(-now-here) as my (here-and-now-concrete) Other and its appearance in the text of my putting it into words constitutes a fundamental problem that will command important developments of Levinas's thought after *Totality and Infinity*. In the form of the relation between the Saying (*le Dire*) and the Said (*le Dit*), it is one of the main topics in *Otherwise Than Being*. In *Totality and Infinity*, we are confronted with a double language: the universalist discourse that is practiced insists continually on the necessity of a speech that involves the speaker in a relation of transcendence toward a concrete Other with whom the speaker is confronted. The strange and extraordinary contradiction between these two discourses is maintained, but we must understand that the basic and transcendent language is the "apology," that is, the logos or discourse that departs "from" the one and is directed to the Other who faces the one, whereas the reflective text of the book is a secondhand and second-rate language from which the absolute Other and the engaged ego have disappeared.

The separation that is essential to the relation of transcendence is not possible unless both terms "absolve" themselves— as absolutely different and independent—from their being tied together by their relation. For (the) ego, this means that its mode of existence must be identical with itself independently from or "before" any encounter with an Other. This self-identity of Me is more than a logical tautology; it is the concrete activity of self-identification through which I establish myself as inhabitant and owner of my world. The concrete way of my being what I am—in the supposition that we can make an abstraction from all encounters with other people—is the egoism of my enjoying, ruling, and transforming the world in accordance with my needs. This egoism is, thus, a condition for the possibility of transcendence and dedication to the nonego that is the Other. Herewith Levinas has "deduced" the theme of section 2, "Interiority and Economy" (79–158/107–83), in which the concreteness of the Same is shown to lie in the economy of a hedonistic autonomy.

The separation and "absolution" or absoluteness of the (human) Other will be brought to the fore in section 3, "The Face and Exteriority" (159–225/185–247). In subsection 2 of section 1, part A, Levinas already contrasts the separation with various forms of relative otherness, such as that of spatial distance, tools that can be handled, perception, and representation, which integrate all beings as moments of an overview. The irreducible Other is a stranger who cannot be reduced to a role or function within my world; he/she is not even a member of "my" community but rather the life of someone who comes from afar and who does not belong to it. If the Same is the life of an egoistic I, how then can I and the Other still be related? What is the structure of this most radical relation? How must it be qualified? To what extent does the face-to-face escape from the text in which the observer's perception and philosophical thought try to say their truth?

In order to prevent a fundamental misunderstanding of the constellation sketched above, it might be helpful to state here, by way of anticipation, that Levinas's philosophy does not fix the opposition between a narcissistic ego and a moral law of altruism that should be urged upon its egoism. Ego is *at the same time* turned and returned to itself by the spontaneous egoism of its being alive (a *zooion* or *animal*) *and* transcendent, that is, exceeding its own life by desiring, i.e., by a nonegoistic "hunger" or generosity for the Other. This duality is *not* the classical twofold of body and spirit. The reflexivity of ego's self-identification is as corporeal, sensible, and affective as ego's orientation and dedication to the Other. Being good without having hands and material goods is empty, while all "spiritual" goods that promise satisfaction fall under the law of hedonistic economy. Being good means giving your life or letting it be taken away, but to suffer and even to die for another implies that I would enjoy the good things that are taken away from me.

In the three following subsections, Levinas sets the "metaphysical" structure of the transcendent relation off against Hegelian (3. "Transcendence Is Not Negativity," 11–12/40–42), classical, and Heideggerian ontology (4. "Metaphysics Precedes Ontology," 12–18/42–48) and compares it with Descartes's analysis of the cogito and its innate idea of the infinite (5. "Transcendence as the Idea of the Infinite," 18–23/48–52).

Levinas agrees that the play of yes and no in *Hegelian dialectics* cannot fathom the extent and the height of the distance between the Same and the Other. Taking his lead from Being (*on*) and Nonbeing (*mè on*), or "Nothing," Hegel reduces all the versions of their opposition to an onto-logical totality (spirit, history, logos, reason, self-consciousness, being), without respecting the radical and absolute otherness of *to heteron,* which cannot be reduced to a lack, a shadow, or an imperfection of *to auton* and still less to an adventure of Being. The whole of *Totality and Infinity* can be read as one long refutation of the attempt to understand the difference between the Same and the Other as an opposition within the unique horizon of a totality (which, in that case, would inevitably be the Same of the all-encompassing ontology).

The fourth subsection starts with a general critique of traditional philosophy, which Levinas—in opposition to *Heidegger*—does not characterize as metaphysics but as ontology. His main purpose here is to show that Heidegger's thought is still a version of classical ontology. The pages in which this is argued (15–18/ 45–48) belong to the clearest pages Levinas wrote on Heidegger. Without defending all the elements of his interpretation, I will formulate here the leading thread of his critique.

Classical philosophy, being a discourse about the beingness of beings, did not and could not do justice to singular beings in their *"tode ti"* (this-here-now), for the essence of ontology is the comprehension of things, events, etc. by means of a *mediation,* i.e., by means of a comprehension that perceives or conceives them in the light of a third, anonymous term, a universal concept, or a horizon. By thus understanding the singular event or thing as an instance within the surrounding framework of some generality—Being, history, idea, spirit, substance, etc.—ontological thought reduces and forgets that which constitutes this-here-now as this unique something. It does not respect it in its ownness but drowns it in an anonymous whole or universal.

Heidegger's thought of Being is a very important version of ontology. Indeed, according to him, *Dasein* understands phenomena in the light (the "phosphorence") of Being and in the space (the "clearing") opened up by it. The horizon of Being has taken over the mediating function of the classical concept or idea. Being, too, is neutral and impersonal, embracing and encompassing, an active and transitive "exist-ing" that makes beings be. It grants them their *conatus essendi,* their perseverance and maintenance in being, as Levinas will say in later works, and it grants us the openness and the light that are necessary in order to grasp them as phenomena that appear. *Verstehen* is, thus, understood as *comprehension:* a totalizing seizure of things, events, and relationships as moments belonging to an anonymous totality. The famous *Seinlassen* ("to let be"), which suggests receptivity on our part, is, in fact, an approach by which the thinking subject maintains the position of a center for which the universe of beings unfolds itself within the horizon of an—albeit more aesthetic than trivially hedonistic—economy. It lacks respect for the surprising unity of the singular, and especially for the shocking emergence of a human other.

This emergence is, indeed, shocking because it calls the spontaneity of my egonomy and egology into question. The condition of respect is the acceptance of this fundamental criticism. It procures the basis of metaphysics as a critique of ontology. The ownness of the Other reveals the greed and the violence of egology and ontology if these are not founded in, and surpassed by, metaphysics. Metaphysics respects the unique; ontology is subordinate to it. To be true to the critical "appearance" of the *tode ti* of the Other, I must let the Other criticize my spontaneous will to power, I must not flee from the face-to-face that accuses me. To do justice to the Other, the "liberty" of ontological "transcendence" must be subordinated to the vocative of my being spoken to by the Other and my speaking to him/her. If I talk or write a book *about* the Other (or about our relation), this can only be an appendix to the truth of our face-to-face. The reduction of the Other to an element of my text about him/her can only be redeemed by offering this text to him/her.

Freedom or justice? Even if we stress, with the later Heidegger, that understanding or thinking is obedience to Being, he still conceives of it as an unfolding of the possibilities of my modes of being as "I can." As long as understanding is practiced as approaching beings from some wider horizon (such as Being, the clearing, the granting event of appropriation), it does violence to the irreducible, nonmediatable, and absolutely immediate "fact" of the Other who refutes my egocentrism, as well as the all-encompassing character of the horizon. The secret of Western ontology is its basic sympathy with political oppression and tyranny. In this sense, the celebration of *physis* as an impersonal and generous mother without face could conspire with the vulgar guide for terror that was *Mein Kampf*. A society based on ontology cannot be just, although it might try to create a balance out of the *polemos* to which the liberties of its monads inevitably lead. Originary respect, metaphysics as critique of spontaneously violent autonomy, is the only possibility of a just society.

To conclude this summary of the fourth subsection, I would like to make only one observation with regard to Levinas's interpretation of Heidegger's philosophy. One could object that, since Being is not a being at all, it can neither be a third, mediating term nor distort or tyrannize any appearance or beingness. To this, Levinas could answer that in this case it is not only useless and misleading but also false to write about Being as if it were anything at all. Even the no-thing-ness posited by Heidegger as that which grants the possibility of beingness and understanding still is or gives a "space," a "horizon," a "light." If "Being" were nothing other than the "name" for the fact that there are phenomena, and that we are able to receive their message or to understand them in a meaningful way, then there would be no reason at all to suggest that this "fact" or this "ultimate condition" should be treated (and treated in a solemn, venerating, almost religious way!) as if it were some One or One-ness or some "It" that grants.

Whether Levinas's critique of ontology would be valid if ontology were able to do justice to the uniqueness of humans and their absolute alterity for one another, i.e., if the "Being" of ontology were neither anonymous nor a denial of human separation and plurality, I will not try to solve this question here. It should be noticed, however, that Levinas himself, in *Totality and Infinity*, very often or almost always uses the language of ontology in order to criticize it—for instance, when he finds "the metaphysical desire" in "a relation with being such that the knowing being lets the known being manifest itself while respecting its alterity and without marking it in any way whatever by this cognitive relation."

After *Totality and Infinity*, Levinas had to choose between two possibilities: *either* he could have tried the way of a new analogy of Being by developing an ontology in which the personal, the intersubjective, and the human alterity would *not* have been forgotten or repressed,[16] *or* he could try to exorcise all ontology from his writing and reflection, *or else*—if the second way was not possible, either—he would have to use ontology in

---

16 In *TI* 53/80 Levinas seems to consider the possibility of an analogy of Being, from which any univocity would have been excluded, but he maintains his rejection of "ontology," understood as a philosophy that denies the equivocity of the term "Being," as applied to God and created beings, by gathering them into one totality. Elsewhere, e.g., in *Philosophie et Religion* (1977), 539, he rejects any form of analogy between God and Being because it is unable to maintain their abyssal difference.

order to overcome it by the refutation of its ontological meaning. What he chose was, in fact, a combination of the second and the third way.

Levinas's discussion of the idea of the infinite, as analyzed in Descartes's third *Metaphysical Meditation,* has been introduced in the essay that was analyzed in Chapter Two above. I can, therefore, be brief in rendering subsection 5, "Transcendence as Idea of the Infinite" (18–23/48–52). After a few hints about the possibility of finding something similar in Plato's *Phaedo,* Levinas tries to show that Descartes defended a truth that is essential for metaphysics but is forgotten or rejected by most or all contemporary philosophers. This truth is hidden in Descartes's meditation on the idea of the infinite, an idea that is as originary as the cogito itself and even more originary than the idea of the cogito (i.e., self-consciousness). In contrast to all philosophies for which the finite is the ultimate, Descartes maintained—with the whole patristic and medieval tradition, not mentioned by Levinas—that the infinite is originally present in consciousness, rejecting thereby every attempt to construct or compose its idea on the basis of other finite ideas. There is no doubt that Descartes did not see any difference between the infinite and God (the God of his Catholic faith), but Levinas separates the formal structure of the idea of the infinite from its concrete content.

Retrieving the expressions with which Descartes qualifies the infinite,[17] Levinas characterizes it by the terms "exterior," "absolving" or "having absolved itself" from the relation (i.e., from our idea of it), and "overflowing" our capacity of thinking it. In "having" the idea of the infinite, one "thinks more than one can think." An immediate "too much" has always already awakened and oriented human consciousness and has undermined, made impossible, the full circle of its reflection upon itself. All beings and their beingness are seen as finite because they are preceded in our consciousness by their relation to the infinite. This has, thus, nothing to do with the "bad infinite" of an endless series or a quantitative or qualitative "more" or "most" or "highest" or "total" or "ultimate."

Separating this structure of a relation ("idea") that relates the cogito originarily to the infinite *before* all possibilities of experience or reflection, Levinas asks: Where, in which phenomenon and in which "intentionality," does this relation

17 See above, pp. 57–61, 81–82, 107–10.

"appear" concretely? Not in the religious awe or gratitude before God but rather only in the encounter with another, in the human face-to-face, is the "experience" in which that relationship becomes concrete. The infinity of the other's face, that is, its exteriority and absoluteness, its impossibility of being ranged among the phenomena of my world and of being seen as a figure against a wider background, is the only possible revelation of the infinite as described before. The word "face" can be replaced by "expression" or "word" or "speech" (*la parole*). Face, speech, and expression are the concrete manners by which the irreducibility of the Other comes to the fore and surprises me, disrupts my world, accuses, and refuses my egoism. In order to bring out the exceptional and disorderly character of this infinite, Levinas uses the word "epiphany" and "revelation" instead of "phenomenon" and "manifestation" or "appearance." The only adequate response to the revelation of the absolute in the face is generosity, donation.[18]

In reading part B of section 1, entitled "Separation and Discourse" (23–53/53–81), we discover that Levinas's titles do not help very much to get an overview of the structure according to which his book has been composed. There seems to be no systematic scheme but rather a series of fragments that have been (re)arranged after their writing. And yet, the fragments form a coherent text not broken by abrupt disruptions or startling turns. One of the difficulties is, however, that they move rather quickly from one topic to another in order to show a certain coherence between them and to convince the reader that the traditional views must be rethought in their entirety. Levinas's meditations perform a spiraling thought, starting from the main themes of philosophy, such as truth, freedom, language, knowledge, respect, and so on. By following that movement, the reader is confronted with constellations rather than with single phenomena; many repetitions, which most often are also further developments of insights expressed before, make a patient reader acquainted with a surprising but revealing approach and challenge.

In order to give some hints for a possible path in the seeming arbitrariness of the analyses contained in part B, I resume the

---

18 For a judicious critique of Levinas's interpretation of Descartes's *Infini*, see J.-F. Lavigne, "L'idée de l'infini: Descartes dans la pensée d'Emmanuel Levinas," *Revue de Métaphysique et de Morale* 92 (1987): 54–66.

questions that should be answered first, if the new beginning, as stated in part A, must command the rethinking of all the problems of philosophy. If neither Being in its relation(s) to beings nor any other form of "totalitarian" principle is the starting point of philosophy, but rather the metaphysical relation of transcendence, it must become clear how I, "the Other," and our relation should be characterized and how they form one constellation. As was said before, "the Other" has two meanings, united by an "and"; both *Autrui* and *God* are invisible, absolute, and high, but *Autrui* is in a way the "visible" invisible, whereas God does not appear at all (4/34). We may, therefore, expect that Levinas will proceed to a clarification of the elements that are constitutive for this relation: in the first place, the position of Me ("the I"), the peculiarities of the Other (in both senses), and the special structure of their relation. In a sort of anticipatory way, Levinas indeed gives here a first analysis of these "elements" by stressing the following aspects.

For a nondialectical relation, it is necessary that I be not a moment of the Other or of a synthesis that reduces "us" to its moments but that I, on the contrary, pose myself as an independent will. Ego's freedom expresses itself by its mastery of a world that is its own. This does not go together with a behavior that testifies to its being immersed in a surpassing whole, as conceived in the primitive religions of magic and mythology. An independent and completely secularized I has gotten rid of all gods and sacred powers; it is atheistic because it is free. As "psychism" or "interiority," it lives a private life and has time for the satisfaction of its needs and for delaying the threats of hunger and death. This time of self-centered mastery is not the temporality of works and functions out of which the time of history is made, for in history, no individual survives, except as names of certain works that have become mere elements of culture. Ego's economy, thus quickly sketched, will be analyzed extensively in section 2 (79–158/107–85).

The Other is not an element of history, either, but the reason for this is a different one. As coming from afar and from "on high," the Other breaks through the network of phenomena, relations, forms, and figures that can be conceived as composing parts of a universe. The Other cannot be possessed or overpowered, not even by the most spiritual thought or imagination that gives him a place or function in a conceptual or representational whole. Ego's mastery is practiced in calling back—by means of memory and reflection—objects and themes that have already passed and gathering them through the recovery of reflection. But the Other cannot be treated in such a way, since it presents itself as someone who cannot be grasped or objectified. The Other's face is not a form; it is naked, and this is precisely the reason why it commands and obligates. The only possible response to the Other's invocation is respect and donation. The Other's emergence is the first and definitive refutation of my egoism and therewith the fundamental dispossession that is needed for the possibility of universalization and objectification by putting the world of things in common.

The face-to-face of a living discourse is the concrete way in which the fundamental relation is practiced. It is neither mediated nor otherwise preceded by an originary "we" or "being-with"; on the contrary, all forms of association or community are founded in the relation of the Same and the Other. The straightforwardness of the face-to-face forbids the ruses and the violence of all rhetoric that is directed at catching or changing the other by approaching her/him obliquely. Discourse in search of truth is not the mere monologue of a lonely observer or thinker who spreads the world of things and humans out before his synoptic eye, for all language and all search of truth are preceded by the response of the One to the Other, who commands in an asymmetrical relationship that cannot be surpassed by any higher perspective. To search for the truth is primarily to be true to the metaphysical relation that excludes indifference as well as domination or fusion, and even—as Levinas often says—"participation."

The "atheism" of the will, as a necessary condition for ego's independence, goes together with true religion. The question of how "the Other" must be understood receives an answer in several formulas by which Levinas tries to explain that the relation to the human Other and the relation to God coincide completely and without fail. The *only* way of having a relation with God—so is his conviction—is to respond to the interpellation of the human face, to be good. This correspondence is neither a form of participation nor a parallelism between two worlds; God does not incarnate himself in human beings, but there is no other relation to God possible than the generous approach of the human Other in his/her misery. *Autrui* is the absolute that orients the world and its history.

In contrast with part B, part C of the first section (54–75/82–101) does form a coherent chapter whose content corresponds adequately to its title, "Truth and Justice." Its importance for an insight into Levinas's "method" can hardly be exaggerated. While discussing the classical practice and conception of philosophy, Levinas shows here the epistemological implications of the metaphysical transcendence that was ignored therein. If "truth" stands for a thought that moves within the parameters of the Same, "justice" summarizes here the adequate response to the revelation of the transcendent Other. The thesis defended by Levinas says that "truth" is not possible unless preceded and supported by "justice." The metaphysical relation is the first "condition of the possibility" of truth.

The argumentation contained in these pages is a good example of the approach most often practiced by Levinas. He starts with an analysis of the approach adopted in the traditional practice and theory of philosophy, indicates some fundamental assumptions that are neither obvious nor reflected upon by it, and shows a fundamental lack in traditional philosophy. Then he points to a fact that was overlooked or forgotten, and he explains why the classical approach was possible at all. This leads to an explanation of the relations between the forgotten or ignored fact (the relation of transcendence from One to the Other) and the ways of classical ontology, which should be converted and transformed by their subordination to transcendence.

True knowledge, as sought in Western philosophy, is the realization—on the level of theory—of the free will, whose autonomous and atheistic structure has been described before (in subsection 1 of part B). As psychism or interiority, this will is the spontaneous conquest of the world by a solitary ego. Its ideal is a complete comprehension of the universe, that is, the full possession of all things as shining forth in the evidence of self-justified concepts. Justification means in this context that the thinker, in the interiority of his understanding, reconstructs or "recreates" the world which he found before he started to think. The empirical a posteriori should be transformed into the a priori of a self-assured mind. Of course, the mind meets with the resistance of many limitations, but these might be overcome by participation in the spiritual life of the ultimate Substance, Spirit, Logos, or God. Or, if such theologies are not possible, the thinker will take refuge in resignation, without abandoning his central place and the project of his universal search, as happens in the contemporary philosophies of finitude.

The world of classical ontology shows two fundamental deficiencies. First, it is an equivocal world without valid indications of meaning and orientation. A universe of total silence, without any speech, is a chaos of appearances without orientation. Nothing is certain or important in it. One cannot know where to begin and how to approach it because it has no beginning or "principle." In this sense, it is "anarchic," as Levinas says in *Totality and Infinity*. (Later on, he reserves the word "anarchy" for the constellation of transcendence.) It is a "world" in which everything is possible but also uncertain because no interpretation can even begin to develop. (One might also say that it is a chaos of too many interpretations: How could they escape from gratuity or arbitrariness?) Bewitchment, the ruses of Descartes's "evil genius," has an easy play in it. Its seductions can only be withstood if there is an absolute orientation and if the chaotic rumbling of appearances can be transformed into the givenness of given data, events, or things.[19]

The second deficiency of the ontological world lies in its not having a place for the "phenomenon" of moral guilt. All its limitations are experienced as provisional or as tragic features of human finiteness; it has immunized itself against the discovery of those resistances by which the human will is accused as unjust.

The emergence of the Other is at the same time that which changes mere appearances into givens and that which awakens the consciousness of the anarchic thinker to its shame. The Other offers me phenomena by talking about them or letting me talk about them to him/her; the Other turns my mind to the ethical dimension by refuting and accusing my ruthless spontaneity and thus gives me an orientation toward infinity. Donation and morality *precede* all objectification and meaningful reference; transcendence precedes and supports (a certain) ontology; justice precedes and conditions the knowledge of the truth.

The presence of the Other abolishes the atheism of the will's monopoly. As for the medieval knight whose fighting force is justified by making him a defender of powerless innocents, ego's freedom is "invested" by the demands implied in the Other's proximity. I am saved by the acceptance of the critique that comes from the Other's face.

---

19 Under the name "il y a," Levinas has described the senselessness of this chaos in *EE* extensively (93–105/57–64). In *TI* it does not play a main role, although it is essential to the understanding of its descriptions of Being, enjoyment, the elements, ethics, and creation (cf. 66, 115–17, 165/93, 140–42, 190–91). *AE* comes back to it (cf. 207–10/*OB* 162–65), and in the preface of 1978 (11–14) to the second edition of *EE*, Levinas refers to it as a still-valid part of his early book.

"Creature" is Levinas's name for a freedom that is not a *causa sui* but still is free either to continue its egoistic conquest of the universe or to submit its freedom to transcendence. Freedom is founded and preceded; it is not its own beginning. Its redemption lies in its association to others. If ego remained alone, it would not be capable of the distance needed for objective thought and representation. To be a being and to have a meaning is to be addressed by words, to be instructed or taught. The word of the Other is the origin of truth.

The last part of section 1, "Separation and the Absolute" (75–78/102–5), forms an inclusion with its first subsection and resumes the "principle" of transcendence once more. In the language of ontology, Levinas writes that the idea of (i.e., the relation to) the infinite is "the ultimate structure of Being" (75/102), but he also appeals to Plato's insight that "the place of the Good" is "above all essence" as the most profound and definitive teaching of philosophy (and not of theology) (76/103). Once more, he opposes the separation demanded by the desire for the Good to the nostalgia for the absolute synthesis of classical philosophy. The infinite does not overwhelm or absorb but opens a space for free and adult independence. This is the structure not of participation, but of creation.

| Interiority and Economy

As we said before, this section unfolds, through the phenomenological method of intentional analysis, the self-identification of the Same in the concrete form of a self-centered existence, which is at the same time independent as well as separated *and* capable of entering (of having-always-already-entered) into the relation with the Other. The section is thus dedicated to "the relations that come to the fore within the Same" (82/110). In a sense that will become clearer in the course of the following analyses, this section claims to be a correction of Heidegger's description of *Dasein's being-in-the-world*, and a careful comparison of both is an urgent and tempting task. However, in order to show as clearly as possible the core of Levinas's intentions and analyses, without from the outset burdening this commentary by a discussion of the exactitude of his interpretations and polemics with regard to Heidegger's works, I will concentrate on the positive and nonpolemical side

of this new description of ego's being-in-the-world. A warning
with regard to Levinas's use of the terms Being (*être*) and
being (*étant*, but also *être!*) and to his way of asking the
question of Being might, however, be helpful for a thorough
understanding.

When Levinas, in *Totality and Infinity*, writes about being
and/or ontology, he thinks in the first place of "the universe
of beings" (*das Seiende im Ganzen* or *das Ganze des Seienden*)
and its Being, that is, the "beingness" that encompasses a
hierarchy of various modes of being, such as objectivity
(*Vorhandenheit*), instrumentality and *Zuhandenheit*, animality, mondaneity, historicity, etc. With regard to the description of ego's *world*, the horizon within which Levinas
achieves his analyses of the phenomena is thus "metaphysical" in the Heideggerian and the traditional sense of the
word: his descriptions try to characterize the modes of being—
the *ousia* or "essence"—of eating, habitation, labor, representation, and so on and their horizons. Levinas, however,
neither shares the ontological presuppositions of traditional
metaphysics nor those of Heidegger's early and later philosophy, and this difference, which is made explicit especially
in sections 1 and 3, cannot be silenced totally in section
2. As "horizon," the relation between the Other and me
codetermines implicitly the meaning of all the phenomena
that compose ego's being in the world. Since the Other,
exteriority, and the metaphysical relation are not thematized
explicitly in this section, it presents us with a still rather
abstract retrieval of the traditional egology, but from another, more radical perspective. The point of departure is
not a transcendental or psychological consciousness or self-
consciousness but rather the presence of the I to itself
whereby it is someone who establishes him/herself as pos-
sessor and commander of a world. This self-presence is called
"interiority," "psychism," or "inner life." Indeed, its structure and mode of being are the mode and structure of *life*
as an autarchic *Bei-sich-selbst-sein*, a self-sufficiency and a
self-deployment that do not care for other beings except
insofar as they are needed for it. If we would take "life"
to include the intersubjective relationship through which the
Other obliges me, it would be composed at least of the
structures described in sections 2 and 3 and summarized by
section 1 and the conclusions in the last section. "Inner life"
or "interiority" as monopolistic economy is an abstraction,

but it is a necessary moment of human existence, since it constitutes the egoity needed for "the interval of separation" (*TI* 82³/110²⁻³) and the primordial relation.[20]

The first subsection of section 2, "Intentionality and the Social Relation" (81–82/109–10), characterizes the relations that play within the horizons of the Same by distinguishing them from the metaphysical relation relating the Same and the Other. Their categorial structures are not identical, since the relations of and within the Same are monistic, whereas the metaphysical relation is heteronomous. As a supplement to the first section, the first page of the second section traces once more the typical features of the metaphysical relation before the relations of the Same are described. The metaphysical relation is set off against Husserl's "principle of principles" and Heidegger's being-in-the-world. Whereas intentionality and being-in-the-world reduce transcendence to the immanence of an all-embracing unity, the metaphysical relation is a real transcendence. The relations of and within the Same, as unfolded in the following pages, are all immanent and are therefore called *"analogous"* to transcendence.[21] They resemble the relations of the phenomenological intentionality and of Heidegger's being-in-the-world, although—as their description will show—in this respect, too, there are fundamental differences.

On the basic level of (human but still "elementary") life, the subject is present at itself—thus constituting a circle of vitality—by a peculiar relation that can neither be understood as the relation of a subject to one or more objects nor as the handling of tools or other beings that are ready-at-hand. This

---

20 The abstractness of section 2 is stated explicitly on 112³⁴⁻³⁸/139¹⁴⁻¹⁷ and, very clearly, on 282/305: "To posit Being as Desire and as goodness is not to first isolate an I which would then tend toward a beyond. It is to affirm that to apprehend oneself from within—to produce oneself as I— is to apprehend oneself with the same gesture that already turns toward the exterior, to extra-vert and to manifest—to respond for what it apprehends—to express."

21 In partial contrast to the passages quoted in note 16 above, Levinas states here an analogy between transcendence and certain forms of intentionality (which he considers to be essentially immanent). Similarly he seems to permit the reader of *TI* 281–82/305 to understand the metaphysical relation as "primary analogatum" of all modes of Being: "The face to face is not a modality of coexistence . . . but is the primordial production of being to which all the possible collocations of the terms point (*remontent*)."

is described in the second subsection, "Living from . . . (Enjoyment): The Notion of Accomplishment" (82–86/110–14). Ego is
concerned and takes care of itself before it becomes conscious
of itself. The primordial relation by which a human subject is
constituted as a subject is its living "on" or "from"—and its
enjoying—food, light, soil, water, sleep, work, and so on. It is
not easy to translate the idiomatic French expression "nous
vivons de bonne soupe, d'air . . . ," but Levinas's description
makes it clear that the concern of a solitary ego is a prereflec-
tive and preconscious turning back to itself that cannot be
explained within the framework of theoretical self-consciousness. To live is a specific mode of commerce with things of the
outside world, having to do with other beings that are not
absolutely other because they can be swallowed, used, enjoyed,
integrated in knowledge or practice. I am involved in an
exchange with worldly things and elements that contribute to
the realization of my possibilities. To live is to deploy and
maintain relations with "other," exterior beings thanks
to which I can persevere in my being. Some of these "exterior"
things are necessary to my maintenance, others are only pleasant or nice, but of all of them I can say that I enjoy them or,
on the contrary, that I suffer from them. Insofar as they all
function within the horizon of my being and staying alive,
what is their common structure? And what is the structure of
such life? It is neither the structure of the representation of
objects nor that of useful tools which function and signify as
parts of an instrumental or referential network. Nor is life as
such oriented to an end that would be different from its own
continuation. It is first of all and essentially *enjoyment,* and its
"intention" is happiness. Handling a hammer has a utilitarian
purpose, but it may also—although by another "intention"—
be experienced as pleasurable. Pleasure or enjoyment, however, do not refer to another goal or end outside them. Life
lives for itself. It "exists" or "is" its own "content" in a transitive and reflexive sense of the words "is" and "exist." The
original pattern of independence is this orientation toward
the happiness of a pleasant life. A primary, self-centered, and
sound hedonism is the spontaneous building up of a position
that develops naturally into the egoism of unhindered
autonomy.

The motivation of enjoyment must not be sought in some
reasonable thought, such as the one that tells me: "If I do
not eat, I'll die"; the tendency to pleasure and enjoyment is

completely spontaneous, it is the upsurge of life itself; but it is also true that the *experience* of enjoyment includes phenomenologically a moment of *restoration* (of our force, energy, vitality, mood, etc.). To live is to feel that one lives and that life strives at intensifying itself by enjoying its own vitality.

With regard to the food, the air, and the means "on" and "from" which we live, we experience them as being integrated into our enjoying ourselves. Their otherness—a nonabsolute but relative and integratable otherness—is "transmuted" in the Same of ego's economy. They are assimilated. In experiencing this sort of otherness, I experience, at the same time, the possibility and the desirability of their being transformed into parts or appendices of my own being. Enjoyment is always appropriation, assimilation, stilling of a need. Hunger is the paradigm: a privation that needs fulfillment. To live is a transitive way of existence, similar to the consumption of food on the basis of a need that promises a vital joy. In consumption, I experience not only my relation to the consumptive good but, at the same time, my relation to this relation. Not only do I enjoy food, but I enjoy my eating and feed myself with it; and not only do I enjoy my enjoyment, but I live (on/from) it; my life "is" and lives enjoyment.

The circularity of life's enjoying itself is typical for the pretheoretical and prepractical consciousness of a solitary ego taken on its most basic level. The difference with a representative or utilitarian attitude is clear. Fulfillment, not the maintenance of a bare and naked existence, is wanted. This circular, but neither specular nor speculative nor reflective, structure could be called the basic "concern" or "care" of human existence. This is not to say that this structure is limited to the basic needs of a corporeal existence. All other enjoyable things, such as work, music, study, making love, prayer, and so on can be experienced and "lived" as pleasure-giving and enjoyable beings. The circle of life is as wide as the totality of all human possibilities. Everything can enter into life as love of a "good," i.e., enjoyable life.

I will skip Levinas's discussions of Sartre ($84^{28-30}/112^{24-26}$), Aristotle (84^{34}–$85^{13}/112^{30}$–11^{38}), the Stoics ($85^{22}/113^{16}$), Heidegger ($85^{25-28}/113^{18-21}$), and Plato ($86^{13-28}/114^{4-14}$) and finish my summary of Levinas's description of life as enjoyment by rendering an important remark about its temporal structure. "Being" (beingness) is seen by Levinas as an anonymous duration that does not have any beginnings or ends of itself. Acts do have beginnings or origins and ends or limits, but the dimension of life is more primitive than the level of acting. Enjoyment is, however, the experience of a time span in which the continuous flow of Being's time is arrested for a while. Every experience of happiness is the experience of an interval in which I feel myself as independent and sovereign with regard to the anonymous continuity from which it emerges. Instead of being taken away by the river of Heraclitus, I feel that my life is being gathered, recollected for a while.

In the third subsection, "Enjoyment and Independence" (86–88/114–15), Levinas shows that the enjoyment of life through consumption of "earthly" *and* celestial "nourishments"[22] procures the human subject with its basic independence. Independence through dependence! Mastery on the basis of needs. A *happy* dependence. A human need is not a simple lack or mere privation, for it is experienced—and even enjoyed—as the possibility and promise of enjoyment. In the pleasure of satisfaction, the need, which was its painful condition, is remembered as a condition and source of plenitude. We are happy to have needs. To be alive is to be happy because of a fulfilling surplus of satisfaction, but it is also suffering because of lacking happiness. Enjoyment of life constitutes the independence and the very ipseity of the human subject—as long as we make abstraction from the intersubjective relation. It achieves the separation of an autonomous existence that feels at home in its world. Thus, needs and their fulfillment constitute me as *the Same*.

The fourth subsection, entitled "Need and Corporeity" (88–90/115–17), continues the analysis of the ambiguity characteristic for the human subject as having needs, that is, as being corporeal. Dependence on (nonabsolute but relative) otherness and independence from it are the two sides of a freedom that shows its mastery in possession, consumption, and exploitation but can also degenerate into a beastly slavery. Rooted in the world, the subject can also detach itself from it. The upright position of the body manifests its capability of handling the world and changing it through labor. Levinas uses here "the world" as a name for the totality of all the beings an ego encounters "before" it meets with the unique and absolute otherness of another human. Confronted with this "world" of

---

22 Cf. Gide's *Les nourritures terrestres.*

consumptive and useful things and constellations, the corporeal subject experiences itself as an "I can"[23] or, as Merleau-Ponty would say, as a "corps-sujet" for which the world spreads out. In this position, I am not just a part of nature but someone who has a distance enabling her to defend herself against the anonymous threats of the surrounding universe and to delay pains or unsatisfactory satisfaction. Such a delay and the distance that is a condition of it are possible only as a "having time": I have time for postponing the fulfillment of my needs, for instance, in order to cook my prey. But where does this time come from—and therewith my distance and detachment? The answer is that this is an anticipation: the emergence of the (absolute) Other provides me with it.

Although the title of the fifth subsection, "Affectivity as the Ipseity of the I" (90–92/117–20), seems to promise a further analysis of the affective elements of the enjoying subject, its text rather stresses its singularity. It gives a phenomenological answer to the old question of how we can determine the individuality of a this-now-here (*tode ti*) as such. The experience of a fulfilled need is the experience of isolation. Enjoyment makes solitary (you cannot feel my pleasures and pains) and confirms the enjoying subject in its identity with itself. Being at home with myself, I am separated from all others, a unique and original substance that does not let itself be absorbed by the continuity of the universe. The self-sufficiency or autarchy of a satisfied ego is its contraction and recoiling in itself—an interiorization but also an exaltation by which it lifts itself above "Being" (in a very flat sense of the word *être*). The experience of uniqueness, discretion, and originality, which constitutes the ipseity of an ego in enjoyment, cannot be reduced to the concept of individuality or singularity as it is understood by the philosophical tradition. The structure of a happy ego, identified by enjoyment from within, is not the structure of an individual instance that—together with other similar instances—falls under one species or genus. To be an ego is not to share a common nature or essence with other instances of the genus "human being," for it is, first of all and still without any rapport to similar beings, the center of the world, a demand for pleasure and a solitary power of exploitation to which all beings are submitted.

---

23 Cf. Husserl's *Ich kann* (*Ideen* 2:257ff.) and Heidegger's *Seinkönnen* (*SuZ*, §54).

The phenomenological analysis has thus reached a point where its conclusions with regard to ontology become perceptible. In his intent to overcome ontology, Levinas points out (1) that the traditional conception of the individual and the scheme of genus-species-individual does not apply to the phenomena as described in this chapter and (2) that enjoyment, happiness, life, and the vital autarchy of the I cannot be explained in terms of Being alone, since the exaltation, i.e., the abundance, the surplus, and the heightening of enjoyment are "more" than Being. The polemical implications of this insight do not, however, touch Heidegger's conception of Being, since Heidegger would immediately agree that enjoyment is a particular mode of Being very different from studying an object or fighting against an enemy. The notion of Being attacked in this subsection is rather Sartrean or Wolffian; it has been emptied of all interesting qualifications, thus becoming a flat, worthless, or even completely indeterminate element of all beings. It is, however, very important that Levinas shows that the constitution of the ego on the level of its self-isolating enjoyment can be understood neither as a form of representation, nor as the handling of a tool or the contemplation of an object, nor as a longing for some *telos*, either. Its structure is original and unique, and perhaps Levinas is the first philosopher who gave a phenomenology of the living being—the *animal* or *zooion*—that we all, without exception and still uniquely and originally, are.

The phenomenology of enjoyment goes on in the second subsection of part B, but Levinas inserts first two subsections in which he reflects upon the methodological implications of his descriptions. The sixth subsection of part A, "The I of Enjoyment Is Neither Biological Nor Sociological" (92–94/120–21), seems somewhat out of place, since it is dedicated to an analysis of the metaphysical relation between me and the Other, which is needed for a real plurality of persons. It is, however, true that the separation of the independent ego, as shown in the above pages, is a condition for that relationship.

Part B (94–116/122–42) announces an analysis of "Enjoyment and Representation," but this topic is treated in its first subsection only, while subsections 2–5 give a further development of the phenomenology of life and enjoyment given in A.2–5. In the first subsection, "Representation and Constitution" (95–

100/122–27), Levinas gives a sharp analysis of Husserl's conception of phenomenology and its key principle, "intentionality." Its secret is the presence of representation. All intentions are either varieties of representation, or they are essentially supported by representing acts. In representation, the noema is an object that in principle fits adequately in a noesis. This implies that the constituting subject has its noema in perfect presence before itself and masters it in the form of a positing in front. This is a triumph of the Same: the gesture of a freedom without passivity, a presencing by which all a posteriori givenness becomes an a priori knowledge.

The contrast with the "intentions" that "constitute" the second subsection, "Enjoyment and Nourishment" (100–103/ 127–30), are obvious. The enjoying subject needs its dependence upon an exteriority that can be assumed but not constituted. It lives "from" and "on" its own passivity and is a conditional freedom, an acceptance and welcoming that enjoys its being dependent on a world by which it is preceded and sustained.

This section is one of Levinas's many attempts to show that the traditional conception of knowledge, reality, human essence, and world are not the most fundamental and universal. Just as the metaphysical relation between the Other and me escapes from it, so also does the relation between the living I and the realities it enjoys. Of the latter, part A elucidated the subjective pole; the following sections of part B give more attention to that which procures us enjoyment.

The third subsection, "Element and Things, Implements" (103–8/130–34), shows the peculiarity of the enjoyable, no less different from things than from the ready-at-hand analyzed by Heidegger in the beginning of *Sein und Zeit.* To enjoy life is neither a vis-à-vis with regard to objects nor a participation—by handling tools or following signs—in a network of references; it is much more primitive, but all instrumentality and representation are rooted in it. To enjoy is to be immersed in an ambiance of elements, to breath the air, to bathe in water and sun, to be established on the earth. Elements are not things, because they are too indeterminate for that, too formless. Therefore, they cannot be possessed. Without limitations, without beginning or end, they come from nowhere; they emerge from an anonymous nothingness. They lack contours and qualification; rather than being substantial, they are pure qualities without supports. Since we bathe in them, they are not really exterior, but they are not interior, either. Their indeterminateness precedes the difference between the finite and the infinite and makes them akin to the *apeiron* of Greek philosophy. Without face they have a certain depth.

A comparison of the enjoyment of the elemental with the structure of *Zeughaftigkeit* as analyzed by Heidegger (106–8/133–34) shows that the former does not imply the instrumental, utilitarian, and rational features of the latter and lacks all concern for a goal outside or beyond its own enjoyment. Enjoyment is completely careless, even about health or perseverance in existence. The egoism of hedonism is utterly frivolous. *Sensibility* is the name for that dimension of the human subject thanks to which it is able to have this pleasurable commerce with the elements (108–14/135–40). Against the traditional conception of the senses as the means through which we are able to know things, Levinas shows that the basic sensibility, in which all other intentions and relations are rooted, is an affective commerce with the elements, a naive and spontaneous feeling at home in a world that has not yet taken the form of an order of things, objects, instruments, and rational relationships. Feeling and affectivity, our bodies as carried by the earth and immersed in water, air, and light, do not constitute a sort of obscure or mutilated form of knowledge; they have a structure of their own that cannot be ignored or neglected, not even on the most sublime levels of religion and morality. The importance of Levinas's description of sensibility lies in its overcoming the old dualism of body and spirit. In enjoying the world, I am a body that feels itself as an affected and affective, corporeal and sensitive I, not as a disincarnate, invisible, or ethereal consciousness. My autonomy *is* a dependent independence, the satisfaction of my needs. The realm of the elements is an ambiguous one. Being a paradise when we enjoy it, it is also threatening, since nobody can possess it or guarantee its favors. Sensibility is an incurable unrest dependent on the contingencies of a future that remains uncertain. After moments of happiness, in which we feel no care, the menaces of the world come back. This experience is told in the mythologies of the elementary gods. They express *"the mythical format of the element"* (114–16/140–42). Against its threats, we can fight by trying to submit the world through labor. This is our answer to an uncertain future, as long as there still is an interval of time. Our insecurity may seduce us to a pagan worldview, but its myths will not open us to a real transcendence because our relation to the elemental does not open us to real otherness.

Part C, "I and Dependence" (116–25/143–51), resumes and refines some of the analyses summarized before, but its subtle and beautiful descriptions bring little positive news. In the first subsection, "Joy and Its Morrows" (116–18/143–44), the insecurity of our happiness is related to a dimension that is still more primitive than the elemental: the dimension of "there is" (*il y a*), which is the most indeterminate and qualified beingness, almost nothing, which we experience as an anonymous rumbling and rustling in the background of the world, inspiring horror and vertigo. Our intervals of happiness form discrete knots that interrupt the monotonous time flow of the "there-is." In the second subsection (118–20/144–47), Levinas insists on the fact that our *love of life* precedes—as a sort of paradise—all experiencing of pain and disgust. The naive innocence of our enjoyment is demanded by the metaphysical relation, which, however, is an accusation of our egoism. Without the beginning in a paradise, without the individualism of a *carpe diem*, ego's adult independence, and therewith the separation of ego from the Other, would be impossible (cf. "Enjoyment and Separation," 120–25/147–51). This becomes still clearer in part D, "The Dwelling" (125–49/152–74).

The phenomenological "deduction" of the home in the first subsection, "Habitation" (125–27/152–54), is a further development of the distance, indicated before, by which the hedonistic subject is independent, thanks to its dependence with regard to the elemental world it enjoys. The insecurity and the threats that endanger the subject cannot be fought off unless there is a possibility of withdrawing from its involvement in nature, a rupture with the elemental realm by which the subject conquers a standpoint and a centerplace from which it can reach out into the world in order to possess and dominate it. This rupture, which is also a rupture with the mythical gods of nature, requires a retreat and a recollection: a house in which I withdraw and establish myself for a different sort of economy.

A house has some similarity with a tool, but, rather than a sort of thing or instrument or implement, it is the condition for all human action and reference. As a place where I can withdraw and recollect myself, it is characterized by intimacy. Being-at-home in this place means that one is at home in a familiar surrounding whose walls enclose an interiority, while the windows open up upon an exterior world into which one goes for conquering or labor. The intimacy and familiarity

proper to a home presuppose that it is already human, although—in this stage of our description—it is not yet necessary
to introduce the metaphysical relation of one human to the
absolute Other. It demands a certain "femininity" (subsection
2, "Habitation and the Feminine" [127–29/154–56]). Since Levinas warns his readers that "the empirical absence of the
human being of 'feminine sex' in a dwelling nowise affects the
dimension of femininity which remains open there, as the very
welcome of the dwelling" (131/158), we must understand that
the "feminine" presence by which a building becomes a home
is a metaphor for the discrete and silent presence of human
beings for one another that creates a climate of intimacy indispensable for a dwelling that simultaneously protects and opens
to the world of enjoyment, possession, and labor.[24]

The rupture with the elements and their gods (cf. subsection
3, "The Home and Possession" [129–31/156–58]) manifests itself most clearly in the complete secularization and humaniza-
tion that is achieved when the subject seizes what it needs
from the outside world. Whence the importance of the hand,
analyzed carefully in this context (132–36/159–62 and 141–42/
166–68). Levinas almost identifies here possession and labor
(cf. subsection 4, "Possesion and Labor" [131–36/158–62], and
subsection 5, "Labor, the Body, Consciousness" [137–42/163–
68]). Both are ways of grasping by which the grasped is transformed into a thing whose limits give it a form, having a use
and belonging to a certain place. Thus, the realism of formless
elements changes into an order of things: solid substances that
can be identified, handled, and exchanged or transported as
furniture dependent on human plans. The gods are dethroned
by the human hand.

A laboring subject is a body that through its needs still
depends on the contingencies of the world, but its distance
permits it to delay dangers and death. It has time, a time of
its own to procure for itself defenses and satisfaction; its labor
manifests that it is a will. Body, hand, and will form the unique
constellation by which the human subject is itself, separated
from any other.

For several reasons, the last subsection of part D, "The
Freedom of Representation and the Gift" (142–49/168–74), is
particularly important. In it culminates the series of figures
that constitute the economy of a solitary ego, but, at the same

---

24 See also *DL* 48–50.

time, it shows the necessity of surpassing that economy. More even than labor and possession, the *representation* of things shows the human possibility of treating the (relative) otherness of worldly beings as objective, presentable, and thematizable things. Representation, the source of all theory, looks at things and objectifies them by making them present. From the perspective of their having happened or emerged, it looks back upon them. Theory is essentially the remembrance of a past from its future. The stand of the representing subject manifests its freedom with regard to all exteriority. On the one hand, this stand is conditioned by the "intentions" formerly described (enjoyment, dwelling, seizure). On the other hand, it is uprooted and liberated from immersion in the world. But how is such a freedom possible?

This freedom presupposes an awakening that can only be given by the absolute otherness of the human Other. For how could I free myself from immersion into my needs and enjoyments? The uprooting presupposes that I have already heard the call or seen the face of a commanding Other. By revealing the violence of egoistic economy, the Other questions, criticizes, and refutes it. This provides the ego with the possibility of distancing itself from that economy. If I open myself up to the Other's claim, I and my home become hospitable; it is, however, also possible to persevere in the monopolization of the world and to choose the egoism of a Gyges.[25]

The objectifying language in which representation becomes a thematizing discourse dispossesses me of my monopoly and achieves the basic universalization by separating things from their being here and now involved in hedonistic egoism and making them into objects of a common speech and view.

In the last part of section 2, "The World of Phenomena and Expression" (149–58/175–83), Levinas unfolds the radical contrast between the universe of works, signs, symbols, and history on the one hand and what he in this book still calls "being as it is in itself"[26] on the other hand. This part thus stands

25 Cf. Plato, *Politeia* 359d–360d; and Herodot, *Historiae* 1:8–13; Levinas refers to it very often, e.g., in *TI* $32^{15,20}/61^{5,10}$; $62^{28,30}/90^{10,12}$; $144^{30}/170^7$; $148^{14,16}/173^{12,14}$; *AE* 185/145.

26 The Platonizing expression "être καθ' αὐτό" is found on many pages of *TI* but (almost?) always misspelled (e.g., 158/183). As a synonym, Levinas uses also the Kantian expression "chose en soi" (the thing in itself, e.g., 156/181).

between the world of egological representation with its objectifying language, which belongs to the economy of section 1, and the truth revealed in section 3. But it contains also a radical critique of the foundational claims of phenomenology.

The analysis of the work (*œuvre*) is the point of departure for the characterization of a universe that is composed of signs, texts, art products, and political works (such as, for instance, the founding of a state). The study of history focuses on these works in order to characterize their content and style and to reconstruct the constellations or "worlds" to which they belonged. By doing so, we get acquainted with anonymous worlds; with persons only to the extent to which they are exponents or functions of those constellations.

To know a person means that one pierces the masks formed by his or her texts, works, performances, gestures, and so on. These do not express who this or that person is, but they give only an impression of his or her appearance. Thus, Levinas opposes the *expression* to the *work* and the *phenomenon* of a person to his or her (true) *being.* To explain this difference, he very often quotes the phrase of Plato's *Phaedrus* opposing the written text to the speaking author, who can attend to his own discourse and "help" it personally, if necessary.[27] Instead of a product that can neither look nor speak, it is a being *an sich* or "in itself" that looks and speaks to others ($156^{38}/181^{29}$). It is neither the textuality of literature or history nor the language of the structuralists or Heidegger's *Sprache,* which would "speak" before we use it, but, indeed, the face of someone who expresses him or herself in speech. Instead of calling this expression a phenomenon, Levinas reserves the words "revelation" and "epiphany" for it. When, in *Totality and Infinity,* he insists on the fact that the *being* of a person (or even his/her "being καθ' αὐτό" [*TI* 158/183]) is not phenomenal in works but revealed in expression only, one could surmise that he, too, wants us to pass from phenomenology to ontology. However, since he reserves the title "ontology" for Heidegger's philosophy, and since—as we will see—the ultimate is not Being but the relation of the Same and the Other, Levinas moves in another direction. The ontological terms still used in *Totality and Infinity* will be replaced more and more by other words in order to avoid a falling back into the customary ways of understanding. In *Otherwise Than Being,* the opposition between phenomenon and expression will be replaced by the difference between the Said and the Saying, and

---

27 *Phaedrus* 247b–277a and *TI* 45/73; 69–71/96–98.

Being will have joined the *phenomenon* as belonging to the same order of the impersonal.

| The Face and Exteriority

After the abstract description of the isolated ego as the identification of the Same given in section 2, Levinas passes to an analysis of the Other as it presents itself concretely in the face of another human. Over against the "interiority" of egoistic psychism and its economy, the third section describes the dimension of "exteriority" opened up by otherness. The opposition between the interior and the exterior, as called forth in the titles of both sections, must not be heard as a rehearsal of the traditional opposition between the ego and its world or as between the subject and the objectivity with which it meets; for *that* opposition was part of the economy described in section 2. Through its needs and its enjoyment but also through representation and objectifying knowledge, the solitary ego is related to the "exteriority" of elements, equipment, things, and objects, but *this* "exteriority" cannot resist ego's encompassing capacity of appropriation and integration. The exteriority revealed by the face is that by which the alterity of the Other escapes from the dimension where interiority and exteriority, subject and object, mind and matter, traditionally are opposed and put into contradiction or mediated dialectically as moments of a differential whole.

The introductory part of section 3, "The Face and Sensibility" (161–67/187–93), is an epistemological analysis of the peculiar sort of "knowledge" by which we are aware of another's face. What sort of "experience" or "perception" or "thought"—in brief, what sort of "intention"—is presupposed and demanded for being able to receive the revelation of the face? In contrast with the gnoseological characteristics of sensibility and representation, as put forward in section 2, Levinas now specifies his question as a question about the difference between the Other's epiphany and the discovery of phenomena by the immediate sensibility of enjoyment and by perception, as thematized in the tradition of philosophy. Both perception and enjoyment are here taken together under the name "sensible experience" (*expérience sensible*). In a discussion of various epistemologists, Levinas tries to show that both sensibility and the peculiar awareness of the face differ—but in different ways—from representational knowledge. The accent lies in this part still on sensible and representational knowledge; it can, thus, be read as a transition from section 2 to section 3.

According to the sensualistic theories of Condillac, for example, all knowledge is based on atomic "sensations" that—in some mechanical way—"compose" a formless "collection" of punctual states of mind that are purely qualitative and subjective. The classical refutation of sensualism by Husserlian phenomenology argues that it is impossible because it denies its necessary experiential basis. Indeed, we are always already confronted with things, substances, or objects and never with free-floating qualities alone. Qualities are always given in unity with things qualified by them.

Levinas's critique of this refutation starts by stating that it is given from the perspective of perception and representation. It is typical for this perspective that it sees sensibility as an inferior, handicapped, or primitive approximation of representation; however, sensibility is primarily not an unsuccessful attempt at acquiring knowledge but is rather *affectivity* and, more precisely, enjoyment. As such, it is the experience of pure qualitativeness without substantial support, immersion in the elements, a form of sensation that precedes all distinctions between subject and object. To a certain degree, sensation should be rehabilitated as an a priori formal structure and a transcendental function *sui generis*. As enjoyment, it precedes the scission of consciousness in an I and a non-I, but it is *not* a content of consciousness, as both the sensualist philosophers and their critics would have it. Their error was that they identified the non-I with objectivity and did not see that it also encompasses that which is sensed by enjoying it and living from it. This error is connected with the traditional privilege given to *vision* and *touch* among the human senses. Eye and hand, optical and grasping gestures, dominate our contact with things. According to Western philosophy, all experience seems to be constituted by them. They are present—even verbally—in its ideas, con-cepts, con-ceptions, visions, com-prehensions, per-spectives, views, etc.

The structures of seeing and grasping are very similar. To begin with vision, its scheme is found in an eye seeing something (a thing or part of it) in the light that is needed for seeing at all. The light is not a thing but that which makes it possible that things appear. The light shows the thing within the surrounding or against the background of a space, which should be a sort of void (at least insofar as other things in it are not focused on, i.e., insofar as they disappear behind their leaving the space to the thing that is seen). Thanks to the no-thing-ness of light and "space," we see things as manifesting themselves by setting themselves off against an openness. This openness (Being?) is not a pure nothing but rather the negation of all qualifiable beings. It can only be the impersonal limit-, contour-, and structurelessness of an *apeiron* or "there is" (*il y a*), the "silence of the infinite spaces" of which Pascal speaks, a treacherous semblance of nothingness, a hiding place of mythical powers without face, an indeterminate and opaque density without orientation or meaning, a senseless and therefore terrifying chaos. As a way of dealing with the elements in the function of human needs, enjoyment is the beginning of meaning; vision and grasping, too, reveal meaning, but they do not abolish—rather *main-tain*— the quasi-nothingness that is the condition of all thingness.

Vision passes into seizure as representation passes into labor when they conquer a world of inhabitation, instruments, and objects, but they do not break or transcend the horizons of immanence. From their perspective, all beings are seizable and comprehensible as parts of a universal panorama. All meaning is, then, a function of the system in which they have their place. All things are approached laterally, as if by ruse; nothing is encountered face-to-face. Vision and handling form a refuge for any subject that, not satisfied by the fulfillment of its needs, has not discovered the possibility of being freed from its immanence by the Other's infinity. By representation and projection, the hand and the eye consummate the economy of egology. Light and "clearing" cannot provide this liberation because they remain "interior"; transcendence to the "outside" has another structure.

In two short passages, Levinas shows how a similar structure is also found in science and art. Especially the latter passage (176/192–93) is important because it contains an implicit criticism of all those theories which pretend that art— and not morality or religion—can liberate human freedom and overcome the crisis of Western egology.

Part B of section 3, "Face and Ethics" (168–95/194–219), could be considered the central part of the book. Although the introductory section 1 has already anticipated its topics, it is here that the concretion of the Other in face and speech receives its main description.[28] Levinas shows how the extraordinary relation opened by another's looking at me and speaking to me causes a discontinuity of the encompassing world and context that is common to us. The gathering of beings, universal and totalizing beingness, and the history of works are disrupted. Ego's autonomy is shocked and put into question; its ruthless spontaneity is converted into shame and conscience is awakened. The asymmetry instituted by the encounter has the structure of the idea of the infinite. The other's face (or speech) is not similar to a work or to language as structure or text or literary tradition; its infinite resistance to my powers is not a power—as if we were still in the dimension of Hobbes's war of equal wills—but an *expression* that forbids and commands me ethically. The first revelation of an astonishing otherness that cannot be reduced to a moment of my world is neither the splendor of the cosmos nor the task of my self-realization; it is the living interdiction of killing this vulnerable, defenseless, and naked other in front of me. This revelation gives me an orientation and bestows a meaning on my life (cf. the subsections 1 and 2, "The Face and the Infinite" and "Face and Ethics" [168–75/194–201]). In the third subsection, "Face and Reason" (176–79/201–4), Levinas draws some conclusions from his description for the "logic" of "first philosophy." The sincere and univocal character of the face, by which it is an expression and neither a phenomenon nor a symbol or a mask, precedes not only its possible hypocrisy but also all actions or words. The face differs, thus, essentially from any text or work or fact of culture. Therefore, it does not call for a hermeneutical approach but rather for a very different response. The "visage" differs even from vocal speech or the faculty of seeing: blind and mute persons can also "look" at me, "regard" me, and "speak" to me.

Instead of initiating a hermeneutical circle, the face claims the responsibility of the one to whom it "appears" or to whom it speaks. This is the first teaching, which precedes all possibility of remembrance and reminiscence. The equivocities

---

28 "Face" and "speech" (*parole, langage,* or *discours*) are here *partes pro toto;* the other can "present him/herself in person"—but in a way different from Husserl's "bodily presence"—by many parts or gestures: "In the face the being par excellence presents itself. And the whole body—a hand or a curve of the shoulder—can express as the face" (239–40/262).

of poetics and hermeneutics belong to a different dimension than the appeal to a straightforward responsibility aware of the (moral) impossibility of murder.

Levinas contrasts the prose of moral responsibility with the charms of the more dramatic incantations and intoxications of poetic and mystical enthusiasms. The face-to-face is a sincere and sober response more concerned with not doing violence than with aesthetic enjoyments. The instruction brought to me by the emergence of a face is neither a dogma nor a miracle but the initiation of a meaning.

In the fourth subsection, "Discourse Founds Meaning" (179–84/204–9), Levinas shows that speaking is radically different from "the language" conceived of as an impersonal system or heritage, of which some claim that "it speaks." Without the face, there would be neither a beginning in language nor any signification, for the language would not be voiced and addressed by someone to someone. The rather difficult discussion with Merleau-Ponty's theory of language included in this section (180–81/205–6) can be clarified by a comparison with Levinas's essay "Meaning and Sense" (*CPP* 75–108).

In the fifth subsection, "Language and Objectivity" (184–87/209–12), Levinas takes up certain themes of section 2 (especially D 6, 142–49/168–74) in showing that the emergence of the visage is a condition without which thematization and objectivity would not be possible. Alluding to the fifth of Husserl's *Cartesian Meditations*, on the connections between objectivity and intersubjectivity, against Kant's and Heidegger's philosophy of originary finiteness, and with Descartes, Levinas defends the primacy of the infinite and its concrete presentation in the other's face.

All theory thematizes (i.e., represents and objectifies), but objectification is essentially the designation of beings in a discourse addressed to other humans. Without another being there in front of me, I could not free myself from immersion in the elementary enjoyment of my surroundings. The other's presence, however, gives me the possibility of offering something to him or her. By offering to someone what I until then enjoyed alone, the elements change into things, they receive another orientation, leave my economy, and become gifts, symbols of welcoming, addressed and presented, possibly common and universal. Objects are born when I place things in the perspective of other persons. Detached from their hedonistic and egocentric function, those things receive an intersubjective meaning and existence. Donation is the necessary condition of distance and objectivity. The absoluteness (or infinity) of the other cannot be constituted on the basis of an objectifying activity such as representation, thematization, or theory; the infinite is presupposed for it; objectification is a subordinate reality.

Subsection 6, entitled "Autrui et les Autres" ("The Other and the Others") (187–90/212–14), is the only part of *Totality and Infinity* where Levinas sketches the "principles" of something like a social philosophy and thus answers an objection familiar to all readers of his book. If *autrui* (this other who faces me or talks to me) reveals the infinite that commands my economy, what, then, about all the other others, what about human society and humankind as a whole? Does not Levinas's "moralism" of the face-to-face destroy the possibility of a social philosophy that is more than an analysis of "you and me"? What, then, is the place of politics? The traditional foundation of modern social philosophy starts from a perspective characterized by, at least, the following assumptions: there is a multiplicity of human beings; as individual instances of the genus "human being," they are fundamentally equal autonomous subjects having equal rights as far as their existence and necessary satisfaction are concerned. The main problem of social philosophy is the question of how a multitude of independent and equal individuals can form one more or less harmonious and peaceful whole.

Levinas's attempt to "deduce" the principles of a social and political philosophy from the asymmetric relationship that constitutes the intersubjectivity of the Other (you) and the Same (me) does not concentrate on the participation of human individuals in the life and the ethos of a people or nation; he focuses on the question of how the primordial relation of the other to me gives birth to my being related to all other possible others. This question remains here subordinated to the perspective that was indicated in the title of section 3 B, "The Face [i.e., Autrui] and Ethics" (168ff./194ff.): What does the Other in the form of *autrui* reveal, and how does he or she relate to me? Very succinctly stated, the answer does not contain the principles of a political constitution but rather shows how the dimensions of society and politics emerge from the asymmetric relation of intersubjectivity, which—as originary relationship—precedes all sorts of universality and community. The dedication of the Same to the Other "founds" *the being-with-one-another* (their *Miteinander-sein*) or the original *We* (and not the other way around); the relation of transcendence does not imprison you and me in the intimacy of an exclusive love but opens me up to all others by obligating me to orient our common world to all the others' well-being. My responsibility for this other here and now who faces me is not confined to him or her; it does not have the clandestine and exclusive character of love and intimacy, but neither is it the application in this case of a general norm that would be valid for all the individual instances of the general class "human beings," whose equal rights would be due to their forming a community or having a common essence. My responsibility for you extends itself necessarily to all human others; it implies my responsibility for social justice and worldwide peace.

In the text of subsection 6, we can distinguish several arguments. The *first* argument states that the visage of the other ("you" who regard me) reveals not only the other's obliging height but also and ipso facto "the third," that is, any other human being. The demanding presence of the other's face *is* the presence of the third. "The third regards me in the eyes of the other." *Autrui*, this other, is in fact simultaneously the revelation of any possible other. "The Other" is also the name for everybody who is not I. *Autrui* is not my beloved or a special friend of mine, for everyone can approach and surprise me in a similar, contingent but infinitely obligating way. "The third" is equivalent to that which makes you ("my other") commanding for me: neither some virtue or special feature nor your belonging to a particular society, people, or family but only your being poor and naked, an exile and stranger without power or protection. The destituteness of the other's nudity, his/her being neither a particular person nor an indifferent instance of a general class of beings, is the secret of my discovering myself as demanded and dedicated without ever having chosen it. The claim by which you awaken me to my responsibility stems from your being a miserable other, not from any specific or particular feature. The other is at the same time unique—and thus incomparable—and nothing special—and therefore in a very special sense "universal." The demands revealed in your face, here and now, are the demands for universal and privatizing love. Insofar as any other other ("the third") is present "under the species" of your face, all others are equal. Universality and equality are "founded upon" the original asymmetry; they are not the starting point, as if our acquaintance with a general class "human being" would be the starting point for ulterior specifications such as love, justice, friendship, concern, etc.; the other's (your) coming to the fore reveals the unicity of *all* others.

From the fact that the third is revealed "in" and "through" the face of the other, it follows that I am related to many others who urge me with equal absoluteness to dedicate myself to them. This destroys the monopoly of one other's demands: I must divide my time and energy in order to respond to more than one revelation of the infinite. I must compare those who are incomparable, treat unique others as instances of *one* universal essence. Here lies the origin of a form of justice that demands and presupposes the structures of logical and ontological universality: in order to do justice to *all* others—and not to neglect any one of them—we must originate a political, economical, judicial, and social system that balances and guarantees at least the minimum of the absolute demands expressed by the other's presence.

Would it not have been possible to deduce this conclusion directly from the fact that the phenomenological analysis of the visage, necessarily and ipso facto, is an analysis of the essence of the visage and therewith an analysis of all possible visages? Such an argument would have stressed that there are many others *besides* the other who, here and now, is facing me. Probably Levinas avoids this argument because of its assumption that the universal concept of all human others—a sort of general class of human beings, in which I am the only missing instance—is contemporary with, or even anterior to, the encounter of the other's uniqueness, here and now. However, he uses this argument, at least implicitly, when he himself assumes that the other's face reveals not only this unique other but a third and a fourth and an nth other, all equal to the first one insofar as they are all *equally* unique, naked, and devoid of particular properties. For how could one discover that the other whose absoluteness puts an infinite claim on me simultaneously hides and reveals a multiplicity of equal others if the existence of other faces and their essential

equality to the first face was not discovered *before* or
at the same time? Still, Levinas can maintain that the
revelation of the third as "universal" other is a *subordinate* moment within the revelation of you, here and now,
as the "primary" unique other if it is true that the latter
"contains" the first. This presupposes, however, as he
will repeat several times in *Otherwise Than Being,* that
the third is "not an empirical fact,"[29] (but, rather, an
essential structure of "the other"). Although we probably cannot maintain that the encounter with the first
other (you) precedes *all* acquaintance with the universality of the other's demanding unicity, the advantage
of Levinas's procedure lies in his showing the unique
character of the asymmetric relation between the other
and me, which is neither blurred by its multiplication
nor reduced to being an indifferent instance of some preceding general concept such as "human otherness."[30]

A *second* argument is given in the statement that
the other who faces me (you) is the servant of another
(the third: "he" or "her") who is the other for "my
other." Whereas the first argument—by a (trans)phe-
nomenology of the face—started from the fact that the
nudity of the face did not exclude but, on the contrary,
included all other faces, it is not easy to find a phenomenological basis for this second argument. The argument
runs thus: *Autrui* ("you" or the other whom I encounter)
is not alone insofar as he/she already serves another (the
third), whom I have not encountered. You, who oblige
me, are another ego, that—just as I am—is under an infinite obligation because you are faced by another other.[31]

This argument presupposes that I see you at the
same time in two "functions": (1) you are an absolute

---

29 Cf. *AE* 201, 204/158, 160.

30 The argument that starts from the fact that there are other Others
besides you, the unique Other here and now, is made explicit by Levinas
in *AE* 200ff./157ff.

31 Similarly, we read in "Paix et proximité" (Les cahiers de la nuit
surveillée, no. 3: Emmanuel Levinas [Paris: Verdier, 1984]), 345: "Le
tiers est autre que le prochain, mais aussi un prochain de l'autre et non
pas son semblable. Qu'ai-je à faire? Qu'ont-ils déjà fait l'un à l'autre?
Lequel passe avant l'autre dans ma responsabilité? Que sont-ils donc,
l'autre et le tiers, l'un par rapport à l'autre? Naissance de la question"
("The third is other than the neighbor but also a neighbor of the other

claim with regard to me; this is why you are other and neither a repetition of my ego nor another instance of a universal concept such as "subjectivity," "consciousness," "reason," "will," or "ego" and (2) you are, just as I am, a subject that has been surprised by an other who reveals to you the infinite by making you infinitely responsible for this other. In the first function, you are absolutely different from me; in the second function, however, you are completely equal to me—not identical—because we are both constituted as unique egos by the infinite claim of a unique other, yet equal. The characterization of you (my other) as an ego who is equally responsible for your other(s) is not contained in Levinas's description of the other. If this were the case, the asymmetry of you and me would at least be interwoven with the fundamental equality of our being ethical subjects of an endless obligation.

Levinas indeed states this equality and adds to it our being associated in the infinite task of serving the other(s), but he wants to make sure that this association is posterior and not—like Heidegger's *Mitsein*[32]— anterior to your and my being oriented and obliged by the (your and my) other. You (the other who is already serving another other) associate me with your task and you join me in my task. (Indeed, it does not make any difference which other I must serve, since the revelation of the infinite lies in the nakedness of the other as such and not in any particular feature.) And thus the first form of being-*with*-one-another is based on your and my being-*for*-the-other. Against Heidegger's claim that concern for another (*Fürsorge*) would be a particular form of *Miteinandersein*, Levinas maintains that the infinite concern of the Same for the Other is the infinite origin of all forms of being-with, togetherness and society. However, here, as in the first

---

and not similar to him. What must I do? What have they done to one another? Who precedes the other in my responsibility? What are the other and the third then with regard to each other? That is how the question emerges"). In the same essay, Levinas connects equality to our Greek heritage and proximity to the biblical heritage (345–46).

32 Cf. *TI* 39/67–68 for Heidegger's conception of intersubjectivity as beginning in a "coexistence" or *we* preceding the relation of the other and I.

argument, it seems inevitable to assume beforehand that both you, "my other," and I are different as well as similar; since both of us are egos, we are "the same." For how could we otherwise state that the other ("you"), just as I am, already is demanded by another other (the third—him or her). But if this assumption is valid, why should we not then begin by stating that all others are—just as I myself am—identical with me insofar as they, too, are egos subjected to the other's claims? In fact, Levinas implies this statement in every sentence that describes or analyzes the features of "the" ego, "the" Other, "the" unique, "the" Same, and so on. The universality proper to the language of logic and ontology cannot be detached from the encounter of you and me as long as we treat it as a topic or theme for a theoretical text.

If everybody is infinitely responsible for everybody else, it might seem that the much stressed asymmetry between the Other and the Same disappears—unless we stress that I (this unique I who speaks or writes here and now) am more responsible and, therefore, more guilty than all others. This would bring us close to the sentence that Levinas so often quotes from Dostoyevski's *Brothers Karamazov:* "We all are responsible for everything and everyone in the face of everybody, and I more than the others."[33] However, the meaning of "more" in this sentence is not immediately clear, and it does not suffice for a rejection of all symmetry because, if it is true, it is valid for all possible egos, who, therefore, must confess that they are more obliged than all other egos.

As soon as I know that you, my other, are claimed in the same way by any Other, the detour by a third seems to become unnecessary: the reason why I say that you are responsible is either identical with the reason why I become aware of my own responsibility (in fact, this is the case when I write a text for you— and all other readers—about the responsibilities of any ego); or I must describe the relation between "my other" (you) and "the other's (your) other" as a relation that, in this respect, is identical to my being related

---

33 Cf., for instance, *Ethique et Infini,* 95.

to you. Therewith, I would show that "the other" (you) is obliged by any other, from which it follows that all others are reciprocally obliged. In the name of its essential asymmetry, Levinas constantly denies the reciprocity of the metaphysical relation, but this rejection seems to rest on an illegitimate identification of the category *reciprocity* with another category that could be called *"double asymmetry"*: when A is infinitely obliged by B, B can still be infinitely obliged by A. This reciprocity does not necessarily entail that A is allowed to claim as much from B as the existence of B claims from A (nor that B may claim from A the same sacrifices the existence of A demands from B). Reciprocally the existence of A and of B as others demand much more from the ego (of B or A) to which they reveal themselves than that which these egos are allowed to claim for themselves.[34] I can, and sometimes must, sacrifice my life for some other, but I can never claim that another should sacrifice his or her life for me, for this would be a sort of murder. Notwithstanding the difficulties that emerge from the second argument, its advantages are that it expresses clearly (1) that the infinite obligation by which ego is related to the other is a relation of universal justice and not of exclusivity and (2) that the basis of human sociability is found in a multiplicity of unique others who cannot be reduced to indifferent instances of a general concept "human being" or "Other."

The *third* argument given in the text of subsection 6 can be seen as a further analysis of the second one. It is contained in the statement that "autrui me commande de commander" ("the other commands me to command"). You, who are the demanding presence of the other, you command me to be your servant, but since

---

34 Levinas states a certain form of reciprocity in writing the following lines: "And if the other can invest me and invest my freedom, of itself arbitrary, this is in the last analysis because I myself can feel myself to be the other of the other (*me sentir comme l'Autre de l'Autre*). But this comes about only across very complex structures" (*TI* 56/84). However, this reciprocity should *not* be thought as a "separation of Me" that would be "the reciprocal of the Other's transcendence with regard to me" (*TI* 24/52). In any case, reciprocity (e.g., in the form of Buber's I-Thou) is not original (*TI* 40/68).

you yourself are a servant, you order me to assist you in your serving the third. Thus your commanding me specifies only your associating me to yourself, which was stated in the second argument. However, since I am a free, autonomous ego and not a slave, I, too, am in command.[35] Against Sartre and certain neo-Hegelians, Levinas wants to make sure that to be dedicated as a servant does not have anything to do with alienation or slavery. His apology for the other's highness does not invert the roles of master and slave but shows that to live and die for the other accomplishes the ultimate meaning of a free and responsible mastery of oneself (188/213). Levinas does not explain here what or whom the other orders me to command, but in all probability we may complete his phrase by relating the latter "command" to the development of the judicial, political, economical, and technological institutions that are demanded for a world of general justice.[36]

The peculiar structure of this third argument, too, is motivated by the attempt to avoid starting from the thesis that the other and I are equal insofar as we are equally responsible for all other human beings. By putting the other (you) and me under the same obligation, this thesis would, indeed, seem to destroy the asymmetry of the originary relation. It would rather look like a Kantian thesis about the universal imperative by which everybody is ordered to respect everyone else,

35 Cf. "Le Moi et la Totalité" ("Ego and Totality") (*Revue de Métaphysique et de Morale* 59 [1954]: 370–71/*CPP* 43): "But if this recognition were a submission to him, the submission would take all its worth away from my recognition; recognition by submission would annul my dignity, through which recognition has validity."

36 In "Ego and Totality," however, the fact of the other commanding me to command is explained in the following way. Since my respect for the other is not possible, unless I am in command of myself and capable of producing a work by my own capacities, the command by which the other commands me cannot involve humiliation but must simultaneously command a work from me and command me to command him/her, who commands me (*CPP* 43, French edition, 371). Here Levinas himself formulates the reciprocity, which I called a "double asymmetry" before. The essay presents this "reference from one command to the other command" as constituting the union that is expressed in our use of the pronoun "we." The *we* is, thus, not the plural of I but—so we may complete his sentence (*CPP* 43)—the solidarity constituted by our mutual respect, command, and productivity.

with this difference, however, that Kant's notion of respect for the humanity (*die Menschheit*) in all human
beings, I myself included, would be replaced by a *being-
for* whose "noema" would not be the human essence,
reason, or any other universal value but rather the
unique other that a unique ego in a contingent time-
space "here and now" would encounter. The asymmetry
of the encounter could be saved even if we would start
from the assumption that everybody, as "an ego," "experiences" another as imposing an infinite responsibility.
However, if the universal experience of asymmetry is
true, it seems to lead to the contradictory conclusion
that all people are simultaneously "higher" than all
people. Must we avoid this contradiction by declaring
the "experience" of asymmetry to be a subjective appearance, or can we maintain the truth of this asymmetry as the secret of morality by showing that the
immediacy of the relation to the other cannot be expressed in the language of a general overview of all
people involved, i.e., the language of universality and
ontology? Levinas contends that the order of universal
justice and reciprocity, as symbolized by the equality of
the primary other and the third, is a consequence of the
primordial relationship of transcendence and that the
language of universal classes and individual instances,
as it is used in traditional philosophy, is a secondary one:
the language of theory. Theory, logic, philosophy, and
all thematization are preceded by a more originary language to which the language of philosophical universality owes its capacity of being spoken to other
speakers. The speaking of speakers, through which they
address themselves to one another, presupposes, however, another, more originary universality: not the universality of genera and species but, as we will see
further on, that of a sort of kinship: the community of
human beings is constituted as a "fraternity" (cf. section
4, 227ff./254ff.).

   The "deduction" of the third and the obligation of
universal justice from the metaphysical relation of the
Same and the Other has left us with a series of difficult
questions that all are related to the "logic" of Levinas's enterprise and its relation to Western "onto-
logic." In a way, one can say that Levinas, by showing

a transition from the originary relation to general justice and theory, wants to indicate the relative function, value, and truth of Western ontology and its logic. At the same time, however, he stresses the fact that concern for "the third," i.e., dedication to the cause of universal justice, is the core of the prophetic message that entered Western civilization not primarily by the way of Greek philosophy but rather through the biblical message. The prophets—neither the kings of Israel nor the emperors of the heathens—were the protagonists of a justice that extends itself to the whole of humankind. The nakedness of the other symbolizes also the other's being unprotected, exiled, and dissociated as a stranger who still must be served as the presence of the infinite. The third, i.e., all others, is present in my being related to you. All others prevent our relation from closing itself up into exclusive love or friendship. Insofar as one respects the presence of the third and remains open to the dimension of a humanity of universal justice and peace—insofar as one's practice remains open to a future of prophetic eschatology—one continues to give a prophetic message of world peace and a special sort of universality.

Although this analysis of the few pages (187–90/212–14) dedicated in *Totality and Infinity* to the passage from intersubjective transcendence to social universality is already rather extensive, the importance of the question—which may function as a test case for the strength of Levinas's position—might justify that I make a few observations about the answers given in some former and later publications. The only philosophical essay in which Levinas, before the publication of *Totality and Infinity*, had given a more extensive analysis of society as such is "Le Moi et la Totalité" ("Ego and Totality," *CPP* 25–46). It had been preceded by the short but dense article "Liberté et Commandement" ("Freedom and Command," *CPP* 15–24), which also treated certain aspects of social life but focused primarily on the question of to what extent an individual will can resist tyrannical violence. Often referring to Plato's *Republic*, this article builds up an argument for the necessity of politics, the state, and positive laws as the necessary conditions for the possibility of individual freedom, which, in its turn, conditions morality. However, rather than being an investigation into social institutions, the article is a meditation on the interpersonal relations involved in violence and resistance to violence.

"Ego and [Social] Totality," too, begins with the question of how we can overcome the moment of violence that seems to be inherent in every human individual's freedom. Freedom is here understood in the sense that is developed in section 2 of *Totality and Infinity,* namely as the spontaneity of an independent life. To live means to behave as the center of a universe that is defined in terms of needs and satisfactions; in living on account of (or "from") the surrounding totality of beings, one confounds one's own individuality and particularities with that totality. Life is the practice of the Same as the active determination of all otherness, without being determined by any other. It is a cynical behavior reducing all otherness to being elements of the vital substance.

Seen as an activity within the self-realization of an isolated human life, thinking is a way of situating oneself within a totality of elements, beings, and relations, while maintaining a distance toward it. The illusory innocence of this spontaneity is, however, demystified by the emergence of the other, who miraculously awakens the vital consciousness to the guilt of its ruthless egoism. This awakening—primordial shame—is the first possibility of an interpersonal relationship.[37]

The relation to which the other calls me is not the closed "society" of love. God is not to be found in romantic love (*amour*) or in friendship but in the *law of justice,* that is, in the nonintimate relationship to the other, who is called here—in opposition to the second person of the beloved Thou—"the third." I would neglect the third and do injustice to him or her if I

---

[37] Levinas often uses the words "social" and "society" to indicate the dual relationship between *autrui* (who demands the dedication of "my whole soul, heart, all my forces") and me. It might be helpful to distinguish systematically between social (or collective) and intersubjective (or interpersonal) relationships.

were to abandon myself to the dual privacy of love. In order to do justice to the third, i.e., to all people, the institutions of a political body are necessary warrants. The third is, indeed, not helped by good intentions or remorse and shame alone; what counts is deeds of concern, objective goodness, and fair distribution of material goods: a *work* of economical justice.

It is important to notice that Levinas's intention in writing this text is the same as the one expressed in subsection 6 of part B interpreted above: social justice is necessary and essential; it cannot be justified by a dual relationship alone and thus not by the originary relation between ego and other because this would develop into an exclusive association excluding all others from its infinite demands. However, the expression "the third" has a different meaning in these texts: whereas *Totality and Infinity* presents the "second" as the first and original other (who, as such, is not a beloved or friend but a naked other without other qualification than his/her otherness), "Ego and Totality" identifies "the third" with the other and the "second" with the beloved person who is too intimate to deserve the name of "other."

The insight that universal justice is "better than" love does not entail the triumph of impersonality! The relation to the other as not beloved but respected third is a relation of goodness with regard to the singularity of this unique one who needs and claims my dedication. The domain of social justice, i.e., the institutional totality that is demanded, is not a purely anonymous realm ruled by universal laws. If that were the case, the individuality of its members would be destroyed. The social totality demanded by the claims of justice is composed of relations relating concrete egos who maintain their unicity while forming a community. How is this possible?

A community of free individuals is one whole, but its unity is not that of a general concept. It implies the possibility and the reality of one's will being the "cause" of another's willing what the first one wants this other to do. The fact of one's will having power over another is, however, the core of violence or injustice. The social totality we are looking for is, thus, a community in which injustice is possible and necessary. This strange conclusion must be understood in the following way. Every form of society is based on a certain injustice: the injustice of an identification by which people's wills are equated with the works that are produced by their activities. Someone's *expression* is, however, different from his or her *work (œuvre)*. Face and speech express the other, but works are not expressions, although, as phenomena with an original style, they show certain characteristics of their producer. They rather betray—at least in part—the will from which they stem. A work can be separated from its author and become part of a history from which the author is absent. As a moment of an anonymous history, the work has a meaning of its own, different from the meaning intended and effectuated through it by its author. The meaning of a work is a function of the social order and its historical economy. From the perspective of society and history, human individuals count as authors of works; in a philosophy that does not permit another—e.g., the moral—perspective, they cannot refuse to be identified with their products. Thanks to their works, individuals can enter into relations with colleagues or other citizens, but they can also be forced, corrupted, or seduced through the manipulation of their works by others. A society that is based solely on the production of work in the broadest sense of the term is defenseless against the power of money, blackmail, violence, and injustice. The secret of all philosophy that considers society and history to be the supreme perspective is war and exploitation.

The only possibility of protecting the human will against violence and corruption lies in a society that would be capable of suppressing all opportunities of betrayal. But is this not a utopian desire? World history seems to prove that people and events are united by the powers of violence and injustice. Any social universe seems defenseless against the interplay of conflicting interests and liberties. As based on the products of human activities, the judgment of history is an unjust outcome, and if the social totality is constituted by violence and corruption, there seems to be no hope for a just society unless justice can be brought into it from the outside. This is possible only if society and world history do not constitute the dimension of the ultimate. The power of nonviolence and justice lies in the dimension of speech and the face-to-face, the dimension of straightforward intersubjectivity and fundamental ethics, which opens the closed totality of anonymous productivity and historicity. However, the irruption of the ethical into the anonymous is not possible unless those who are facing and speaking to one another also participate in the interplay of the political and economical network to which human productivity gives birth. Ethics, economy, politics, and history cannot be separated. Although the ethical dimension transcends the dimension of world history, it must politicize itself in order to develop into a concrete and universal justice.

Thus, in this article, too, Levinas has shown that a society without ethics necessarily will be unjust, but, more clearly than elsewhere, he shows that the "totality" (i.e., the society as a collectivity whose social structures hide the unique and personal character of the face-to-face relations among its members) is *also* a necessary condition and integral element of the justice demanded in the face-to-face. Morality judges history, and not the other way around. But ethics is not serious if it does not concretize itself in judicial and political institutions. All forms of justice are, however, preceded by the ethical inspiration that is found in the immediate response of unique individuals to unique others who express themselves through eyes and words.

In *Otherwise Than Being* (200–207/157–62), Levinas gives a new analysis of the constellation *I-the other-the third.* He takes up the analysis of *Totality and Infinity* and develops it further within the broader question of how the relation of transcendence (which is thematized in *Otherwise Than Being* under the name of *the Saying*) and the inevitable dimension of thematizing, universalizing, and objectifying discourse (*the Said*) are connected and interwoven, as is shown in all our communication (*TI* 195ff./153ff.). The enigma on which Levinas concentrates here is the necessary union of the infinite responsibility for the other (*autrui* or the *prochain*—i.e., the nearest one or the "neighbor") with the theoretical and practical (moral and political) forms of universalization, as, for instance, developed in the judicial system or in ontology.

The thesis defended in these pages states that the transition from transcendence to universality (or from the Saying to the Said) is necessitated by the emergence of the third. If I were only related to one other human, our intimacy would not be bothered by any question about universality; neither general justice nor philosophy would pose any problem for me because I would be taken entirely by my responsibility for you. It is the third—and this is not a contingent empirical appearance but rather a structural component of my proximity to you—who introduces the necessity of universalization, objectification, totality, and even calculus, into the relation of transcendence that constitutes me as a subject.

Thus, in contrast with Hegel's deduction of reason, universality, and self-consciousness from the encounter of two consciousnesses, Levinas claims that without a third person there would not even be consciousness (in the emphatic sense of a panoramic and totalizing openness). But would not the Saying always imply a Said, and would this not necessarily include at least some "objective" elements about which the sayer would state or promise or say something? Is not the "something" (the *ti*) of Aristotle's *legein ti kata tinos* (saying something about something) inherent to all Saying, at least in its affirmative function? By stating that "consciousness is born as presence of the third,"[38] Levinas wants to show that the face-to-face and the dimension of politics and philosophy are, indeed, interwoven and inseparably intermingled but also distinct and incommensurably different.

His starting point is here again a threefold characterization of the third: "The third is (a) other than the neighbor (*le prochain*), but also (b) another neighbor, but also (c) a neighbor of the Other (*l'Autre*)" (200/

___
38 *TI* 203/160. Cf. 200/157: "If proximity ordered to me only the other alone, there would not have been any problem," and 201/157–58: "The entry of the third is the very fact of consciousness."

157). If, in agreement with the bulk of *Otherwise Than Being*, we substitute *le prochain* for *l'Autre* (or *Autrui*), we can state the following equivalences between the pages we are examining here and the subsection of *Totality and Infinity* on *Autrui et les Autres* explained above: (b) the third as another other or *prochain* for me corresponds to the third as presented in the first argument of that subsection; (c) the third as *prochain* of "my" other corresponds to the third as analyzed in the second argument; (a) the third as other than (or different from) the (i.e., "my") *prochain* is not thematized explicitly in *Totality and Infinity*, but the difference is presupposed in all the arguments. Indeed, the third comes to the fore as a virtual (and thus anonymous) face behind or "in" your face, and he/she has to be discovered as "also an other" (*autrui* or "nearest one"). Since the possibilities and difficulties of (b.1) the third as other other and (c.2) the third as my other's other have been exposed above, we can limit our further analysis to (a) the structure of the third being as the other (or neighbor) of "my" other (or neighbor). For me (the subject of a relation to the infinite in the other *and* of a relation to the one who is the infinite for this other), the emergence of a third means that my infinite responsibility for the other makes it impossible to concentrate on the needs and desires of the third, although this virtual and as yet still anonymous other is already calling for a "same sort of" responsibility. I cannot be infinitely responsible for the third because I am infinitely responsible for the other. Since I am responsible for the other—and, thus, for his/her life—I am also responsible for his being related to his other, who for me is the (or a!) third, but I cannot identify myself with the other's infinite responsibility for his/her other unless I let my care and attention for so many others be divided and, thus, limited by their multiplicity.

The simultaneity of many others distances me from the infinity of my responsibility. The contradiction caused by an infinite claim that is multiplied can only be overcome by the opening up of a dimension in which *all* others are served, respected, and treated justly: the dimension of universal justice. The infinite "principle" of transcendence (or—as Levinas

calls it in *Otherwise Than Being*—of proximity) neces-
sitates its own universalization and therewith a certain limitation. This is the "origin" of justice as the
concern for a universally just order. This justice
demands comparison (of unique and incomparable
others), coexistence (of those whose "truth" can only
"appear" in a face-to-face), gathering, equality (of the
differents), administration, politics (which necessarily
includes totalization), and so on. As a dimension of
universality and totalization, this is also the dimension of ontology or philosophy in its classical form.
And since this philosophy can be characterized as
the quest for the origin (in the form of *archè, causa,*
or *principium*), the relation of transcendence and
infinity, as necessarily passing over into universal
justice, can be called "the origin of the origin" (204/
160).

The importance of Levinas's new attempt to connect justice, politics, ontology, universality, and totality with transcendence and the infinite lies in the
fact that they are thereby rooted in, and preceded
by, a "more originary," *"pre-"* or—as Levinas prefers
to say—*"an-archic"* infinity (or "origin" or "non-
origin" or "an-archy"), and not in an (onto-)logic of
the universal (or the total). The finitude of politics
and philosophy—and, in general, of human history,
culture, ethos, and concrete existence—is shown by
relating them to the epiphany of the other, which
is the concrete form taken by the infinite. They
receive their meaning from their Beyond, which
shows itself now as "more interior" or "more essential" than their essence. General justice is impossible
if it does not originate "anarchically," in the responsibility of the unique one-for-the-(unique) other, but
this responsibility includes the universality of politics
and ontology. This unbreakable bond "between the
order of being and of proximity" by which "the face
is both the neighbor and the face of [all] faces" (204/
160), clarifies the first argument of *Totality and
Infinity,* according to which it was "in" the other's
face that the third and all other faces presented
themselves. Because of the third as "the incessant
correction of the asymmetry of proximity" (201/158),

a reinterpretation becomes necessary: "The face obsesses and shows itself between transcendence and visibility/invisibility" (201/158); it confronts us with the "ambiguity" and the "ambivalence" (199/156) of an enigma that unites unicity and multiplicity, equality and difference, symmetry and asymmetry, the finite and the infinite, politics and religion, phenomenality and transcendence. The treason (*trahison*) that the idea of the infinite suffers by becoming a dimension of the world is its necessary translation into the concreteness of human action.

A very important consequence of the development exposed in *Otherwise Than Being* is that the universalization of the otherness by which every other other (who is also an other of the other) reveals his/her claim to justice encompasses also my life; "my lot," too, "is important" (205/161). "I, too, am an Other (*Autrui*) for the Others" not because of a primordial equality of all human individuals who share one common essence but thanks to the "pre-original" structure of transcendence, i.e., "thanks to God" (*grâce à Dieu*). As members of a society that is founded on transcendence, we are related by a relation of *reciprocity*: "the reciprocal relationship binds me to the other man in the trace of transcendence." This community is called here *"fraternity."*[39]

Levinas stresses that justice, together with the whole constellation of universal rules and totalizing gestures (in politics and theory), is "in no way a degradation" or "degeneration" of the infinite responsibility for the Other; he even denies that it is a "limitation of the anarchic responsibility" (203/159). But he concedes, on the other hand, that the apparition of the third tempers the hyperbolic intensity of transcendence and brings it under the measure of a well-balanced justice (204–5/160–61).

---

39 *AE* 201–2/158. Cf. also the succinct summary in *TI* 229–30/252: "An order common to the interlocutors is established by the positive act of the one *giving* the world, his possession, to the other, or by the positive act of the one justifying himself in his freedom before the other, that is, by apology.... It is the primordial phenomenon of reason, in its insurmountable bipolarity."

In his 1985 essay "The Rights of Man and the Rights of the Other,"[40] Levinas discusses the modern ethos of universal human rights, which functions as the standard and measure of all law and rights, in order to show that it presupposes a prejuridical and prepolitical peace. Since the multiplicity of human individuals causes a perpetual conflict over their rights unless an effective administration of justice prevents or conquers a general war by imposing many compromises, the peace that is thus established remains uncertain and risky: it depends on the benevolence of the political powers in place. This situation shows clearly that the effective realization of justice presupposes a prepolitical or "extraterritorial" goodness different from the general justice whose essential limitation, this time, is stressed. Before the alternation of political war and peace and at the roots of a just society lies the fraternity of those who are responding to one another's incomparable uniqueness by being hostages for the other. The essay thus gives a new version of the thesis forwarded in the preface of *Totality and Infinity:* peace and justice, i.e., good politics, are not possible except on the basis of the ethics of a prophetic *Shalom.*

After subsection 6 on the foundation of a social philosophy, on which I have chosen to comment in some detail, Levinas reformulates in the seventh subsection of part B, "Asymmetry of the Interpersonal" (190–91/215–16), the results of his descriptions given in the preceding subsections. As coming from beyond "the world" (or as not being a part or moment of the economy of an isolated ego), the other is not a "phenomenon." Indeed, the concept of "phenomenon" has been defined by Husserl and Heidegger within the horizons of "the (life-)world," and it is in solidarity with all the assumptions of a philosophy confined to "the world" as ultimate horizon. Even the category "being"—as understood within the context of Western ontology—does not fit here: I, who am responsible for the other, am *less* than "a being," thus I am structurally determined by the other's infinite claim and judgment, according to which I am always in default; but at the same time, I am *more* than "a being" because, as infinitely

40 Cf. "Les droits de l'homme et les droits d'autrui," in *Hors sujet,* 173–87.

responsible, I am free and thus master of the resources without which my responsible autonomy would not be possible. Correlatively, the other is both *more* and *less* than a being by the simultaneity of the height and the nakedness revealed in the face.

One of the difficulties with which any reader of *Totality and Infinity* has to cope lies in its ambiguous use of the word "being." Very often it expresses the true and "real" reality toward which any "first philosophy" is oriented. The other can then be called a being *par excellence* or *kath' hauto*. In other places, however, "being" and "ontology" serve to characterize the egological and totalitarian nature of Western philosophy, which should be surpassed by something "higher" and "other" than, or beyond, being. As Levinas himself recognizes in "Signature," in *Totality and Infinity* he still speaks the language of ontology,[41] but there are also pages in which he has begun to overcome it with a terminology and conceptuality more adequate to the "Otherwise than Being," which is the central purpose of his later book. Levinas's critique of the category "phenomenon" as contained in subsection 7 shows that he has started to surpass not only ontology but also the phenomenological method, to which he owes most of his own approach. However, since his overcoming of phenomenology is wholly based on the practice of intentional analyses in a style akin to that of Husserl and Heidegger, we might call his philosophy "transphenomenological" rather than "antiphenomenological."[42]

The last subsection of part B, "Will and Reason" (191–95/ 216–19), starts as a refutation of idealism in the name of the thesis that "the essence of discourse is ethical." It (1) attacks the Kantian identification of (practical) reason and will; but (2) it continues also the analyses of section 3 on the essence of theory in light of the visage; (3) it shows how "reason," understood as a synonym for responsibility and responsible thought, must be distinguished from the will as the capacity of freely assuming or refusing responsibility; and (4) it shows that ethics differs radically from politics, therewith continuing the meditation of subsection 6 on a just society. In brief, Levinas continues to unfold the meaning of reason, will, ethics, politics, thinking, communication, and so on, as renewed by the revelation of the face.

---

41 *DL* 379/*Research in Phenomenology* 8 (1978): 189.
42 Cf. S. Strasser, "Antiphénoménologie et phénoménologie dans la philosophie d'Emmanuel Levinas, *Revue philosophique de Louvain* 75 (1977): 101–24.

Idealism, as exemplified by Plato and Heidegger, sees the human subject as a moment of an anonymous order composed of mutual relationships ruled by universal laws of reason. The will is defined as "practical reason," i.e., as the ability to be affected by rational universality, whereas a good will is a will whose motivations and actions are entirely determined by that universality. From this follows the identification of ethics (as acting according to universally valid laws) with politics (as acting for the general good of a realm of ends). The multiplicity of wills is in this framework explained by sensibility: although human beings are rational, they are also *animalia*, striving for vital happiness. The unicity of their individuality is reduced to the indifference of many cases of a genus. Their essence appears thus as composed of rational will (or willing reason) and irrational, obscure, egoistic animality. Since this conception cannot understand communication except as a participation of different individuals in the anonymous universality of common ideas, discourse has no meaning in it. Subjectivity is not, however, constituted by the sole sensible aspect of the will, for subjects are also separated by the uniqueness of their nonexchangeable responsibility. The will names a responsible subject that cannot refute the responsibility by which his/her unicity is constituted; one can, however, refuse to assume it. If human individuals were no more than indifferent cases of universal reason, the infinite could not reveal its surpassing the universality of genera and species. Only the uniqueness of desire and responsibility—and not a defense of arbitrary choices—can reveal a *surplus* over being, as expressed in Plato's "Good." It is the Good that constitutes the subject as responsible and, thereby, as willing and rational.

Part C, "The Ethical Relation and Time" (195–225/220–47), is a turning point within *Totality and Infinity*. Prepared by the subsection on the will (B.8) summarized above, it shows which consequences the discoveries of parts A and B concerning the "metaphysical" (or "ethical") relationship have for politics and history, and especially for the questions of war and peace announced in the preface.

The pluralism revealed by the metaphysical relation is based on asymmetric relations of separate and free subjects whose existence is constituted—at least partially—by that relationship. As free and finite subjects, they can maintain the originary peace demanded by that relation, but they are also able to destroy it by violence and warfare. The multiplicity and finitude of their freedom cannot be explained within the context of the traditional conception of freedom as a diminished *causa sui* whose finitude would be caused by material and social limitations only. According to modern social theory, the human constituents of a society would limit each other's freedom, and this limitation would be the first form of violence. However, limitation is not necessarily a kind of violence, and the concept of limitation implies the concept of totality. Violence, but also commerce, presupposes existences that refuse to be part of a totality; to the extent to which they are free, they transcend all sorts of community. As a relationship between subjects who confide in themselves, war shows their separate independence; but insofar as they thereby take a supreme risk, they manifest also their utter dependence. Violence supposes that one can grasp someone who could escape or withdraw. The interwovenness of independence and dependence constitutes human freedom as a finite freedom. As simultaneously exposed and offered to others and separated or independent from them, a human body has the liberty of parrying attacks or of rusing against an enemy or, to be brief, of postponing death. The postponement of death, and not its anticipation, is the secret of human freedom. And therewith the concept of *time* is introduced. Finite liberty is to still have time— a move against the inexorable violence of death—the "not yet" of death. Violence or war is, then, to urge death upon someone who still exists and tries to delay death. Such a being is a body that possesses a distance, interiority, and consciousness. The "will" is a name for being mortal but not yet dead. Temporality (mortality *and* postponement of death through time) precedes and constitutes human freedom. Nothing is definitive; there is still time. The delaying of death is possible only because of the Other, who—by constituting my responsibility—gives me time. The Other ("the metaphysical") distends the tensions of my present by delivering me from the immediate violence of mortality; by opening the dimension of time, the infinite makes me free.[43]

In the second subsection, "Commerce, the Historical Relation, and the Face" (201–8/226–32), Levinas continues his analysis of

---

43 It is noticeable that this subsection contains also a clear formulation of the paradox that will be one of the main questions in *AE*: "The very utterance by which I state it [i.e., the incommensurability of transcendence and the 'truth' of a total reflection] and whose claim to truth, postulating a total reflection, refutes the unsurpassable character of the face to face relation, nonetheless confirms it by the very fact of stating this truth—of telling it to the Other" (196/221).

the will by opposing it to the *works* (including also the deeds and texts), of which he already had given an analysis in *Totality and Infinity* (150–51/175–77) and in the essay "Freedom and Command" (see above, 159–60). As the embodied unity of independence and dependence, the will is simultaneously the possibilities (the "I can") of Merleau-Ponty's *"corps propre" and* a biological structure that is delivered to manipulation and corruption. On the one hand, the will is free self-enjoyment; on the other hand, it is always on the verge of being used, abused, corrupted. Through its works, the will becomes part of a history of products, monuments, texts, literature. If fulfills a function and makes a name, the name of a destiny. By its functioning, it loses, however, its uniqueness. If the hermeneutical approach is the ultimate, it does the same as more practical ways of reduction, such as manipulation, corruption, or enslavement: they kill the transcendence of the will. Violence is the reduction of the will to work, a narrowing of the metaphysical to functions, monuments, and texts. History is the story of how persons performed in dramas, but it does not expose the time of unique wills that never wholly coincide with their products. As showing how oeuvres composed traditions and a heritage, history is essentially a necrology. Is there not another history, another time, and another judgment possible in which the unicity of the will is actually respected? Is there not a jurisdiction beyond the will's betrayal by its work?

Having shown that the will, as a free body, is a vulnerable consciousness between the immunity of independent initiative and the weaknesses of its exposition to the forces of nature and seduction, Levinas elaborates in a third subsection, "The Will and Death" (208–13/232–36), on its *mortality* as a typically human mode of temporality. As a postponement of the last event, the will is met by the inexorability of its disappearance. We are afraid of death because it puts an end to any further delay. The annihilation whereby death threatens a human life cannot be explained in terms of the categorical pair *being* versus *nothingness,* as if they formed the ultimate horizon of the world. For death is neither a being nor nothing; rather, we experience its threat as that of a murder coming from some sort of enemy. It comes from a dimension beyond life and world: from the dimension of invisibility and otherness over which we do not have any power. Therefore, death is not our last or ultimate possibility, and we are not able to accept, to anticipate, or to welcome it. Our fear originates in the will as still having (some) time by delaying the ultimate and absolute impossibility of all possibilities, but the inexorability of death refutes any view on human being according to which it is primarily an "I can," a possibility of possibilities. The invisibility of death does not lie in the nothingness with which it confronts us but in its not permitting us to grasp it, fight with it, and protect ourselves against it. Death always comes too early and as a nonwelcomed murderer. Since we cannot conceive of it as a possibility of our own, we cannot want it.

And yet, this enemy can receive a meaning precisely because it is not a moment of the world or any other totality composed of beings and their negations. The absolute passivity revealed in our ultimate impossibility belongs to a life that is directed to a meaning beyond its own destruction. This meaning cannot be found in a life "after death" of some immortal soul, since this idea itself sticks to the ultimacy of the categories being and nothingness as constituting world and time. To live for a time beyond one's own life is to live for the other(s), and this is made possible by mortality; the necessity of losing one's life belongs to the structure of being-for-other(s). Thus, the egoism of a fearful life can be converted into the obedience of having time for others; the absolute violence from which nobody can escape can become the source of indestructible goodness. To lose one's life for the other(s) *is* to be meaningful in living for a time after one's own life. If death—and suffering—were a purely individual event, it would be meaningless; its having a place within the horizon of the metaphysical (i.e., intersubjective) relation saves it from absurdity.

"The supreme ordeal of freedom" (or "of the will") "is not death, but suffering" (216/239). For whereas death terminates the ambiguity of humanity's finite freedom, suffering is the extreme experience of the discordance discovered in mortality as human temporality. This is shown in subsection 4, "Time and the Will: Patience" (213–17/236–40). Since time is the ability of free consciousness (or "the will") to postpone death, it is also the possibility of keeping a distance from all fixations that would identify the will with a certain instant or present. As long as there is time, nothing is definitive; the will can always take or change its position with regard to what the subject has done, thought, become until now. It has a distance toward the presence thanks to the many possibilities for a future that are still open. The future is not a prolongation of the present but rather the possibility of having a distance from it.

Suffering reduces this distance and the difference between present and future—as well as between fact and possibility or between fixation and freedom—to a minimum. In it we are backed up and glued to what we are, without possibility of fleeing it; a feared future has caught us, annulled our capacity of withdrawal, almost taken away our distance, and submitted our consciousness to utter passivity, without permitting it to die. A heroic will is a will that "stands" this "impossible" situation without giving in. It conquers by patience, i.e., by a disengagement within its forced engagement, thus still saving an ultimate mastery in the midst of almost total passivity. Patience is the experience of the limit of our will. Suffering, much more so than death, reveals the ambivalence of finite freedom and self-consciousness. But suffering, too, receives its meaning from "the order of discourse," that is, from its being endured for the Other. Even hate, as expressed, for instance, in torture or persecution, is better than complete isolation because it frees us from the egoistic absurdity of suffering for nobody, and without such a deliverance desire and goodness remain empty words.

The last subsection of section 3, "The Truth of the Will" (217–25/240–47), gathers the analyses formerly given into a central question that receives here a first, still partial answer, while it will dominate the last section of the book that leads "beyond the visage." It is the question of whether a philosophy of history in the traditional style of modern (especially neo-Hegelian) philosophy can solve the problems that arise from the tensions between politics and morality, and, if not, how this can be effected. Here, toward the end of his book, Levinas will clarify what he means when, in the preface, he calls his enterprise "a defense of subjectivity" as "founded in the idea of the infinite" and writes: "We oppose to the objectivation of war a subjectivity born from the eschatological vision. The idea of the infinite delivers the subjectivity from the judgment of history to declare it ready for judgment at every moment and—as we will show—called to participate in this judgment, impossible without it" (xiv/25).

Subjectivity, in the form of a separated "inner life" or "interiority," has been shown in sections 1 and 2 to be indispensable for the revelation of the infinite in its otherness. This necessity expresses itself in the fact that all speech and discourse is an address directed to others, as well as an *apology:*

> Conversation (*discourse*), from the very fact that it maintains the distance between me and the Other, the radical

> separation asserted in transcendence which prevents the
> reconstitution of totality, cannot renounce the egoism of
> its existence; but the very fact of being in a conversation
> consists in recognizing that the Other has *a right* over
> this egoism, and hence in justifying oneself. Apology, in
> which the I at the same time asserts itself and inclines
> before the transcendent, belongs to the essence of conversa-
> tion. Goodness . . . will not undo this apologetic moment.[44]

As necessarily apologetic, a human subject demands justice, not so
much happiness—although this, too, pertains to the free position
of an ego—but rather recognition of its unicity as a responsible
subject dedicated to others. The ego demands its recognition by a
judgment that does not neglect or destroy its truth. Since its truth
lies in its relations to the infinite, the true judgment must "situ-
ate" ego's unicity "with regard to the Infinite" (218/240).

The true judgment confirms the apology but cannot coincide
with a subjectivistic and narcissistic cry of protest; it must come
from the Other(s) and recognize responsibility and goodness as
they are. The "judgment of (world) history," which has become
famous since Schiller's and Hegel's identification of the *Welt-
gericht* with *Weltgeschichte,* does not do justice to the unicity of
responsible subjects because it is based on the *works* and the
institutions left behind by those who realized but simultaneously
betrayed their freedom therein. By identifying them with their
political or cultural productions, history denies the truth of their
unique responsibility with regard to marginal figures, such as
the foreigner, the widow, and the orphan. These are wholly neglected by world history because their works are too common to
be interesting. And what about the millions and millions of
people slaughtered and forgotten after being used for the building
of empires and monuments? If the universality of reason and the
importance of political or cultural heroism were the sole standard
of recognition, the "small" goodness of most people, the infinitude of the Other, and the ultimate meaning of subjectivity would
not count at all. The "great" history of "the world" is a cruel
tyranny; universal reason obliterates the election of irreplaceable
representatives of the Good.

Without denying that the dimensions of politics and technology—and their specific temporality—are necessary for the

---

44 *TI* 10/14. Cf. 91/118: "The I is an apology: whatever be the trans-
figurations this egoism will receive from speech, it is for the happiness
constitutive of its very egoism that the I who speaks pleads." Cf. also
TI 34/62–63.

realization of authentic justice, Levinas states that the preoriginal and preuniversal or "an-archical" responsibility of apologetic subjects necessarily implies another time and history than those which are celebrated by modern philosophy: a time and history which reveal the truth of the metaphysical relation between unique subjects and the infinite constituting them as responsible beyond all works. If such a history of the infinite is possible, its judgment reveals the invisible. As an eschatological judgment, it is pronounced by prophets, not by kings or scholars; as such, it may be called a "judgment of God."

Where and how does such a history of the invisible Good reveal its truth if it can neither be found in a "life after death" nor in the egoistic protestations of a bitter ego? The true judgment is revealed in the eyes of the other, who sees me and speaks to me, although I cannot reduce the other's epiphany to an image, a concept, a work, or a text. The other's eyes and voice express—silently and discretely—the true judgment by making me discover my unlimited and incessantly growing responsibility and, thereby, revealing the meaning of my suffering and death. The goodness demanded by this judgment and its accusation of my guilt call me forth to a justice without end beyond the universal justice of a well-ordered world. The more I am just, the more I am guilty, for the nonchosen responsibility that constitutes me does not diminish but grows by its fulfillment. By revealing my debt, the judgment of the infinite confirms my apologetic position, not in the form of a consolation but as an ongoing transformation of the egoistic fear of my death into a fear of causing the other's death. My apology receives a different meaning by being cited before the tribunal of the Good beyond "justice." Ego's "inner life" is declared unique and indispensable by urging it to a moral creativity that does not despise or neglect the political and technical conditions of universal justice but surpasses them by a limitless dedication to the "unimportant" marginals. Such a dedication cannot remain conscience. As a condition of its possibility, it presupposes a specific temporality and a particular form of fecundity, which the last section of *Totality and Infinity* must clarify.

| Beyond the Face

Although the encounter with the infinite in the face of the other does not permit a "higher" or "more absolute" horizon of which it would be a moment only, the *aporia* to which the contradiction between the cruelty of world history and the demand for a fair judgment leads cannot be resolved without appealing to another time and "history" beyond the actuality of this or that encounter. In this sense, Levinas can speak of a dimension "beyond" (*au delà*) the face. The main purpose of section 4 is the disclosure of this dimension as the condition of an ultimate justice beyond intimacy and political institutionality. The apology by which the subject tries to justify itself before the other cannot "stand" the cruelty of reason's history without submitting itself to it unless it reaches beyond its own death through a special sort of fecundity. Around this thesis, the whole of section 4 has been composed. It contains, however, much more than the necessary argumentation for that thesis. The extensive description of erotic love with which the section begins is, by itself, a splendid piece of phenomenology, but its relation to the main thesis consists in one thread only, namely in the erotic experience of an indeterminate future. Simultaneously, it is part of a meditation about the kinship and the difference between the erotic form of intersubjectivity and the metaphysical relationship between the One and the Other; and, thirdly, it offers certain elements for a philosophy of the family and its being "an-archically" prior to the realm of politics.

The introductory pages (229–31/251–53) restate the leading question from the perspective of ego's apology: How can I escape from the tyranny of rational but impersonal (world) history and be judged "in truth"? The answer, given in part C, "Fecundity" (244–47/267–69), is prepared by two parts on love and eros, the first of which (A, "The Ambiguity of Love," 232–33/254–55) stresses the equivocal character of love as a sort of synthesis, or—as Levinas prefers to say—as something "between" the transcendence of the face and immanent enjoyment, between the desire for the Other and the need for concupiscent self-satisfaction. As choosing someone for whom one is predestined, without choice, love is a sort of incest with the other as a "sister soul": simultaneously less than discourse and "more." In loving, one enjoys the beloved in reaching beyond her toward a future that is "not yet," an "obscure light" beyond the beloved's face. This desire of "a future never future enough," in contrast to, *and* in union with, the needy and consumptive part of love, is the moment with which Levinas's phenomenology of love relates to his phenomenology of fecundity and the question asked in the introductory pages of this section.

The long description of love in part B, "Phenomenology of Eros" (233–44/256–66), can hardly be summarized in a few lines.

As part of the final section, its main importance lies in the observation that erotic life tends to a future that is not yet, a peculiar sort of future differing radically from any projection of possible works or deeds. This "not yet" emerges in love because it intends neither objects, things, or possibilities nor the face of the other as such. Since love differs essentially from simple enjoyment, the other's face and language must be present in it. To love someone is to enjoy the other's enjoyment, but it is the enjoyment of someone who speaks (although in the act of loving she might be silent or laugh or play). The appearance of the beloved differs from the face: she is frail, vulnerable, tender, but simultaneously indecently exhibited and exorbitantly material: the equivocal union of pure eyes and lascivious nudity, a voluptuous body with a naked face. The tender is the carnal, different from both the physiological body and the expressive body of the other as other. Neither is it Merleau-Ponty's *corps propre* as the incarnation of "I can." Since the beloved is someone having a face, the exhibition of its nudity is always a sort of profanation: to love is to be concerned for the vulnerability of the beloved but also to participate in the profanation of her secret, a secret that is brought to light without abolishing its nocturnal clandestinity. The secret is exposed as secret but is not disclosed. The beloved cannot be grasped: by caressing, the lover searches and forages without end for some mystery that cannot be captured. At the same time, erotic love is always a profanation and, somehow, a violation of never-lost virginity. The searching and tending of love and its abandonment to the nonsignifying density of passion and com-passion point to a not-yet that cannot be willed, projected, or achieved. Love's impatience does not anticipate but abandons itself and lets itself blindly be drawn toward an emergence beyond any act or possibility. Love is searching for "the infinitely future." In loving the other's love—in the intimacy of a voluptuous union without fusion—a future beyond all possible decisions announces itself: a transubstantiation of the lovers' momentary identification into a child.

For the right interpretation of Levinas's phenomenology of eros as it is given in *Totality and Infinity,* two questions must be answered: (1) Is it meant as a "neutral" description or, perhaps, as the description of the typically masculine perspective? and (2) Does this description limit itself to eros as intimately connected with determinate physiological conditions? The first question might be answered by Levinas's explicitly stated equivalence of the one who is loved (*l'aimé* in the *masculine* or *neuter* form!) with "the feminine" (*le feminin*): "To love is to fear for another, to come to assistance of his/her frailty (*faiblesse*). In this frailty, as in the dawn, rises the Loved (*l'Aimé*), who is Beloved (*Aimée*). As epiphany of the Loved (*l'Aimé*), the feminine is not added to an object or a Thou antecedently given or encountered in the neuter (the sole gender formal logic knows). The epiphany of the Beloved (*l'Aimée*) is but one with his/her regime of tenderness" (233/257). The loved one is essentially frail, tender, carnal, ambiguously naked and nude, and, thus, "feminine," whether he or she is a man or a woman. Still, one might maintain that Levinas's description of love, the beloved, and the lover are typically masculine. This would certainly not offend an author who does not swear by the neutrality of "formal logic." As for the femininity of the house, which was thematized in Levinas's phenomenology of dwelling in section 2 (cf. 127–29/ 154–56 and 157–58 above), there, too, "the feminine" was used in a metaphorical sense (which, of course, does not yet answer the question of whether it is a good metaphor, and why or why not).

An answer to the second question is indicated in the last line of section 3. Levinas states there that fecundity and paternity, as thematized in section 4, do not coincide with their biological concretizations; they "can be sustained by biological life," but they can also "be lived beyond that life" (225/247). If this means that, for instance, education, or writing, or fighting for human rights are equally forms of paternity, the whole metaphorics of fecundity seems to be detached from its biological connotations. Must we, then, also detach the "eros" from erotic love in its narrow meaning and understand "father," the "feminine," "beloved," and "son(s)" as examples or illustrations of a history that is not essentially connected with procreation or the family? In any case, we should bear in mind that the fecundity introduced here in the name of a true judgment beyond world history cannot coincide with the history of heroic deeds or social institutions: it must save the apology of moral subjects who have a future beyond their own life thanks to others in whom they can recognize a new emergence of their own moral subjectivity.

In part C, "Fecundity" (244–47/267–69), a new temporality, the time of "transubstantiation," is analyzed. The future of the "not yet" experienced in the erotic union reveals itself as a child. Since a child cannot be projected or anticipated as a possibility that should be realized, the relation between father and child (again another "sort" of Other!) cannot be understood as the fulfillment of a possibility or the achievement of a work. The father is identical with, and radically different from, his child: the desired one is the father's future but is neither projected nor anticipated. In discontinuous time, the child *is* the father, for whom it is, at the same time, a stranger. Due to fecundity, as a relation to a particular future, one can be saved from endless repetition and senescence by new youths. The fixations of old age and death are refuted by a time whose discontinuity conquers the boredom of aging by the birth of others who are "mine" without being a possession. In his child, the father is another beyond the fulfillment of possibilities, the achievement of an "I can," or the actuality of a destiny. Desire is not arrested in a child, for the father desires his child as a renewal of his own desire by another (and yet the same) desire for another (and the same) future of responsibility. Fecundity is, thus, the engendering of goodness by goodness in a time of the infinite without end. Because of this "infinite time," human subjects transcend death, not by dissolution or extasis into an ocean of Being but through the discontinuity of transcendence to others who achieve a transubstantiation of their generators.

Possibly alluding to Plato's interpretation of philosophical education as "procreation in beauty,"[45] Levinas gives an example of a nonbiological form of fecundity when he writes that "philosophy itself constitutes a moment of this temporal accomplishment, [as] a discourse always addressing itself to another" (247/269). The teacher transcends his own life and death by being changed into his student, reader, or successor, who, after him, speaks in a new way to others. As a specific relation to the future, fecundity shows that there are levels and modes of Being having another structure than the continuous time-space of a totality. In testifying to the irreducibility of a fecund pluralism, the time of transcendence—the temporality of desire and the Good—refutes any *hen kai pan* and the pantheism that goes with it.

Part D, "The Subjectivity in Eros" (247–51/270–73), repeats and develops what the former sections already have shown and stresses how the erotic *initiation* (which is not an initiative) liberates the aging subject from its self-identification vis-à-vis the other. The child is the other in which the father, who is the origin, has his own new beginning. "I am an other," who is a new I. Discontinuous time is the possibility of recommencing *in infinitum.*

---

45 Cf. *Symposium* 206b ff.

The four pages of part E, "Transcendence and Filiality" (251–54/274–77), give the somewhat revised text of the paper "Pluralism and Transcendence," which Levinas presented at the Tenth International Congress of Philosophy (Amsterdam 1948).[46] Starting from the question of how transcendence is possible, Levinas states that the logic of Western philosophy does not permit us to conceive of a substantial transcendence by which the I transcends itself without losing its own identity. Since that logic is based on the presupposition that the bond between Being and the One is indestructible, plurality is always subsumed by a final synthesis. Being is, then, conceived as monadic and monistic; and since transcendence, from this perspective, must be seen as a relation between a multiplicity of monads, it is considered a second-hand and superficial reality. In a discussion of Brunschvicg, who represents classical rationalism, and of Heidegger, the great renewer of philosophy, Levinas argues that the paradigmatic function given to modes of being such as consciousness, knowledge, becoming, temporal continuity, power, and possibility do not enable us to conceive of transcendence as an originary principle of ontology; and he forwards the thesis that the erotic or sexual relationship, understood as fecundity, makes this possible. Against Freud's libidinal interpretation of sexuality, he indicates some elements of the phenomenology developed in *Totality and Infinity* and concludes that fecundity is the transcendence between me and the son, who is and is not I.

The ontological framework in which Levinas treats here another question than the one announced in the introduction of section 4 and the thesis, formulated on 253/276, that transcendence is primarily found in eroticism and fecundity—a thesis which seems to contradict the core of *Totality and Infinity*—give us a glimpse of the thought process achieved between Levinas's lectures of 1947 on *Time and the Other*, closer to his 1948 paper, and the later work in which the responsibility for the destitute and unfamiliar stranger is sharply distinguished from erotic love and familiar relationships.

In "The Other and the Others" (III.B.6), analyzed extensively above (166–75), Levinas had already affirmed that society, as the organization of human solidarity and universal equality, presupposes a specific community of humankind in the form of universal fraternity (189–90/213–14), but how and why this is the case was

---

[46] Cf. the proceedings of this congress, published by North-Holland Publishing Company, 1949, 1:381–83.

not shown. In part F, "Filiality and Fraternity" (255–57/278–80), we read an attempt to "deduce" the fraternity of all humans as a condition not only of any well-ordered society but also of the realization of successful goodness in the face-to-face. That the fecundity from which this fraternity is "deduced" cannot be understood in a purely biological sense is stated explicitly on several occasions.[47] Neither can fraternal universality be understood within the frame of species and genera because that would contradict the unicity and the alterity essential for human parenthood.

Since the father is and is not his son, who, as other, lives and desires independently, although he also resumes the past represented by his parents, the son's freedom is neither absolute nor made but a created freedom. As a son prolonging his father's life, he also revolts against it. The history of fathers and sons is, thus, a drama in many acts: the time of fecund discontinuity is open to surprising turns and authentic renewals. Every son is, as other of the father, unique. This unicity, again, cannot be understood in biological terms, for it presupposes an election by the father. His desire invests the son with a responsibility that is at the same time new and similar to the father's responsibility. Election constitutes the son's ipseity, through which the father receives another future than that of his own repetitious senescence. Freed from its biological limitations, *paternity* is "being capable of another fate than its own" or a "way of being other while being oneself" (258/282), while *fraternity* is "the very relation with the face in which, at the same time, my election and equality, that is, the mastery exercised over me by the other, are accomplished" (256/279).

Seen as a gathering of unique sons, the human race is a family composed of "brothers," that is, of responsible but created freedoms turned to one another's face. Their coming from "(the) fathers" constitutes their unity, quite different from the generic unity of a universal essence instantiated by many individuals. The explanation of humankind as fraternity implies a reinterpretation of the metaphysical relation that is the central topic of

---

47 "If biology furnishes us the prototypes of all these relations, this proves, to be sure, that biology does not represent a purely contingent order of being, unrelated to its essential production. But these relations free themselves from their biological limitation" (256–57/279). On 189–90/213–14 the transbiological meaning of fraternity is implied in the thesis that *all* humans are "brothers."

Totality and Infinity: neither isolated individuals related to others by dual relationships nor members only of social totalities,
we form an originary—or preoriginary—community of unique
"brothers." Although it is clear that the concept of such a fraternity presupposes transcendence and the face, some sentences
suggest that the latter are also conditioned by the former, for
instance, when Levinas writes: "The human I is posited in fraternity: that all men are brothers is not added to man as a moral
conquest, but constitutes his ipseity. Because my position as an
I is *effectuated* already in fraternity, the face can present itself
to me as a face" (257/279-80).

When Levinas, in the last lines of part F, states that "the
erotic and the family" open the dimension of a future in which
desire and the Good can triumph, he does not clarify to what
extent the categories of the erotic and the family are taken in
a restricted sense or rather are meant as metaphors for moral
or religious communities, spiritual families, traditions, and prac-
tices. "Sisters" are not mentioned, and "maternity" is mentioned
only once, with hardly any explanation (255/278). The "paternal
Eros" (256/279) reminds us of Plato's transformation of love into
a passion for good education.[48]

In stressing several aspects of Levinas's text that cannot be
understood in a biological or strictly familial sense, I do not want
to suggest that biology, sexuality, procreation, and family life
are unimportant elements in the history of responsibility and
goodness, which Levinas opposes to the cruelty of world history;
rather, I would like to stress that the end of *Totality and Infinity*
presents us with new tasks for philosophy. If the family (or the
"family") is not an organic part of the state or the city but rather
a prepolitical and "prehistoric" dimension with a time of its own,
we must ask exactly how the biologically conditioned family,
several sorts of spiritual families, and especially the filiations of
which the history of morality is composed relate to one another
and to the history of politics, culture, civilization, and positive
religion.

The closing pages of section 4 give an answer to the question
that emerged at the end of section 3 by showing that the time
of fecundity—the infinite but discontinuous time of others' taking
over the responsibility of desire—makes a true judgment about
good and evil possible. Such a time differs radically from the
continuous temporality that is typical for consciousness and

---

48 *Symposium* 206b ff.

memory, for several possibilities of fulfillment, and for the production of works. Memory unfolds the past in the present, and
the fulfillment of possibilities extends the present to the future,
but the distance implied in such deployments is not enough for
real newness or radical change; they only unfold the moments
of a fate or destiny that develops itself inexorably. Since the
other—"my brother"—refuses to become part of a whole, he escapes also from the temporal totalization that would reduce him
to a mere element or means. The other is the origin of a discontinuous time in which no event is definitive. The "infinition" of
fecundity surpasses all possibilities of past and present by its
openness to other destinies. Beyond his own death, a "father"
receives new chances in the existence of his "sons." They give
him—in the strongest sense of the word—a new beginning, thanks
to an interval of time separating his and their life. Beyond death
there is a continuity on the basis of discontinuity. The infinition
of fecund temporality is the time of real death and resurrection:
the past can still change its meaning, and the future is a new
chance for desiring and being good.

A clear example of such a transformation is found in the
possibility of *pardon:* a bad deed or event that cannot be denied
can be purified and inverted. The past is not abolished, but it
might receive a new meaning. If pardoned, a deed can become
part of a "history" that is better than a series of innocent events.
Thus, the infinition of this temporality permits revisions of the
judgments pronounced by world history: the justifications and
condemnations of which the history of works is composed are
overcome by judgments that testify to the ultimate standard—
the standard of the Good itself.[49]

The infinition of time does not, however, guarantee the victory of the Good over all injustices in judging and practice. Our
dream of a completely just and peaceful eternity expresses our
desire for a completion beyond the infinite time of risky goodness
and possible crimes. The eschatological peace announced in the
preface demands still another time: instead of the ongoing discontinuity of innumerable recommencements, such a peace postulates a "sealed" or completed time, an eternity of "messianic"
peace.

How must we understand our desire for such an eternity?
How can we—within philosophy—give an interpretation to the

---

49 Cf. also 207–8/231; Levinas insists on the exteriority of pardon,
judgment, and justice.

prophecies about a messianic time from which the possibility of evil will have been excluded? Is that eternity another name for the extreme vigilance of any conscience that is as pure and as universally responsible as that of the "Messiah"—a conscience not bound by any specific time or context and thus timeless or "eternal"—or must we think of yet another temporality beyond the time of filiality? The phrase with which Levinas postpones an answer to this question ("this problem exceeds the bounds of this book") could mean that an answer demands new analyses, but it might also indicate the extra-philosophical character of the prophetic messianism commented upon by the Talmud and by Levinas himself in various "Talmudic lectures."[50]

Before considering the conclusions with which *Totality and Infinity* closes, we might look back on its course as designed by the succession of its sections, parts, and subsections. Although it is characteristic for this book that it spirals constantly around a whole constellation of new concepts and perspectives, I have tried to detect also a linear progression in it, thereby partially reducing its originality and its difference from more traditional texts of philosophy. Continuing this procedure, which has some didactic advantages, I would like to stress here what may be considered to be the (or one?) main line that gives unity to the analyses of *Totality and Infinity*.

If we consider the first section to be a long introduction that summarizes the whole, we can divide the book in roughly two halves. The first encompasses then sections 2 and 3 A and B, whereas the second half runs from 3 C (prepared by 3 B.6–8) until the end of section 4. Subsection 3 B.6. is a sort of turning point, while 3 B.7–8 prepare 3 C. In the first half of *Totality and Infinity*, Levinas analyses the three moments of the metaphysical relation: ego's economy (2), the other (3), and their asymmetric relation (passim, but especially in 2 D.5–6 and E and 3). The second half develops from this "principle" the key concepts of a "first philosophy" radically different from Western ontology. After a short treatment of the transition from the intersubjective relation between ego and the other to the society of humankind in 3.6, a critique of the will (3 B.7ff.) reintroduces ego's finite

---

50 Cf. *DL* 83–129 and the two books *Quatre lectures talmudiques* (1968) and *Du sacré au saint* (1977), gathered in *Nine Talmudic Readings* (1990).

freedom. Whereas, in section 2, it had been analyzed as the enjoyment of a dependent independence, it is now thematized as the responsible confrontation with its own body, its works, the world, exterior constraints, death, suffering, and history in light of the other's and the others' faces. Since ego's desire and responsibility are the only presence of the Good, they must be recognized somehow if there is any hope that the Good indeed will win. Ego's nonegoistic apology cannot be silenced ultimately. However, because world history, as the history of works, does not recognize the truth of the will and its expressions, a "beyond" of history must be sought—a time of the Good, a "history" in which justice is done to morality and justice itself, a "judgment" recognizing the absolute transcendence of responsibility. This time beyond history is found in a time beyond suffering, and death is to be fecund in "sons" who continue the "tradition" of responsibility and justice by new (and, thus, discontinuous) commencements. Since all human beings are elected as such unique "sons," the time of fecundity (the "tradition of the Good," we might say) is the dimension of humankind as a prepolitical and an-archic fraternity. In this dimension, only a peace beyond the alternation of political wars and peaces is possible. In this time, humanity can still become good.

| Conclusions

The character of the conclusions is not so different from that of the introductory section 1. They can be read as a review of the main topics and theses forwarded and analyzed in the preceding pages: ego's freedom, the Other's exteriority and the infinite, transcendence, language, work and expression, subjectivity, the family and the state, and so on. A striking feature of these last pages is, however, their outright ontological character. Although some of the passages, like many of the preceding pages, express the necessity of a thought beyond ontology,[51] "Being," "truth," "the truth of Being," and the "logic" of Being play key roles, and Levinas's metaphysics seems to present itself as a new form of ontology. (Since the overcoming of ontology, which is already underway in *Totality and Infinity,* becomes one of the most important aspects of Levinas's works, I have tried to avoid the language of ontology as much as possible. However, the text of

---

51 See, for instance 267^{30}, 268^{27-30}, $269^5/291^{31}$, 292^{25-29}, 293^{3-4}.

Totality and Infinity itself still uses two different languages, and this is one of the reasons for its difficulty.)

A second feature of the conclusions lies in their focus on the concept of *exteriority*. While the preface concentrated on the question of true peace, and the introductory section 1 dealt with transcendence (desire, otherness, infinite), the conclusions seem to intend primarily a justification of the subtitle of *Totality and Infinity: an essay on exteriority.*[52] The way this is done could be characterized as a plea for *another* ontology rather than as a defense of a thought *beyond* ontology. In light of the first subsections of section 1, we could even interpret these conclusions as the sketch of a new onto-*logic:* an ontologic of the absolute relation between the Same and the Other (or between finite interiority and infinite exteriority), which should replace the Western onto-logic of monistic universality.

This approach is, for instance, rather obvious in the very beginning of the first conclusion, "From the Like to the Same" (265/289–90), where Levinas summarizes his book in the thesis that the "social relation" (another name for the "metaphysical relation" or "transcendence") is "the logical frame of Being" (in which "Being" [*l'être*] encompasses the universe of beings as well as the beingness of all beings). In preparation for the following "conclusions," which focus upon exteriority, this first conclusion contrasts the formal logic of the traditional ontology—said to be a logic of genera, species, and individual indiscernibles—with the logic of *interiority* and self-identification-from-within, which section 2 has shown to be constitutive for the Same, i.e., for the I as relating to the Other in the face-to-face, and therefore also for the *exteriority* of the Other, whose otherness implies a separation from the independent Same.

The overtly ontological title of the second conclusion, "Being Is Exteriority" (266–67/290–91), is repeated twice in the text and paraphrased by the sentence: "The very exercise of its being [i.e., its mode of transitive being] consists in exteriority, and no thought could better obey being [notice the Heideggerian expression!] than by allowing itself to be dominated by this exteriority" (266/290). Levinas resumes here the ontological significance of the face as the revelation of an exteriority that essentially is authority and superiority and, thus, reveals the "truth of being": Being surprises us not only as exterior but as

---

52 Cf. 279/303: "The present work has sought to describe metaphysical exteriority."

a "curvature of the space" under the influence of the divine. Toward the end of this conclusion on the essential superiority of Being, however, Levinas calls this truth of Being a "surplus of truth over Being and its idea," a surplus—revealed in the curvature of space—that "is, perhaps, the very presence of God." Notwithstanding Levinas's opposing, in this section again, Heidegger's ontology, he still seems to adopt the basic assumptions of any ontology, although he already tries to break out—in a way akin to the Platonic one—by trying the thought of a "*surplus* over Being," which, however, is not yet clearly distinguished from "Being *as* exteriority."

Levinas's third conclusion, entitled "The Finitude and the Infinite" (268–69/292), calls that "surplus" "the surplus of the Good over Being" and insists once more on the separation and independence of the finite subject vis-à-vis the infinite. Against the tradition of a philosophy that sees the finite as a negation or as a diminished or limited form of the infinite—and its monistic nostalgia for a return to the all-encompassing origin—Levinas affirms the radical exteriority of the created (not emanated) liberty, whose desire is not nostalgic, since it transcends all satisfaction.

The fourth conclusion, "Creation" (269–70/293–94), continues the characterization of the relation between the finite and the infinite through the consideration of an enigmatic concept that emerged several times in the course of *Totality and Infinity* without being analyzed extensively: the concept of creation. Now, however, Levinas turns against ontology because of its inability to understand the independence and separation of finite freedom from the infinity of God. The "principle" (270/294), which is "the prime intelligible" (270/293), namely the other human (*Autrui*), has revealed that the autonomous atheistic ego owes its freedom to a preceding (preoriginary or preautonomous) heteronomy. Before the possibility of *Sinngebung* or any other initiative—that is, in an absolute passivity without preexisting substantiality or materiality—I have already been constituted a responsible, transcendent, desiring subject, independent, free. This strange structure cannot be understood within the horizons of the logic of totality, which goes together with ontology. Levinas still seems to have a reservation: "If the notions of totality and being cover one another, the notion of the transcendent places us beyond the categories of Being." But the remainder of his conclusion shows that the "if" is rhetorical; according to Levinas, ontology necessarily blurs the separation between God and the finite by seeing the latter as originally contained in the infinite Being from which all finite beings emanate. Instead of such a synthesis (in which God—as "highest being" or summit—becomes as finite as the rest), the concept of a creation *ex nihilo* expresses the absolute exteriority and "atheistic" independence of a finite responsibility.[53]

Having shown how central exteriority is in (1) the constitution of ego's interiority, (2) the Other's height, and (3–4) the transcendence of the finite to the infinite, Levinas returns to the concreteness of exteriority in the encounter with the Other. In contrast to the fourth conclusion, the fifth, "Exteriority and Language" (270–73/294–97), continues to use the ontological language of the first three conclusions. Against the totalizing philosophies from Plato to Heidegger—Heidegger's thought of Being is here characterized most clearly as a philosophy of totality—Levinas defends "an ontology that is not equivalent to panoramic existence and its disclosure" (270/294). The primordiality of vision and its paradigmatic function for intelligibility conditions the panoramic perspective in which the exterior is experienced as adequate to the interiority of ideas. Husserl's theory of *Selbstgegenheit* and the intentional correlation of the noesis and the noema is only a modern version of that tradition. The face-to-face of language as address and invocation expresses the unconquerable exteriority of all discourse and the superiority of the other's speech, which thereby is an instruction (*enseignement*). A different ontology than the traditional one should show that the Being of beings (*l'exister même de l'être* or *l'être de l'étant*, 270–71/294) is the scattering of a panoramic totality into a multitude of beings who are "personally present in their speech" (273/296). This form of presence, self-presentation through the expression of the face, is once more put forward in the sixth conclusion, "Expression and Image" (273–74/297–98), and, as the true signification and key to morality, is opposed to the meaning of intuition, imaging, and *poièsis* constitutive for politics, culture, and history.

The title of the seventh conclusion, "Against the Philosophy of the Neuter" (274–75/298–99), indicates the polemical character of this section. The impersonality of Hegel's reason and of

---

53 Two excellent articles have been written on Levinas's conception of creation: R. Burggrave, "Het scheppingsbegrip bij Levinas: bipolariteit van autonomie en heteronomie," *Bijdragen* 42 (1981): 366–91; and O. Gaviria Alvarez, "L'idée de création chez Levinas: une archéologie," *Revue Philosophique de Louvain* 72 (1974): 509–38.

Heidegger's Being has suppressed the truth of the face-to-face and therewith the possibility of language, morality, and philosophy as the search for human wisdom. Instead, the collective We of politics, the neutralization of the personal in art, and an aesthetic conception of nature have conquered our culture. But obedience to these figures of the Anonymous sacrifices, as do all forms of idolatry, the very essence of the human, which is always personal and unique.

Levinas reminds the reader that the main purpose of section 2 was to show that the human subject in no way can be reduced to any structure, situation, or constellation of elements or nature. Since the interpretation of Being as impersonal suppresses its being also the Being of personal, unique, free, moral, and transcendent beings, it restricts Being to an infrahuman—and certainly not a superhuman—mode of Being. The ontological primacy of the Neuter is, thus, equivalent with the celebration of the faceless as the paradigm of all Being. This is what Levinas calls "materialism," and in this sense he criticizes Heidegger's concentration on the Fourfold as a "shameless materialism" (*un materialisme honteux*) because it is dominated by a *logos* that does not come from anybody and thus can neither be speech, nor language, nor face or call.

The eighth, ninth, and eleventh conclusions, "Subjectivity" (275–76/299–300), "The Maintainance of Subjectivity, The Reality of the Inner Life and the Reality of the State, The Meaning of Subjectivity" (276–78/300–301), and "Freedom Invested" (278–81/302–4), focus on the consequences of the thesis that "Being is exteriority" (the second conclusion) for human subjectivity. These three conclusions can be read as Levinas's retrieval of egology in the frame of his nonegological metaphysics. The eighth conclusion summarizes the analyses of section 2, which were already resumed in the first conclusion, but it stresses how ego's "atheistic" interiority by an individuation from within (and not by participation, emanation, or division) enables the subject to listen to the other and to receive him/her as a guest. The ninth conclusion gives a brief account of the pages that I have called the second part of *Totality and Infinity:* as the sole source of goodness toward the other and of justice to all, ego's unicity is demanded for their victory. Ego's apology is not a clandestine subjectivism in confrontation with the powers of the state but rather the source of a moral future that delivers the subject from fate and facticity. The infinite time of fecundity transcends the dimension of politics by permitting the subject to be another desiring I.

By its very title, "Beyond Being," the tenth conclusion (278/ 301-2) announces that Levinas ultimately chooses to abandon the frame of any ontology. Aristotle's analogy of Being concentrates on the solid thing as exposed to an objectifying eye; Kant's interpretation of the object sees perduration as its essential structure; for Spinoza, Being is equivalent to universalizing thought. If Being must, indeed, be characterized as objective and perduring thingness, the exteriority of the other's face proves that Being cannot be the first and ultimate. To exist [to be?!] as transcendence to the exterior is to surpass existence and death in the service of the Good. Starting from being, the subject transcends its own being. Being surpasses its own perduration. Under the title "Freedom Invested" (278-81/302-4), but without using the word "investiture," the eleventh conclusion summarizes the consequences of Being's exteriority for the notion of freedom. Against the modern philosophies of freedom exemplified in Heidegger and Sartre, Levinas firmly states that human freedom cannot justify itself. Its finitude is not due to its inability to choose or found itself—and this limitation is not tragic at all!—but rather to its being founded and justified through an exteriority that cannot be grasped by vision, knowledge, or any other form of appropriation. If the relation to the face constitutes the ultimate exteriority of Being, then morality or goodness is—in the ontological language used again in this conclusion—"the truth of Being." "To be in truth" is, then, "to encounter the Other without allergy, that is in justice" (280/303). The justification of freedom—which otherwise would be arbitrary, violent, and shameless—comes from "morality" or "the ethical." If *logos* is interpreted as reason, no ontology can have the ultimate answer, for reason's universality is not exterior enough to justify freedom. A metaphysical transcendence is necessary, and this is not found in vision or knowledge but only in respect for *that which is.* "Truth as respect of being, that is the meaning of metaphysical truth"; it may be called "morality," and Levinas can thus write: "In morality alone it [freedom] is put into question. Morality thus presides over the work of truth" (280/304). In this sense of "morality" as the ultimate truth of metaphysics (or "true ontology"), we may conclude: "Morality is not a branch of philosophy, but first philosophy" (281/ 304).

The last conclusion, "Being as Goodness—the I—Pluralism— Peace" (281-84/304-7), gives one of the possible syntheses of *Totality and Infinity* by starting again from "metaphysics as desire" and finishing with the biological fecundity of the family as the model for a "general fecundity" that escapes from the heroic but monotonous realm of unjust politics. The ontological structures of metaphysics are stressed. Being (or "the production of Being") is primarily the metaphysical movement of transcendence, desire engendering desire, Being for the Other, goodness beyond happiness. In a sentence that could be developed into a new sort of *analogia entis,* the face-to-face is called the "original production of Being towards which all the possible collocations of the terms [such as coexistence, *Mitsein,* knowledge, or participation] refer" (*remontent,* 281–82/303). The ego is absolutely needed for the goodness of this transcendence; subjectivity is, thus, not dead at all but necessarily present as free and conscious (independent and enjoying) hospitality. Transcendence implies pluralism but excludes the ultimacy of a panoramic perspective. The plurality of Being as going from me to the Other does not permit the superior truth of a higher perspective unengaged in the infinite demands of the Good. The eschatological peace announced in the preface is not possible within the horizons of the historic war and peace game but only in the discontinuous time of the family and human fraternity.

Autrement qu'être ou au-delà de l'essence, which was published in 1974, can be considered as the second opus magnum of Levinas. In more than one regard, it continues and develops the main ideas of *Totalité et Infini* and answers—mostly in an implicit way—some criticisms that were brought up against the first book.[1] It is, at the same time, an independent whole, which states the problem of *Totality and Infinity* in a different manner and develops those problems from other perspectives.

It is impossible to understand the philosophy of Emmanuel Levinas (or any philosophy) if it is isolated from the prephilosophical life (the experience, conviction, events, and the spiritual climate) in which it has its roots. The interpreter of a philosophy does not, however, need to consider explicitly its philosophical and nonphilosophical presuppositions if he/she and most other readers share them with the author of the interpreted text. One can legitimately state that Levinas's thought is an expression of the spiritual climate of our time,

---

1 The most important, in fact the only, critique with which Levinas argues—in an implicit way—seems to me to be the long essay of Jacques Derrida, "Violence et métaphysique: Essai sur la pensée d'Emmanuel Levinas." This critique appeared first in the *Revue de Métaphysique et de Morale* 69 (1964): 322–54, 425–73, and was reprinted in J. Derrida, *L'écriture et la différence* (Paris: Du Seuil, 1967), 117–228; cf. *Writing and Difference*, 79–153. A respectful dissension, which does not exclude affinity, is to be found in the short contribution under the title "Tout autrement," which Levinas wrote in an issue of *L'Arc* devoted to Derrida (no. 54, 1973) and which is also included in *Noms propres* (81–89).

held in common by all those who were educated in the Greek and European traditions, who went through the Nietzschean crisis of our culture, and who suffered the wars and persecutions of the twentieth century. A particular trait of Levinas's *Lebenswelt* that he does not share with all contemporary thinkers is, however, that he is a Jew who, since his youth in Lithuania and the Ukraine, has been familiar with the Bible and who, since the end of the Second World War, has intensely studied the tradition of the Talmud.

The stress that Levinas lays on morality and religion has caused some misunderstandings. Some readers consider his philosophy to be too pious or even to be a sort of theology. Yet few contemporary philosophers have criticized the praxis and the idea of traditional theology more radically than has Levinas; and, although no philosophy can or may free itself from its prephilosophical, and therefore naive, convictions, Levinas has stressed more than once the fact that he is not a theologian but a philosopher, one who tries philosophically to explain and to justify only a part of his convictions and positions.[2] Is this self-interpretation accurate? The answer to this question must be found through a philosophical analysis of the works themselves. We should thus read them as philosophical works that have won a place in contemporary philosophy. Notwithstanding their surprising originality, they belong to the tradition of Husserlian and post-Husserlian phenomenology. The relation between Levinas's philosophy and phenomenology is, however, a very special one because it is at the same time a radical critique of the main phenomenological presuppositions. A thorough acquaintance with Husserl's and Heidegger's thought is necessary to understand his "method," but it demands a special explanation beyond this. Although Levinas does not dwell very much on methodological reflections, concentrating instead on direct

---

2 Cf. TH 110: "My point of departure is absolutely non-theological. This is very important to me; it is not theology which I do, but philosophy." In a conversation of 1 May 1975 on the occasion of his receiving an honorary doctorate in Leiden, Levinas repeated: "I have never even thought that I was doing theology. Whatever my experiences and prephilosophic sources may have been, I have always had this idea (a bit mad perhaps): that I was doing or was endeavouring to do philosophy, even in commenting on the biblical text which called this forth." This conversation has been published under the title "Questions et réponses," in *DDVI* 128–57.

descriptions and analyses of human "phenomena" and relations, the themes of his work are so fundamental that these
analyses are themselves a sort of *"Fundamentalbetrachtung."*
However, as we will see later on, even the words used
here ("fundamental," "phenomena," "phenomenology") are
inadequate to characterize Levinas's way of thinking, for
they belong precisely to that manner of thinking which he
radically questions and criticizes.

Right from the beginning of his work—in his dissertation[3]
and in his early studies on Husserl and Heidegger[4]—Levinas
formulated a certain critique that he has since developed and
deepened: Western philosophy is an ontology; it is therefore
incapable of talking about transcendence. It transforms not
only God but also human beings, even the thinking subject
itself, into moments or "adventures" of Being.

Totality and Infinity described ontology as a philosophical
totalitarianism or as an egology and made way for a philosophy of the infinite by means of descriptions of the human
visage. The philosophy "beyond the *ousia*"[5] developed in
Totality and Infinity was called "metaphysics." As far as I
can see, the word "metaphysics" itself does not come up in
Otherwise Than Being, but Levinas does again criticize Western ontology, including Heidegger's thought concerning Being. Again he investigates the possibilities of a philosophy
of transcendence. It is possible that he avoids the word
"metaphysics" in order to prevent the impression that he
has any intention of restoring the old metaphysics attacked
by Husserl and Heidegger. Along with Nietzsche, Levinas
is convinced that every philosophy or conception that attempts to explain our world and existence in the light of
an other-world (*Hinterwelt*) is definitively exhausted. The
God who dwelled above the earth is dead. Actually, he was
never really God. The way in which he was talked about,

---

3 *La théorie de l'intuition dans la phénoménologie de Husserl* (Paris:
Alcan, 1930). The second (1963) and the third (1970) editions are distrib-
uted by Vrin. See also note 1 above.

4 "Martin Heidegger et l'ontologie," *Revue Philosophique de la
France et de l'Etranger* (1932) and "L'œuvre d'Edmond Husserl" in the
same journal (1940), reprinted in *EDHH* 7–76.

5 This expression, quoted in Greek in *Totalité et Infini,* is translated
in *Autrement qu'être* by "au-delà de l'essence" (in which "essence" must
be heard in the Heideggerian sense of all-ruling Being). The Platonic
text to which it alludes is *Republic* 509b.

thematized, and demonstrated killed him more radically than the so-called atheism of those for whom the human person was always the most important being.[6]

In *Otherwise Than Being*, we find a whole series of words that were scarcely or never used in *Totality and Infinity* (such as *subjectivité, proximité, obsession, substitution, otage, persécution, illéité, énigme*), whereas key words of the earlier work (such as *totalité, extériorité, séparation, investiture, hauteur*) seldom or never appear in the later one. A partial explanation of this difference in terminology can be found in the fact that Levinas has chosen another perspective in *Otherwise Than Being* for his approach to transcendence and the infinite. In *Totality and Infinity*, the central place was taken by the Other and its visage; in *Otherwise Than Being*, Levinas meditates on the "position" and the meaning of the subject; of the self who meets the other.

The two books do not differ only in their problematic and focus. The critical interpretation of Western ontology has developed and become more radical; ideas and formulations that in *Totality and Infinity* were still too dependent upon the ontological tradition are now purified, and critical objections against the content of the first book are answered. Whereas *Totality and Infinity* attempted, with Plato, to think beyond the totality of all beings[7] and closed with eschatological questions, *Otherwise Than Being* goes back to a sort of (under)ground: it attempts to trace down the underlying "fundament" and subject of the various relations that it describes.

The first chapter (3–25/3–20) gives an outline of the whole book. It begins with the question of how it is possible to think transcendence. This question is already suggested by the title of the book: How is it possible to think or to speak beyond (*au-delà*) Being? One can read this first chapter as an analysis of what one may with certain reservations call the "conditions of possibility" of the thinking of transcendence. In order to think transcendence, one has to think "something" that "is" otherwise (*autrement*) than Being or beyond (*au delà*) Being. This statement presupposes a certain concept of "Being." The

---

6 Cf. *AE* 10/*OB* 8 (against the idea of a *Hinterwelt*) and the last paragraphs of the book: "In this work which does not seek the restoration of any ruined concept...; after the death of a certain god inhabiting the world behind the scenes (*les arrière-mondes*)" (*AE* 233/*OB* 185).

7 Cf. *Phaedo* 61e; 117c; *Symposium* 212a; *Republic* 484c; *Phaedrus* 250c.

word "Being" stands here for the whole Western philosophical tradition, in particular as it was interpreted and recaptured by Heidegger. "Being" (*das Sein*) is the realm or the order of the active essence or *Wesen* (in French *essence* or—with a neologism—"essance," having a transitive connotation), in whose "phosphorence" the phenomena appear and from which they receive their truth. In order to think that which is beyond or otherwise (than Being), we must first reflect upon the thinking of Being itself, i.e., upon ontology and upon the way of Being of the essence that comes to the fore within its boundaries. It is, however, impossible to free our thought altogether from the structures that reign within the frame of ontology because another order—a world "behind" Being—does not exist. The only possibility of transcending Being and ontological thinking would be a movement by which we point to that which "is" differently than any being and transcends even Being itself: a sort of "An-denken" expressing itself not in a superficial way but "an-archically" (*anarchiquement*). Such a discourse would not claim, as ontology does, to manifest the origin or *archè* of its "object." Rather, in close contact with the only world that exists, the world as lived by human individuals in history, it would search for the conditions and the presuppositions of ontology and its grounding *archai.*

Various points of departure present themselves for a description of Being's reality. Characteristic of any ontological description is an inner coherence, a systematic unity under the light of Being, within which all beings and all formal elements of Being are gathered. The way in which Levinas describes the order of Being is a sort of structural analysis of ontology. He considers the ontological meaning of consciousness, reason, sensation, corporeity, subjectivity, freedom, death, war, peace, etc. and makes it clear that neither a single being, nor the totality of beings, nor Being itself is capable of taking up the role of an absolute primary ground.

The core of Levinas's criticism of ontology was already formulated in his first studies on Husserl and Heidegger.[8] The Husserlian concept of *intentionality* freed philosophy from the constraint of the subject-object schema. Husserl was right in seeing that not every intention is an objectifying one. In

---

8 See A. Peperzak, "Phenomenology—Ontology—Metaphysics: Levinas' Perspective on Husserl and Heidegger," *Man and World* 16 (1983): 113-27.

this sense, he initiated the overcoming of the monopoly of representational thinking. Meaning is not exclusively found in the objectified contents of consciousness: it can and must also be discovered in intentions and implications that do not appear in the same way as a representation does. The anonymous intentions by which representational intentions are codetermined constitute meanings that can be made conscious by a second reflection and thereafter can be represented in a new representation. The making explicit of these implicit meanings, however, is an endless process due to the fact that every intention has an infinity of horizons. Moreover—and this is decisive—there are many intentions that cannot at all be considered as representations.

Although Husserl's conception of intentionality can be interpreted as a universal characterization of all human relations to some X, he himself stressed the primordiality of the *"meinende Intentionen."* His theory of intentionality was thus dominated by the model of knowing. In every intention, he saw a variation of the structure of representing. Living presence (*lebendige Gegenwart*), a presence that can always be re-presented through memory, was for him the key concept of reality. Being is presence, being present for a consciousness that appropriates it by (re)constituting the given in the knowledge of what it is. To abolish the tyranny of the theoretical, it is not sufficient to extend the doctrine of intentionality to practical or emotional intentions, even if these are considered as more fundamental than the theoretical intentions. For it is precisely the representional *structure,* dominating not only intending (*meinen*) and knowing but affectivity and the practical realm, that must be brought into question.

It is in light of representional thinking that the relation between subject and reality is interpreted as the relation of a consciousness and the presence of something given. The given presents itself as a "corporeal" presence (*leibhaftige Gegenwart*) occurring in a certain sort of time, the moments of which can be gathered in the presence of an all-encompassing glance through retention and protention. The position of the subject in this ontological time is that of a free consciousness that is aware of its freedom and wants to realize it by returning to its own self. This self-identification implies a grasping of the phenomena. In the Heideggerian explanation of *Dasein*, the same structure is dominant: the consciousness, which in an active and transitive way "ex-sists" Being, has a hold on itself in light of the collectible time of its relation to the active essence of Being.

The critique that is sketched here has been extended in *Otherwise Than Being* to a series of meditations on various themes of ontology.[9] Being is a gathering and an interweaving of all beings; in it each being and every occurrence fulfills its place and function on a level with every other occurrence and being. Every attempt to escape the dominance of Being, every free action and every form of negativity, is immediately devoured by the rushing "essence" in which everything is equal, irrespective of differences. Mediation and dialectic are the devices by means of which Being fills up all the gaps that negativity breaks open.

The time of Being is the time of its deployment. "Timing" (*Zeitigung,* ripening) is the primordial light, to which phenomena are indebted for their appearance. The way in which Being presents itself is the illumination that keeps the phenomena distinct and brings them forth in their truth. Active essence is essentially the presentation, collection, and interpretation of the phenomena: *phenomenology.* Time, in which Being develops its meaning, can collect itself through memory (retention and protention). Active essence is dispersion *and* recollection into presence.

On the side of the subject, this process is sensation:[10] an experience of the flowing of the inner time-consciousness. The qualitative variations of sensation (*sensibilité*) are experienced as modifications of flowing temporality; they are adverbial modes of the active essence that expresses itself in its verbal form. In art this (ad)verbiality is expressly displayed.[11] It is also possible, however, to grant autonomy to these variations. As a system of names (*noms*), language is suited to the identification of certain things and experiences. These are no longer adverbially experienced but are ascertained by "the Said" (*le Dit*) of a thesis, an account, or an announcement, through which time is collected and a being is captured in words.[12] On the basis of the flowing

---

9 Cf. *AE* 3ff./*OB* 3ff.: The order and "archy" of Being is contrasted in the first chapter as the system of "inter-esse" against dis-interestedness.

10 Cf. the extensive analyses of *sentir, sensation,* and *sensibilité* in *AE* 39ff. and 77ff./*OB* 31ff. and 61ff.

11 Cf. *AE* 44, 49, 51–52/*OB* 34–35, 38, 39–41.

12 *AE* 46/*OB* 36; Levinas uses the expressions *epos, kérygme, fable, doxa,* and *narration* as synonyms.

stream of time in which the truth of Being manifests itself, the phenomenon shows and identifies itself, thanks to the "already said" (*le déjà-dit*) through which it can be grasped and named. Being is inseparable from its being said (*AE* 47ff./*OB* 38ff.). Being and wording belong together; the active essence cannot be separated from a verbally pronounced meaning. If beings appear as identities, they owe it to a noun that encloses them in the *horismos* of a (fore)word which has already been pronounced.

The time structure of the active essence conditions the accomplishment of the highest interest of the subject as consciousness: through collecting and identifying, it orders the entirety of all beings in the pronouncement of a distinct system. In the light of the truth, consciousness constitutes the edifice of reality within which it establishes itself. Thus, consciousness possesses itself and acquires the highest degree of certainty. The subject triumphs after a period of seeming (only temporary) passivity; by means of memory and interpretation, it takes the temporal dispersion, and all events that occurred in it, back into itself. Thinking is remembrance, and thought is a recollection. The order of Being is an eternal return of the Same. This is the Western conception of freedom and subjectivity.

The diagnosis sketched here is not contradicted by the continually repeated attempt of Western philosophy to transcend the order of beings on the basis of one ultimate ground. Indeed the ground, the principle or the *archè*, is necessary as the condition of the free self-possession in which consciousness can take pleasure in itself. For without an unshakable fundament or a sustaining and surrounding ground that is at the same time cause and end, it would be impossible for the subject to oversee the universe of beings and grasp them by a conceptual knowledge. A thematic and systematizing consciousness is grounding and fundamental. It demands an architectonic and contests every sort of anarchy.

In accord with the way of being of the subject that has just been described, ontology interprets Being as a conatus through which beings exist and persist in their being for themselves. Due to the fact that a multitude of beings exist next to and opposite one another, their concern for themselves results necessarily in a war of all against all (*AE* 5ff./*OB* 3ff.). On the basis of the ontological presuppositions indicated above, this battle can only be ended when the fighters give it up for a form of shared and mutual self-interest. The overcoming of violence and the securing of rational peace—the traditional solution of political philosophy—are due to a dialectical *Aufhebung* of the antitheses within the sphere of the ontologically understood reality. Being holds war and peace together and rules over both. The incentive to peace remains selfish—striving toward a secure life in mutual exchange with other humans. The self-interested repression of violence secures rational coherence and association. Reason and politics fight every possible anarchy. The order that they assure is not grounded on the selflessness of *désinteressement* but on selfish interests.[13]

The decisive refutation of ontology is the emergence of the human Other. While *Totality and Infinity* placed the focus on the other's visage, the analyses of *Otherwise Than Being* concentrate on the Self (*le Soi*), which has from the beginning a special relation to the Other. Both books are concerned with the same relation. In the latter work, however, it is treated within the framework of the question, "Who am I?"

If the order of Being and grounding do not give others, the subject, and the Infinite their due, the question arises: Why is it that our discourse cannot liberate itself completely from the terminology and conceptuality of ontology? The answer is: It is due to the fact that the Said (*le Dit*) predominates. The realm of the Said (either as the confirmation of beings or as the verbalization of the active essence itself) is the realm of ontology.

The Saying (*le Dire*), however, which precedes the Said, is "more" than a collection of Being through verbs and nouns. It breaks through the range of the active essence. Its tense is a different one from that of the Said, in which everything becomes united and viewable. The time of the Saying is not to be won back through memory. During the Saying, time passes by; something gets irrevocably lost, and one grows older. But because of this, surprises and adventures are possible—surprises and adventures that stand in opposition to the monotony and boredom of ontological time, in which all things are synchronized by theoretical overviews or practical projects. The time of Saying resists the

---

13 The last of the five introductory devises of *Autrement qu'être* (vi/*OB* vii) is taken from Pascal's *Pensées:* "On s'est servi comme on a pu de la concupiscence pour la faire servir au bien public; mais ce n'est que feindre, et une fausse image de la charité; car au fond ce n'est que haine" ("They have used concupiscence as best as they could for the general good; but it is nothing but pretense and a false image of charity; for at bottom it is simply a form of hatred)." (Brunschvicg, n. 451; Lafuma, n. 210.)

simultaneousness of the Said and precedes it. It is an irreducible diachrony (*AE* 47–48/*OB* 37–38).

To break through the dominance of ontology, it is insufficient to uncover an Unsaid behind or under the Said. The direction of Heideggerian questioning remains caught in a play of the Said and the Unsaid, of uncovering and hiding. As phenomenology, this ontology is necessarily dialectic: a separation and association of the Said and the Unsaid. To transcend this ontology, one must question back in another way: in the direction of another time; in the direction of the diachronical time of Saying, thanks to which the synchrony of the said exists. The new dimension that is thus opened makes speaking about transcendence possible.

The Said is not opposed here to the written or the engraved (*l'écriture, le gramma*). For Levinas, writings are, just as much as a spoken text, elements of the ontological order, in which the living speaking that makes transcendence ring has lost its sound. The written is, however, more clearly identified by simultaneity than a speech. The book is an attempt to fill out and heal all gaps and breaches through a complete and permanent synthesis of what is to be said. The foundering of this effort, however, is manifested by the simple fact that a book demands interpretation and thus refers to people who can explain it through living words.[14]

The permanent presence of the written synthesis—a kind of *nunc stans* from which the whole can be systematically regarded—stands in glaring contradiction to the "unsystematic" meditations through which Levinas tries to expose speaking itself (*AE* 211, 217/*OB* 166–71). Thematization and systematicity, however, are typical modes of ontological understanding. They change their theme into something said. The peculiarity of Saying is different from reflective thinking. Saying is an exceptional form of "intentionality" because it exhibits no noetic-noematic structure. It happens when it is carried out. But one can only reach the Saying laterally—one can only think *back* to it. The anachronism of Saying can be shown only by a special form of philosophical reduction (*AE* 56/*OB* 43). The asking back from

---

14 Starting from the Socratic question, "What is?" Western philosophy has made the "what" and the "Being" of beings the central question and, at the same time, the model of all that is intelligible; it has forgotten, however, that this question, too, is addressed to someone. As a question, it is a call for help—*demande* and *prière* (*AE* 31/*OB* 24)—not (yet) a dialogue, for this presupposes reciprocity. The explicit rejection of dialogue as a primordial relation is found in *AE* 142 and 152–53/*OB* 111 and 119–20.

what is already said to the preceding saying is a most important task of philosophy. The accomplishment of this task is possible due to the fact that what is said maintains a trace of the act of saying to which it owes its existence (*AE* 62/*OB* 190 n.34). Through "reduction," philosophy goes backward into the time before the repeatable time of what is said. We are moving thus in two times, not simultaneously but switching off: we shuttle back and forth between the synchrony of ontological time and the anachrony of a time preceding it. The latter reveals itself in an untimely way via the restlessness of a coming back to that which cannot become a part of the Said (*AE* 57, 232/*OB* 43, 184). So long as we remain within the Said—in the framework of ontology—we have the Saying behind us; but we cannot remember it because it has its own uncollectible time. We point to Saying in criticizing the Said and its time, but the discussion or description of the Saying changes it into a Said, which demands a new critique in turn. As soon as we have said something about Saying, we must take our distance from this Said, too. Saying (*dire*) and unsaying or denying (*dédire*) fashion the halting way in which we think back on the preceding Saying. Every denial, however, is necessarily followed by a new Saying, which as a repetition indeed wants to say what was brought to the fore and then negated. This "saying again" (*redire*) is not a dialectical synthesis but rather a new attempt in the history of the continual Saying that suffers and settles its own (im)possibility.

"Reduction" thus does not lead to any better ontology, nor does it give the last word that could decipher the enigmatic "way of Being" of the Saying. For each last word belongs to the order of Being (*AE* 57/*OB* 44–45). The "truth" of the Saying "exists" in the ever-renewed attempt to bear "witness" (*témoignage*) to the preceding Saying; a "prophetism" (*prophétisme*) that—as the unending critique of the synchronous and the systematic—has some affinity with skepticism.

Otherwise Than Being can be read as a series of "intentional analyses" of Saying through which its implications and conditions are worked out. The attempt to summarize these analyses comes up against a great difficulty: the succession in which the various gradations and levels of Saying are demonstrated is not always the same. At first sight, the fundamental relations appear muddled.

Sometimes Levinas announces a sequence that signifies a deepening, for example in *AE* 232/*OB* 184, where he says that signification is analyzed as *proximity*, proximity as *responsibility* for the Other, responsibility as *substitution.* Precisely the same order of these three characteristics is found in *AE* 229/*OB* 182, where the relation between them is indicated by the expression "is only possible as" (*ne se peut comme*): "The proximity of the Other ... is possible only as responsibility for the Other, and responsibility is possible only as substitution for the Other." Is this a question of the relation between a reality and the conditions of its possibility? But *how* then does the one fit together into the other? Similar difficulties are presented by such formulations as "a signification, which is possible only as embodiment (*incarnation*)" (*AE* 87/*OB* 69) and "Only a subject which can eat can possibly be for the Other or signify" (*AE* 96–97/*OB* 76–77). In both cases, corporeity is "deduced" from significance, which was previously described as a relation of the One-for-the-Other.[15]

Most of the time, however, the various "moments" are placed next to one another, seemingly without allowing a definite order among them. The difficulty hinted at here and the question that rises out of that difficulty might have its ground in the need for an architectonic that is characteristic for the investigating, grounding, and constructing thought of ontology.[16] Levinas, however, is not a master-builder: he is rather a ground-worker who laterally digs passages against and under the Being of the world, laying open a texture of references. In connection to this, a before and after of the various layers present themselves, but they bear and call forth *each other,* without one being able to indicate precisely which one is first or second. In one of the few and short remarks on his own "method," Levinas expresses this as follows:

> The various concepts which the attempt to assert transcendence brings forth evoke reciprocal echoes. The necessities of the thematization in which they are said impose a division into chapters, although the themes in which these concepts come up do not lend themselves to a linear development. They actually cannot be isolated, for they cast their shadows and their reflection onto one another. (*AE* 23/*OB* 19)

The following attempt to present a resumé of the various aspects and levels of transcendence does not pretend to systematize the analyses that are carried out unsystematically. A sum-

---

15 *TI* xvii/28 is, as far as I can see, the only place where Levinas calls his procedure a "deduction." This word must here be understood as having a different meaning from the deduction against which he polemicizes in *TI* 76/103.

16 Cf. *AE* 86/*OB* 68: "The idea of an ultimate or primary sense is ontological."

mary violates the anarchy that belongs to Saying, but every Said does that. As an easy and fast way of introducing a work, it may be considered as tolerable.

As a pronouncing of Being and of beings by means of verbs and nouns, Saying is a speaking to *someone*—signifying or signification in an active and dative or donative sense. When I say something, it is not only and not primarily a matter of passing on pieces of information; rather, it is a matter of the communication itself—more so than and before any specific piece of information. Signification is thus not primarily the labeling of an object or of a truth but a pointing toward itself: signification of the signification.[17] Signification happens in the proximity of the Other. The other to whom I say something is close to me, my neighbor (*le prochain*). *Proximity* is an approach and contact. In approaching, I bare myself. Saying and signification is an *exposure* through which the center is transferred from me to the other. The structure of intentionality, by which consciousness relates the phenomena to itself, is put out of joint.[18] The activity of speaking robs the subject of its central position; it is the depositing (*déposition*) of a subject without refuge. The speaking subject is no longer by and for itself; it is for the other: obligated to response and responsible for the other, without ever having chosen this responsibility. Responsibility for the other without any preceding engagement is passivity in a special, exceptional sense. I am delivered to my neighbor. This passivity without choice can only be thought of as patience and pain or suffering, for otherwise—as enjoyer—I would myself still be the focus and neither handed over nor dedicated to the other. My suffering must even be—at least partially—meaningless. For were I able to grasp its meaning, I would be able to integrate it into my consciousness in the form of some piece of knowledge.[19]

With this analysis, we are far removed from the traditional identification of the subject with the cogito. "I speak" is not the same as "I think." The sovereign self-consciousness, as developed in

---

17 *AE* 153/*OB* 119–20. The second chapter of *AE* is devoted to the analysis of Saying. In this connection, the *time* of saying and the *subjectivity* of the saying subject especially are illuminated.

18 *Désarçonné, AE* 163/*OB* 127.

19 The analyses of proximity that are summarized here and in the following sections comprise the third and fourth chapters. The fourth chapter, "La substitution," is the heart ("la pièce centrale," *AE* ix/*OB* xii) of the book.

Kantian, Hegelian, and Husserlian idealism, is a narrowing of the one (*l'un*) and the only (*l'unique*) who speaks. In this form, it already belongs to the realm of the Said. On the other hand, even Heidegger and the structuralists misjudge the peculiarity of the passivity of the vulnerable self (*soi*) when they—again placing themselves on the level of the Said—conceive it to be completely dependent upon an anonymous "It that speaks" or on "the Language" as such.[20]

Since Socrates, the spiritual life of the West has concentrated on knowing and self-knowledge. Consciousness tried to ground and justify itself; for consciousness, images and ideas were only moments on the way to an enjoyment of its certain self-possession; freedom and *"Bei-sich-selbst-sein"* became the solution; and apology was the mode of philosophizing (*AE* 125–26, 256/*OB* 99–100). In contrast to this, the subject whose radical passivity is exhibited by the analysis of Saying is not consciousness or spirit but the one and only (*l'unique*) who is for-the-Other. This passivity is only possible in the form of a body that is animated and inspired by the orientation of the "One-for-the-Other." The passivity of Saying thus implies corporeity and the senses. Embodiment (*incarnation*) is a "condition of the possibility" and a necessary implication of the various ways of deprivation (such as pain, labor, decline), without which the relation of the One-for-the-Other would be changed into the selfishness of self-assertion. It now becomes understandable why the subject's time can only exist in diachrony and not in ontological synchrony: only in an irretrievable time is it possible to truly lose something or to give (*AE* 66/*OB* 51–52), to become old and to die.

Burrowing yet deeper, Levinas discovers in passivity an *accusation:* the obligation that is imposed on me in responsibility makes me guilty—a debtor—without my having made any choice. Beyond this, the responsibility grows to the measure in which I fulfill it. I can thus never pay off the burden of my guilt. There is always more demanded of me than I can accomplish. I stand under an accusation that I have not earned. In the accusation, Levinas uncovers *persecution* as a necessary presupposition: only a persecuted subject is a subject who—without so desiring, against his will—lives for the Other. The most extreme intensifying of passivity is, however, attained in the concept of *substitution:* the subject is so little its own possession and so greatly of

---

20 *AE* 59–60, 75/*OB* 46–48, 58–59. Cf. Heidegger's famous dictum, *"die Sprache spricht."*

and for the other that he/she is responsible for everything that
has to do with the other—not only for the other's misery but also
for his/her crimes—even for the outrage that the other initiates
against the suffering subject (*AE* 139-44/*OB* 108-13).

The outcome of the analyses that Levinas carries out is a
totally new understanding of the Self (*l'ipséité*). It can neither
encompass itself by an adequate (ap)perception or concept nor
rule over itself in sovereign freedom. As *sub-jectum*, it bears the
entire universe, without comprehending it (*AE* 147/*OB* 116). The
subject has no latitude, no free space to take any distance from
it and rejoin it (*AE* 136/*OB* 107). For this reason, it cannot find
peace in itself. As a sensibly affected body, one stands in an
immediate contact with one's neighbor, with whom one is obsessed (*AE* 126-29/*OB* 100-102). As a mother, I bear the other
within me, without fusing together (132-35/104-7). I cannot
grasp myself in thought; in saying, however, I expose myself.

The ethical terminology of which Levinas's philosophy of the
subject makes use does not point the way to a system of commands and prohibitions. It describes the situation of responsibility that precedes every ethics—a relation that "constitutes"
me even be fore I can ask: "How should I conduct myself?" or
"What should I do?" As an adequate description of the subject,
insofar as it escapes the order of Being,[21] ethical language is pre-
or meta-ontological. As characteristic of a situation that precedes
freedom, it is also pre- or meta-ethical. It does not spring from
a particular moral experience; rather, it answers the radical
questioning of the subject's mode of "being," which questioning
receives an incorrect solution in ontology. The classical dualism
of a spirit according to the model of an autonomous consciousness
and a body that is independent from that spirit is a misunderstanding. Human corporeity is animated by the relation of responsibility. This animation or *inspiration* constitutes the human
psychism (*le psychisme*). The other is "in" me without estranging
me from my freedom.[22] The "essence" of the subject is not *conatus
essendi* but inspired giving (*AE* 180/*OB* 141), not only in a purely
spiritual way—as a giving of the heart—but corporeally: to work

---

21 The vicarious subject is an exception; cf. *AE* 143, 149, 156/*OB*
112, 117, 121-22.

22 Cf. *AE* 69/*OB* 54: "service without slavery"; *AE* 134/*OB* 105: "nor
a slavish alienation, in spite of the gestation of the other in the same
which this responsibility for others signifies"; *AE* 143/*OB* 112: "Psychism is the other in the same without alienating the same."

with one's own hands for the other, to take the very bread from one's lips to still the other's hunger.[23]

These descriptions of the subject have undermined the ontological realm of self-conscious freedom. The Self (*le Soi*) lives on this side (*en deça*) without taking a place among ontologically comprehended beings. As an exception, it is a certain nowhere.[24] It lives in another time, without its own light (*AE* 20–23/*OB* 17–19), poor and vulnerable, not in the position to defend itself,[25] solitary and incomparable but without independence (*AE* 156–66/*OB* 121–29).

Nevertheless, the humility of this subjectivity is the point where the infinite reveals itself. The an-archy into which Being comes via the exception of subjectivity makes possible the revelation of the infinite as an enigma. It is of the utmost importance to make a sharp distinction between Levinas's speaking about the infinite and the theology of the Western tradition. As a thematizing within the frame of ontology, this theology localizes God as a (highest) Object in the eternal order of a "world behind the scenes" (*AE* 4, 6, 10, 193/*OB* 4, 5, 8). His representation through dogmas and formulas of belief destroys the religious situation.

Theological language rings untrue or becomes mystical (*AE* 148, 155/*OB* 196, n. 19; 197, n. 25). As ontological language, it belongs to the fabric of interests that dominate the state and its religious parallel, the church. Being incapable of disinterestedness,[26] theology impedes transcendence. If seen as an object opposite to a thinking subject that desires knowledge, God is the fulfillment of interested (or "erotic") need (*besoin*)—not the Absolute to which true desire refers (*le désir de l'Absolu*).[27] This God is the seducer who apes the infinite; he is an enemy of morality and a principle

---

23 "To give, to be for the other, in spite of oneself, but while interrupting the for-oneself, is to take the bread out of one's mouth, to feed the hunger of the other with my own abstinence" (*AE* 72/*OB* 56). Cf. *AE* 87–91/*OB* 69–72 and *AE* 97/*OB* 77.

24 The exception is a *non-lieu*, *AE* 9, 17, 21, 148/*OB* 8, 14, 17–18, 116.

25 *AE* 129–30/*OB* 102: "The meta-ontological and meta-logical structure of this Anarchy, undoing the Logos in which the apology is inserted, by which the conscience always recovers and commands itself." *AE* 156/*OB* 121: "persecution is a disqualification of apology."

26 *Désinteressement* beyond and beside Being, which is always *interesse*; cf. *AE* 4–6, 120–21, 149, 162–63/*OB* 4–6, 94–95, 117, 126–27.

27 Cf. *AE* 13–14, 68, 120–23/*OB* 11–12, 53, 94–96. See the analysis of desire in *TI* 3–5/33–35; *EDHH* 174–75; *CPP* 56–57; *EDHH* 192–94.

of hate.[28] The nonontologically understood God is nonpresent: he is not a theme, not even in the form of a "Thou" with whom a dialogue would be possible. He cannot be known because as noematic correlate, he would immediately be annihilated in the totalizing knowledge of the subject.[29] Even the question, "Does God exist?" testifies to an irreligious attitude (*AE* 120/*OB* 94). The question belongs in the sphere where interests, security, utility, projects and results, proof and calculations, totality and *conatus* are at home. The God who is brought to speech there is not strong enough to overcome the death of God that characterizes our times.

Thinking about God in the form of a negative theology also remains caught in an ontological framework because its statements presuppose an object (even if it is unknown) to which one could assign (negative) attributes (*AE* 14–15/*OB* 11–12). A philosophy of the infinite must reduce theology by renouncing pronouncements concerning God and laying open an anterior speaking that precedes every possible pronouncement (*AE* 193/ *OB* 151). The concern is "to perceive a God who has not become spoiled by Being" (*AE* x/*OB* xlii).

The infinite reveals itself in an enigmatic and extravagant way,[30] not by means of proofs but by a trace.[31] This trace is the designation and election of the subject.[32] In its Saying, the subject as it is described above is a testimony for God. Levinas does not appeal to a special religious experience that could serve as a foundation to this testimony (*témoignage*): the only "experience" and the only "evidence" is the sustaining of the responsibility that must be understood as glory and glorification of the Good (*AE* 181–94/*OB* 142–52). Glory is the reverse side of the subject's being delivered over; an an-archical disturbing of the hierarchy

28 *AE* 13, n. 7/*OB* 187, n. 8: "The Good would not be the term for a need susceptible of satisfaction—it is not the term for an erotic need, for a relation with the Seductive which resembles the Good such as to be mistaken for it. It is not its other but its imitator." Cf. also *AE* 157, 224/*OB* 122, 177 and the aphorism quoted here in note 13.
29 *AE* 157–58/*OB* 122–23.
30 The equivocal character of the "enigma" (*AE* 11, 15, 23, 57, 118, 120–21/*OB* 10, 12, 19, 44, 93, 94–95) is thoroughly described in the important essay "Enigme et phénomène," which appeared first in *Esprit* 33 (1965): 1128–42 and which is included under the title "Phenomenon and Enigma" in the second edition of *EDHH* 203–17; *CPP* 61–74.
31 Cf. *AE* 14–15 and 118–20/*OB* 12, 93–95. The idea of the trace was first developed in "La trace de l'Autre" (1963). Cf. *EDHH* 187–202.
32 For the *assignment* and *election* of the subject, cf. *AE* 19, 109–12, 115, 134, 146, 157–58, 163/*OB* 15, 86–87, 90, 106, 114, 122–23, 127.

of Being; the undermining of established thinking and of the central position of the I; a life that never comes to the end of its task because the obligations of substitution grow while they are being fulfilled. In the inspiration of the "Here I am" that precedes freedom, the infinite reveals its glory without ever appearing. The only evidence is the sincerity of Saying. In that sincerity, "He" (*Il*) passes by.[33] The thought of the infinite is in fact "something" that is "behind" thought (*une arrière-pensée*) and "too high to push itself into the first position" (*AE* 190/*OB* 149). It declares itself in the prophetic pronouncement, "Here I am in the name of God," which precedes all theology and even prayer. Pure religion does not pronounce itself in the declaration, "I believe in God," for this is already the beginning of a thematization. The coming hither of God is not an approaching of us; rather, it is the responsibility, not chosen by me, by which he touches and chooses me. The trace that refers to him (in a remembrance that always comes too late for his passing by) is the liberation from the interests of the ontological web.[34] This is the manifestation of the goodness of the Good that loved me (by its election) before I could love it. All human goodness is derived and gives thus evidence for the glory of the infinite.[35]

The discussion of the "otherwise than Being" (*autrement qu'être*), by which Levinas attempts to break the tyranny of ontological thinking, is itself a discourse on various concepts and states of affairs that form a particular structure and coherence. No matter how much they differ from the moments of ontology, they still make up a "Said" that—just like phenomena, knowledge, consciousness, repeatable time, memory, certainty, and the relations among them—falls under the laws of ontology and its logic. The anarchy of diachronic transcendence and the nonidentity of absolute passivity change during discussion into elements of an objective whole. The representation of that which is found

---

33 God is not a "Thou," as with Buber and Marcel. His way of more-than-active-essence or having-passed-by is "illéité." Cf. *AE* 15, 120, 148/*OB* 12–13, 193, 196.

34 *AE* 13, 133, 157, 181, 191–93/*OB* 11, 104–5, 122, 142, 150–51.

35 *AE* 13, n. 7/*OB* 187, n. 8: "The good . . . chose me before I chose it. Nobody is good voluntarily. . . . And if nobody is good voluntarily, nobody is a slave of the Good." *AE* 176/*OB* 138: "Goodness in the subject is an-archy itself; insofar as it is responsibility for the freedom of the other, anterior to all freedom in myself but also preceding the violence in me which would be the contrary of freedom, for if nobody is good voluntarily, no one is the slave of the good."

beyond (*au delà*) or before (*en deça*) the active essence of Being assigns it a place within Being. The triumph of the ground and of simultaneousness is irresistible.

Levinas is aware of the inevitability of this metamorphosis, and he himself asks the question of how one can speak of "beyond" and "before" or of "that side" and "this side" of Being when this speaking unavoidably contradicts itself. A first answer may exist in a counterquestion: Did and does not every philosopher entangle herself necessarily in such contradictions when she questions and thinks radically and in this sense pursues metaphysics? The Platonic dialectic of the One, the Aristotelian thought of prime matter, the Kantian explanations of the thing in itself, the always recurring attempts to name God or Being itself—all of these bring forth a result that they immediately must contradict in order to make clear that it is meant differently than it sounds. One can try to use the key words in a transformed, more primordial way along with Heidegger, or state with Derrida that they are merely strategically used, but this only proves the helplessness of a thinking that borders on the unsayable. It uses necessarily the manners of speaking that are possible and comprehensible on this side of the border, but it attempts to bend them in such a way that they—precisely through their inner conflict—point beyond that border. The "realities" that are meant by the use of words such as "transcendence," "anarchy," "passivity," etc. can only be described by means of a misuse of language. Their translation into the language of thinking is always a betrayal (*AE* 195–98/*OB* 153–56).

Levinas brings our attention in this connection to the eternal return of skepticism.[36] Insofar as philosophy asks radical questions, skepticism is "her legitimate child" (*AE* 231/*OB* 183; instead of "bastard child," the translation should read: "legitimate child"). Its classical refutation seems simple and irresistible. What the skeptic claims does not correspond to the implicit conditions of his explicit statement. That which he says (for instance, "It is not possible to discover any truth") contradicts the content of his saying (namely: I state this as a truth). When one compares the two, the contradiction exposes itself.

But should one compare the Said with its Saying? A comparison unites them as if they were two contemporary statements, while they are actually related like a statement and a stating. Only when reflection and memory transform them into two

---

36 Cf. for the following *AE* 9 and 213–18/*OB* 7 and 167–71.

"Saids" that are there at one and the same time does the absurdity of a universal skepticism appear. But is this reflection not the symptom of an imprisonment in logical and ontological assumptions that would first have to be proved? The classical refutation of skepticism assumes that all explicit statements or "truths" are contemporaneous in the *nunc stans* of a synchronized state of affairs. Through its refusal to recognize synchrony as the highest viewpoint, skepticism bears witness to the irreducible difference that distinguishes the Saying and the Said. As a denial of the universe of transcendental apperception, skepticism stands on the side of diachronic thinking, whose "truth" has already been indicated positively. It translates the riddle of diachrony in a way that is unacceptable for philosophy. The fact that skepticism always remains possible and continually returns, without the skeptic being silenced by his own words, shows that the synchronous reason of ontology is not the only reasonable one. Reasonable arguments are not sufficient to bring the skeptic to silence. The monopoly of ontological reason demands the exercise of violence. Western philosophy commits this violence by logic, whereas the state conquers anarchy by political means. Clinics and jails, but also scientific institutions, represent the *logos* of synchrony; humanism, however, lives from the diachronic reason of the One-for-the-Other.

The foregoing discussion does not prove that the thesis of skepticism (its Said) is true, or that it is true in a higher degree than the thesis of its opponents. The "truth" that attempts to pronounce itself in skepticism is rather the necessity, indicated above, of recalling (*dédire*) the Said, and of replacing it by a new Saying (*redire*) that is just as little a final Saying as the previous one was. The enigma of transcendence, which can never become evident, does not come into its own by synoptic expositions in which time stands still but only by continual attempts through new speeches to rectify the unavoidable contradictions of speaking.

The order of ontological truth, however, can and must be more positively estimated than it was above. The mistake of Western ontology does not consist in its structure and logic but in its pretense of grasping all reality and in that sense of embodying the absolute principle or point of view. The realm of the Said in which knowledge and thematization, calculation and planning, clarity and objective judgments are at home is even demanded and furthered by the transcending goodness. For it is a necessary presupposition of *justice*.

The order of active essence and simultaneity is a condition of the possibility of justice. This comes to existence through the fact that I have to do not only with my neighbor but also with others who exist beside my neighbor. In addition to the neighbor, there is also "the third."[37] If I could limit myself to confrontation with this unique other-here-and-now whose visage bids me to responsibility, there would be no problem. "The third human," however, the neighbor of my neighbor, disturbs the immediate relation of the twosome and its intimacy. As soon as a third enters the picture, my responsibility is divided. It is no longer an unlimited care for only this one neighbor, and I must ask myself: Who comes first? What are my neighbor and the third man to one another? What should they do for one another? What have they done for one another? My substitution for my neighbor involves my responsibility for his/her responsibility toward his/her neighbor. My neighbor and the third person obligate me simultaneously. Together with my neighbor, I am for the third person; with both of them I am against myself (*AE* 19–20/*OB* 15–16).

The infinite obligation now becomes the duty of justice. I must be just in the distribution of my attention and devotion. I must compare and calculate, correct and order, treat others as equals and conduct myself as a judge. This presupposes a synopsis and synchrony and founds the order of law. The order of consciousness and its totality can consequently be derived from saying and substitution. The ethical relation of the One-for-the-Other obligates us to the rational organization of society, in which justice is exercised and violence is suppressed. Thus are the state and reason "deduced" in their ontological way of Being.[38] In this perspective, I may and must understand and even treat myself as being equal to all others. My destiny and salvation are also important: I, too, am one of the many who are neighbors of my neighbors. My responsibility for the other includes now also care of myself (*AE* 202–4/*OB* 158–61).

The radical inequality of the infinite responsibility for the other does not exclude reciprocity on the level of justice but rather "founds" it. On the "primordial" level, however, neither

---

37 *Le tiers.* Cf. for the following *AE* 200–206; 19ff., 152–65/*OB* 157–62; 15ff.; 119–29.

38 Perhaps the author is referring here to the political philosophy of Eric Weil (who is quoted in another context in *AE* 143, n. 17/*OB* 195, n. 17). Cf. Weil's *Philosophie Politique* (Paris: Vrin, 1956), in which the state is legitimized as the necessary overcoming of violence.

reciprocity nor dialogical relations are possible. Levinas does not support a philosophy of dialogue. But the radical asymmetry that is his real "theme" furthers the equality without which no justice is possible.[39]

These analyses do not indicate by "the third" a purely empirical fact, as if this expression meant a third and a fourth being who happen to be there and by their existence urge me to compare them with each other and myself. "The third" is a structure that co-constitutes the proximity of the neighbor. The visage reveals not only the invisible other, who is my neighbor, but simultaneously the visible other, who represents every person. The other is from the beginning the brother of every other. Because I am obsessed by the Other, I cannot escape from the justice that makes me devoted to all human beings. The visage of the other is incomparable *and* identical with every other visage. The third, who shows him/herself in the visage of my neighbor, is the origin of appearance and, thus, of the realm of phenomena and phenomenology.

The relation to the third, through which the realm of the Said is recovered and justified, rectifies the asymmetry of immediate and intimate relations. It legitimates the state and politics as the regulation of symmetrical relations. At the same time, the (pre)-ethical relation in which it is rooted preserves the state from degenerating into a pure technology of social equilibrium. Insofar as politics borrows its inspiration from the radical responsibility of the One-for-the-Other, the law and the state owe their activities to anarchic transcendence.[40] Thus, they are a trace of the Good that has no place within the time of the active essence of Being but passes by without ever being present.

Justice is the only possible legitimation of the orders of synchronous equality and reciprocity. Therefore it is also the justification of philosophy in its ontological form. Insofar as philosophy oscillates to and fro between transcendence and ontology in order to do justice to the radical responsibility for the other, it preserves Being from its decline into the irresponsible and absurd "there is," which is the primordial nonsense.[41]

---

39 Cf. the rejection of dialogical philosophy in *AE* 32, 142, 153, 164, 184/*OB* 25, 111, 119, 198, 145.

40 "Grâce à Dieu," *AE* 201/*OB* 158.

41 For the absurdity of the "there is" (*il y a*), which was described as early as 1947 in *EDHH* 93–113/57–64; cf. *AE* 3–4 and 207–10/*OB* 3–4 and 162–65.

To end this chapter, I should like to attempt some reflections on the method of philosophy expressed in *Otherwise Than Being.* Since the conceptual exposure essential to any "methodology" belongs to ontological thinking, we cannot expect here a self-certain explication of the logos that rules Levinas's texts. The metaontological speaking that Levinas tries here is out of breath even before it has said anything.[42] In the few statements about his "method," Levinas always characterizes it as an "intentional analysis."[43] Although he does not follow the rules of Husserlian reductions and brings the whole of classical phenomenology into question, he remains attached to its spirit insofar as his analyses expose the forgotten horizons (*Abschattungen*) and "manners" that essentially belong to it.[44] "Our presentation of notions . . . remains true to intentional analysis insofar as this means that one brings those notions back into their horizon of appearing—a horizon which is misunderstood, forgotten, or transposed in the object's showing, in its notion, in the glance which is absorbed by the mere notion" (*AE* 230–31/*OB* 183).

In *Totality and Infinity,* Levinas compares his thinking with the transcendental method, but he refuses the technical proceeding of transcendental idealism. I spoke repeatedly above of "conditions of possibility" and gave some examples of it. For example, embodiment is the possibility of the victim and of pain. As such, it is necessary, for that which is made possible through it is necessary. Pain is assumed to be the possibility of endurance in passivity for the Other (*AE* 65–66, 71/*OB* 51, 55). Giving belongs to inspiration and to spirituality. They are therefore possible only in the form of corporeality, for a purely spiritual giving, which does not offer one's own bread and one's own skin, is a lie. "Only an eating subject can signify" (*AE* 86–91/*OB* 68–72). The giving out of absolute passivity, however, also implies enjoyment, for without the selfishness of enjoyment, giving could not be a giving of oneself (*AE* 92/*OB* 73). In every case, an implication is found by looking for something that makes the "object" of description possible. In this sense, we can also understand the use of the word "deduction" in *Totality and Infinity,* to which I referred several times above.[45]

---

[42] This speaking is characterized by "essoufflement," *AE* x, 5–6, 17/ *OB* xlii, 5, 14.

[43] Cf. *EDHH* 130–31; *TI* xvi/27–28.

[44] *DDVI* 139–43.

[45] Cf. *TI* xvi/27–28.

Sometimes the transition between two "moments" occurs even more immediately. The making possible is replaced in these cases with a simple "is" (*AE* 138/*OB* 108–9). For example: The body is that through which the self is receptive. Only when the persecuted is also responsible for the persecution is his passivity integral and absolute. That is why passivity is atonement (*expiation*, *AE* 141/*OB* 111). Without persecution, the I would exalt itself. It is thus a necessary implication of the dethroning of the I (*AE* 143/*OB* 112). Passivity is irritability, receptivity, bareness, vulnerability. Motherliness is the ultimate meaning of vulnerability (*AE* 137/*OB* 108). In this last example, motherliness (*maternité*) is disclosed as an implication of vulnerability. On the other hand, vulnerability is found to be a prerequisite of the relation of the One-for-the-Other—a relation that seems to coincide with the relation of the "Other-in-me" and thus with motherliness. We have thus an example of the "echoing-in-one-another" of which Levinas speaks (*AE* 23/*OB* 19).

In order to maintain the reference to transcendental method, one should disregard its connection to a transcendental and foundational consciousness. Insofar as these connections seem essential, the characterization of Levinas's "method" as a "transcendental" one is less suitable than the much more modest and less suggestive characterization as "intentional analysis." Levinas later on rejected the transcendental method because it seemed impossible to detach it from an ultimate consciousness in search for an ultimate ground of all beings, i.e., from the design of ontology.[46] Levinas's "method" is not founding, planning, and constructing but rather a new kind of "association."[47]

"There is another kind of justification of one idea by another, namely the transition from one idea to its superlative or its emphasis.[48] In this way, a new idea—which is not implied in the first idea—flows or emanates out of its excess. The new idea is

---

46 Cf. *DDVI* 139: The rejection is not absolute, for Levinas also characterizes his "method" as a "transcendentalism that begins with ethics" (143).

47 *DDVI* 141: "to associate the ideas in a new way."

48 *DDVI* 142; *AE* 8, n. 4/*OB* 187, n. 5: "It is the superlative, more than the negation of the category, which interrupts the system . . . as if the logical order and the being which it comes to espouse preserved the superlative which exceeds them: in subjectivity, the excess of *the non-lieu*, in the caress and sexuality—the 'outbidding' of tangency"; *AE* 13/*OB* 11: "by its goodness which is the very superlative." For "emphasis," see *AE* 152 and 161/*OB* 119 and 125.

thus justified—not simply on *the basis* of the first one but through its *sublimation*. As thinking "beyond phenomenology," this philosophy takes its refuge in the superlative and in hyperbolic speaking, the emphasis of which attempts to express the all-surpassing character (*excellence*) of transcendence (*AE* 231–32/ *OB* 183–84). An example of this procedure is the deepening and sharpening of the passivity that exists in Saying. The "passivity that is more passive than all passivity" is an extreme possibility of thinking. Another example is the characterization of pain as "excess of passivity."[49] Why does such a sublimation produce a justification and not simply an exaggeration? Levinas himself refers to the relationship with the *via eminentiae*.[50] But why does one seek an other-than-Being? Because in a certain sense one asks more radically. Emphasis is a way of turning the grounded and the grounding of ontology into transcendence.

In this light, we must also understand the many iterative expressions in *Otherwise Than Being*, such as "denudation of the denudation," "significance of the signification," "infinitizing of the infinite," "communication of the communication," "gratitude for the condition of gratitude," and so on.[51] Thus, Levinas formulates the structure of the nonidentity and of the nonsimultaneity of the subject with it—its "preceding itself" (*se précéder soi-même*). Through the iteration of the expression, an inner duplication of the subject shows itself, a duplication that can be thought of as a self-difference in a quasi-time. Here, too, an intensifying, sharpening description radicalizes the investigated "theme" through a kind of extremism. In an an-archical way, the analysis attempts to shake the movement of grounding through the freeing of a true precedence.

"More I do not know, I do not believe that transparence in method is possible, nor that philosophy is possible as transparence. Those who have concerned themselves with method all their lives have written a lot of books in the place of the more interesting books which they did not write."[52] The idea of a completely transparent, completely self-conscious method and

---

49 Cf. *AE* 112 ("surplus of passivity"), 137, 152 ("emphasis of the overture")/*OB* 88, 108, 119.

50 Cf. *DD VI* 142.

51 *AE* 63/*OB* 49 ("denudation of the denudation," "to give a sign of its significance"). *AE* 119/*OB* 93 ("infinition of infinity"), *AE* 153/*OB* 119 ("communication of the communications"), *AE* 190/*OB* 149 ("gratitude for this state of gratitude").

52 *DD VI* 143.

methodology is characteristic of ontology. The need for such a self-consciousness corresponds to the desire for a sure foundation on the basis of which one can master everything. The monopoly of this need deafens and blinds one to the enigmatic ambiguity of the Other that the philosophy of Levinas attempts to show. The only way of thinking that corresponds to what is sought is a humble speaking that has lost its self-control and that, while doing unavoidable violence to language, endures "the pain of the expression" (*AE* 128, n. 4/*OB* 194, n. 4). It indicates traces without self-assuredness. One always comes too late for what is sought because it has already passed by; it is, however, close to someone who is not caught up in a reflective self-concern.

Before the publication of *Totalité et Infini* (1961) Levinas's production of strictly philosophical papers was modest. He became famous immediately afterwards and, partly because of the many invitations he received, the number of his publications grew very fast, as well as the secondary literature on his work. An almost complete bibliography of both has been published by Roger Burggraeve: *Emmanuel Levinas: The Ethical Basis for a Humane Society*. Bibliography 1929–1977, 1977–1981; 1981–1985; 1985–1989, Center for Metaphysics and Philosophy of God, Institute of Philosophy, Leuven (Belgium), 1990. It includes almost all the philosophical, religious and circumstantial texts of Levinas, most of the translations, the secondary literature, and even a number of studies that are influenced by Levinas.

Since this book has the character of an introduction, I will list here a selection of Levinas's essential texts in the field of philosophy, some of his more explicitly religious writings, and a small selection of English studies on his work. Of his innumerable interviews I only quote a long one that provides an excellent introduction into his thought: *Ethique et Infini: Dialogues avec Philippe Nemo* (Paris: Fayard, 1982; Livre de Poche, 1984); translated by R. A. Cohen as *Ethics and Infinity: Conversations with Philippe Nemo* (Pittsburgh: University of Pittsburgh Press, 1985); and another that gives a host of information about his life and personality: François Poirié, *Emmanuel Levinas: Qui êtes-vous?* (Lyon: La Manufacture, 1987). A very concentrated autobiography that focuses on the philosophical work can be found in Levinas's own "Signature," published in *Difficile Liberté* (see below; an English translation with commentary can be found in *Research in Phenomenology* 8 (1970): 175–89).

| Philosophical Texts
| of Emmanuel Levinas

La théorie de l'intuition dans la phénoménologie de Husserl (Paris: Alcan, 1930; reprinted by Vrin in 1963 and 1970). This is the dissertation on the basis of which Levinas received his Ph.D. from the University of Strasbourg. Its interpretation of Husserl's phenomenology shows the influence of Martin Heidegger. The work has been translated into English by A. Orianne as *The Theory of Intuition in Husserl's Phenomenology* (Evanston, Ill.: Northwestern University Press, 1973).

Having absolved his academic studies, Levinas began to write a book on Heidegger's philosophy, but this project was interrupted when Heidegger, as rector of the University of Freiburg, pronounced his *Rectoratsrede*. A fragment of the planned book can be found in "Martin Heidegger et l'ontologie," published in the *Revue de la France et de l'Etranger* 113 (1932): 395–431 and reprinted, in a revised form, in a collection of essays on Husserl and Heidegger that Levinas published in 1949: *En découvrant l'existence avec Husserl et Heidegger* (Paris: Vrin).

The first essay that expressed a personal and original thought is "De l'évasion," *Recherches Philosophiques* 5 (1936–36): 373–92, in which the central motifs of his later work already present themselves. It was published in book form, with a preface by the author, by Fata Morgana, Montpellier, in 1979 and, augmented by an introduction and annotations of Jacques Rolland, republished in 1982.

Levinas's first personal book, *De l'existence à l'existant* (Paris: Fontaine, 1947; later on taken over by Vrin), contained the program of further developments. Its title alone (not from *Seiendes*/"beings" or "existants" to *Sein*/"Being"/"existence" but the other way around) announced a polemics with Heidegger, whom Levinas has continued to consider the greatest philosopher of our century. The book was translated by Alphonso Lingis under the title *Existence and Existents* (The Hague-Boston: Nijhoff, 1978).

Invited by Jean Wahl to speak about developments in phenomenology and existentialism in the parauniversitarian Collège Philosophique, Levinas gave four lectures on "time and the other" (*Le temps et l'autre*), which subsequently were published in a collective book, *Le Choix—Le Monde—L'Existence* (Grenoble-Paris, 1947). This text was republished separately, and with a preface by the author, in 1979 (Montpellier: Fata Morgana) and by Quadrige-PUF (Paris) in 1983. An English version was published, together with two other translations, "The Old and the New" and "Diachrony and Representation," by Richard Cohen in *Time and the Other* (Pittsburgh, Pa.: Duquesne University Press, 1987).

In 1948 Levinas was asked by Sartre to contribute to *Les Temps Modernes,* for which he then wrote two of his very few texts on art: "La realité et son ombre," *Les Temps Modernes* 4, no. 38 (1948): 771–89, followed by "La transcendance des mots: A propos de 'Biffures' de Michel Leiris," *Les Temps Modernes* 4, no. 44 (1949): 1090–95. An English translation by Alphonso Lingis of the first essay has been published in the *Collected Philosophical Papers,* 1–14 (see below).

Of the essays written between 1949 and 1961, the most important ones are "L'ontologie est-elle fondamentale?" (*Revue de Métaphysique et de Morale* 56 [1951]: 193–203; English translation by Peter Atterton: "Is Ontology Fundamental," *Philosophy Today* [1989]: 121–29), which is probably the clearest and most straightforward formulation of Levinas's interpretation and criticism of Heidegger; "Le moi et la totalité" (*Revue de Métaphysique et de Morale* 59 [1954]: 353–73; English translation in *Collected Philosophical Papers,* 25–46 under the title "The Ego and the Totality"), important for its analysis of social and economic phenomena; and "La philosophie et l'idée de l'Infini" (*Revue de Métaphysique et de Morale* 62 [1957]: 241–53, which contains the outline of *Totality and Infinity* ["Philosophy and the Idea of Infinity," *Collected Philosophical Papers,* 47–60]; see chapters 2, 3, and 4 of this book). Whereas the last essay was integrated into the second edition of *En découvrant* . . . (1967), the two others became parts of the recent book *Entre nous* (1991, see below).

In 1961 Levinas became Docteur ès Lettres with *Totalité et Infini: Essai sur l'extériorité,* Phaenomenologica 8 (The Hague-Boston: Nijhoff, 1961), which made him world famous. In 1969 the English translation by Alphonso Lingis was published by Duquesne University Press, Pittsburgh, in cooperation with Nijhoff, The Hague-Boston. A paper in which he summarized his thought under the title "Transcendance et hauteur" was presented on 27 January 1962 to the Société Française de Philosophie (*Bulletin de la Société Française de Philosophie* 56 [1962]: 89–111). It will appear soon in an English version as part of Levinas's *Basic Writings.*

Having written, from the late 1940s on, a large number of papers and pieces on Jewish religion and spirituality, Levinas collected them in 1963 in *Difficile Liberté: Essais sur le Judaisme* (Paris: Albin Michel, 1963), which was augmented and republished in 1976. It contains also commentaries on Talmudic discussions of messianism and eschatology. An English translation by Sean Hand (*Difficult Freedom: Essays on Judaism*) was published by Johns Hopkins University Press in 1991.

As a regular commentator who uses the philosophical language of "the Greeks" to clarify the Judaic thought of the Talmud, Levinas has published several other collections of "talmudic lessons": *Quatre leçons talmudiques* (Paris: Minuit, 1968); and *Du sacré au saint* (Paris: Minuit, 1977); to which we may add the "talmudic readings" in *L'au-delà du verset: Lectures et discours talmudiques* (Paris: Minuit, 1982): 29–122, and *A l'heure des nations* (1988): 19–124. Of the two first books Annette Aronowicz made one English book under the title *Nine Talmudic Readings* (Bloomington: Indiana University Press, 1990), for which she also wrote an introduction (ix–xxxix).

The second edition of *En découvrant l'existence avec Husserl et Heidegger*, published in 1967, has been augmented by some essays on Husserl and Heidegger written in the fifties and a number of original studies, such as the very important "La philosophie et l'idée de l'infini" (1957), "La trace de l'autre" (1963), and "Enigme et phénomène" (1965). The Husserl studies have been translated by Richard Cohen in *Discovering Existence with Husserl* (Bloomington: Indiana University Press, 1988), while the personal essays of this collection have been published by Alphonso Lingis in Emmanuel Levinas, *Collected Philosophical Papers* (The Hague-Boston: Nijhoff, 1987), together with "God and Philosophy" (a translation of the very important "Dieu et la philosophie" of 1975, republished in *De Dieu qui vient à l'idée* of 1982, see below), "Transcendance and Evil" (a translation of an essay published in 1978), and three essays of 1964, 1968, and 1970 that have become the three chapters of *Humanisme de l'autre homme* (Montpellier: Fata Morgana, 1972).

In 1974 Levinas published his second opus magnum of which he already had published several fragments since 1968: *Autrement qu'être ou au-delà de l'essence* (The Hague-Boston: Nijhoff, 1974). Alphonso Lingis published his translation at the same publishing house in 1981: *Otherwise Than Being or Beyond Essence*.

As a friend of Maurice Blanchot since the time of their university studies, Levinas had written several essays on Blanchot's work. They were gathered in *Sur Maurice Blanchot* (Montpellier:

Fata Morgana, 1975). In 1976 Levinas collected his philosophical and circumstantial papers on other "proper" thinkers (such as Agnon, Buber, Celan, Derrida, Jabès, Kierkegaard, Proust, etc.) in *Noms propres*, published by the same publishing house.

Levinas has continued to publish one paper after another, but fortunately he collected most of them in a series of books: *De Dieu qui vient à l'idée* (Paris: Vrin, 1982 and, with a new preface, in 1986), *Hors sujet* (Montpellier: Fata Morgana, 1987), *L'au-delà du verset: Lectures et discours talmudiques* (Paris: Minuit, 1982), *A l'heure des nations* (Paris: Minuit, 1988), and *Entre nous: Essais sur le penser-à-l'autre* (Paris: Grasset, 1991). A separate publication of the paper *Transcendance et Intelligibilité* (Geneva: Labor et Fides, 1984) deserves special mention.

Finally, there is an English anthology of texts from various periods of Levinas's production: *The Levinas Reader*, edited by Sean Hand (Oxford: Blackwell, 1989).

| Secondary Literature in English

Of the English publications on Levinas's thought, the following list gives some titles that seem to me particularly useful for readers who are not yet familiar with its difficulties. I add three English collections of papers on Levinas and some outstanding essays in which, for more advanced readers, the discussion on the significance of his work has developed. The list closes with three French volumes in which friends and admirers have honored Levinas by responding to his work.

| Introductory Studies

The first monograph on Levinas's work—an excellent one—was written by Edith Wyschogrod: *Emmanuel Levinas: The Problem of Ethical Metaphysics* (The Hague-Boston: Nijhoff, 1974). Also excellent are Alphonso Lingis's introductions to his translations of various books of Levinas (see above). Other helpful studies are:

Bernasconi, Robert. "Fundamental Ontology, Metontology and the Ethics of Ethics." *Irish Philosophical Journal* 4 (1987): 76–93.

————. "Levinas: Philosophy and Beyond." (*Continental Philosophy* 1 (1987): 232–58.

————. "Rereading *Totality and Infinity*." In *The Question of the Other*, edited by Arleen B. Dallery and Ch. E. Scott, 23–34. Albany: SUNY Press, 1989.

Burggraeve, Roger. "The Ethical Basis for a Humane Society," in his forementioned bibliography: 5–57.

Greisch, Jean. "Ethics and Ontology." *Irish Philosophical Journal* 4 (1987): 64–75.

Peperzak, Adriaan. "Emmanuel Levinas: Jewish Experience and Philosophy." *Philosophy Today* 27 (1983): 297–306.

_____. "Phenomenology—Ontology—Metaphysics: Levinas' Perspective on Husserl and Heidegger." *Man and World* 16 (1983): 113–27.

_____. "From Intentionality to Responsibility: On Levinas' Philosophy of Language." In *The Question of the Other*, edited by Arleen B. Dallery and Ch. E. Scott, 3–22. Albany: SUNY Press, 1989.

S. Strasser. "Emmanuel Levinas (Born 1906); Phenomenological Philosophy." In H. Spiegelberg, *The Phenomenological Movement*. Phaenomenologica 5/6. The Hague-Boston, Nijhoff 1982: 612–649.

| Readers

Since most of the essays in the collections listed here present an advanced reading of Levinas's work, they belong to the second list rather than to the introductory literature.

Bernasconi, Robert, and David Wood (eds.). *The Provocation of Levinas: Rethinking the Other*. London-New York: Routledge, 1988. Besides an interview with Levinas and his text on "Useless Suffering," this volume contains a detailed study of the relations between Levinas and Buber by Robert Bernasconi, a paper of John Llewelyn on Levinas and Derrida, and several contributions on Levinas in relation to feminism and psychotherapy.

Bernasconi, Robert, and Simon Critchley (eds.). *Re-reading Levinas*. Bloomington: Indiana University Press, 1991. This volume contains translations of Levinas's text on Derrida ("Wholly Otherwise") and of Derrida's second text on Levinas ("At this very moment in this work here I am"), followed by twelve essays on Levinas, some of which focus on his relationship with Derrida.

Cohen, Richard (ed.). *Face to Face with Levinas*. Albany: SUNY Press, 1986. Besides a "dialogue" between Emmanuel Levinas and Richard Kearney (13–34), translations of Levinas's "Mauvaise conscience et l'inexorable" of 1981 (35–

40: "Bad Conscience and the Inexorable") and Blanchot's "Our Clandestine Companion" (41–50), this volume contains contributions of nine Levinas scholars.

| Suggestions for Further Study

Bouckaert, Luc. "Ontology and Ethics: Reflections on Levinas' Critique of Heidegger." *International Philosophical Quarterly* 10 (1970): 402–19.

Chanter, Tina. "The Question of Death: The Time of the I and the Time of the Other." *Irish Philosophical Journal* 4 (1987): 94–119.

Derrida, Jacques. "Violence and Metaphysics: An Essay on the Thought of Emmanuel Levinas." In *Writing and Difference*. Chicago, Ill.: University of Chicago Press, 1978, 79–153.

Llewelyn, John. "Jewgreek or Greekjew." In *The Collegium Phaenomenologicum: The First Ten Years*, edited by G. Moneta et al., 273–87. Dordrecht-Boston: Kluwer, 1988.

————. *The Middle Voice of Ecological Conscience: A Chiasmic Reading of Responsibility in the Neighbourhood of Levinas, Heidegger and Others*. London: Macmillan, 1991.

Smith, S. G. *The Argument to the Other: Reason Beyond Reason in the Thought of Karl Barth and E. Levinas*. Chico, Calif.: Scholars Press, 1983.

| Volumes in Honor of Emmanuel Levinas

Laruelle, François (ed.). *Textes pour Emmanuel Levinas*. Paris: Place, 1980 (with contributions by Blanchot, Delhomme, Derrida, Dufrenne, Halperin, Jabès, Laruelle, Lyotard, Neher, Peperzak, Ricoeur, Wyschogrod).

Levinas: Exercises de la patience. Cahiers de philosophie, no. 1. Paris, Obsidiane, 1980 (contributions of J. Rolland, Blanchot, and others).

Chalier, Catherine, and Miguel Abensour (eds.). *Emmanuel Levinas. L'Herne*, no. 60. Paris, 1991 (with 17 little known texts of Levinas and 28 contributions by other authors).

INDEX

Nazism, 10–11
Need, 22, 133. *See also* Desire
Neuter, 97, 205
Nietzsche, 125, 211
Nostalgia, 114
Noun, 216

Objectification, 146, 159, 165–66, 180
Obsession, 223
Odyssey, 67–68, 91 n. 11
One-for-the-Other, 222
Onto-theo-logy, 44
Ontology, 12–14, 36–37, 140, 145–46, 160, 182, 185, 202–8, 214–18, 228, 230; categories of, 32–33; language of, 40, 224
Origin, 182
Other, 61–65, 111 n. 62, 112, 121, 134–37, 143, 159, 161; as *Autrui*, 22–30, 144; as God. *See* God; and the Others, 166–84
Otherness, 19–22

Paganism, 103 n. 37, 104, 156
Pantheism, 196
Pardon, 200
Participation, 48–49
Pascal, 103
Passivity, 189–90, 221–22
Past, immemorial, 34–36
Paternity, 195–99
Patience, 190, 221
Peace, 175, 184; eschatological, 127–28, 200; messianic, 127, 200
Persecution, 222
Phenomenology, 14–19, 40–42, 132, 155, 160–61, 185, 210, 215, 230, 233
Phenomenon, 21–22, 41, 62–63, 160–61, 184, 230
Philosophy, 129, 182, 196, 230; first, 46, 65, 123–24, 207; of history, 190; and theology, 210
Physis, 13, 41–42, 131, 139
Plato, 11, 43, 49–50, 67, 99, 128, 131–32, 147, 160, 175, 186, 199
Platonism, 13, 39

Pluralism, 196, 208
Politics, 122, 125, 127–28, 130, 182–83, 186, 191, 217, 230; and ethics, 123, 125, 128; and morality, 190
Power, 97–98, 110, 116, 177
Presence, 33–36, 155; bodily, 214; living, 214
Present, 189–90
Procreation. *See* Fecundity
Prophet, 105 n. 43, 127–28
Prophetism, 175, 219
Proust, Marcel, 6
Proximity, 180, 182, 221, 230
Psychism, 223

Ready-at-hand. See *Zuhandenes*
Reason, 126–27, 180, 186, 193, 217, 229
Reciprocity, 172, 174, 183, 229–30
Rectitude (*droiture*), 70, 110 n. 55
Reduction, 219
Relation, metaphysical, 129, 136
Religion, 144, 199, 226
Remembrance, 34, 216, 226
Representation, 155, 159, 214
Respect, 174
Responsibility, 164, 220–21, 223
Revelation, 109 n. 54, 142, 160
Rhetoric, 144

Sacred, 143
Said (*Dit*), 122, 215–16, 230
Same (*le Même*), 94–105, 120, 136, 149, 152; vs. The Other, 91 n. 12, 99 n. 33, 131, 137
Sartre, Jean-Paul, 125, 173
Saying (*Dire*), 36–37, 226; again (*redire*), 122, 219, 228; vs. Said, 29–30, 136, 160–61, 180, 217–22, 227–28; vs. Unsaying (*dédire*), 122, 218–19, 228
Seinlassen, 139
Self (*le soi*), 25, 217, 222
Self-consciousness, 190
Self-identification, 136–37, 147, 196
Self-realization, 134, 176
Senescence, 196, 198
Sensation, 162, 215